THE MIND'S ARROW

ARCHER COE

Written By:
JAMIE S. RICH

TH

AR

Edited By:
ROBIN HERRERA

Designed By:
JASON STOREY
with
KATE Z. STONE

Illustrated By:
DAN CHRISTENSEN

MIND'S ARROW

HER

COE

THE WAY TO DUSTY DEATH

Oni Press, Inc.
Founder & Chief Financial Officer, Joe Nozemack
Publisher, James Lucas Jones
V.P. of Creative & Business Development, Charlie Chu
Director of Operations, Brad Rooks
Director of Publicity, Melissa Meszaros
Director of Sales, Margot Wood
Marketing Manager, Rachel Reed
Director of Design & Production, Troy Look
Senior Graphic Designer, Hilary Thompson
Junior Graphic Designer, Kate Z. Stone
Junior Graphic Designer, Sonja Synak
Digital Prepress Lead, Angie Knowles
Executive Editor, Ari Yarwood
Senior Editor, Robin Herrera
Associate Editor, Desiree Wilson
Administrative Assistant, Alissa Sallah
Logistics Associate, Jung Lee

Oni Press
1319 SE Martin Luther King Jr.
Blvd., Suite 240
Portland, OR 97214

onipress.com
facebook.com/onipress • twitter.com/onipress
onipress.tumblr.com • instagram.com/onipress

confessions123.com
dcdrawings.blogspot.com

First Edition: June 2018

ISBN 978-1-62010-505-4 • eISBN 978-1-62010-506-1

Library of Congress Control Number: 2017959235

1 3 5 7 9 10 8 6 4 2

Printed in China.

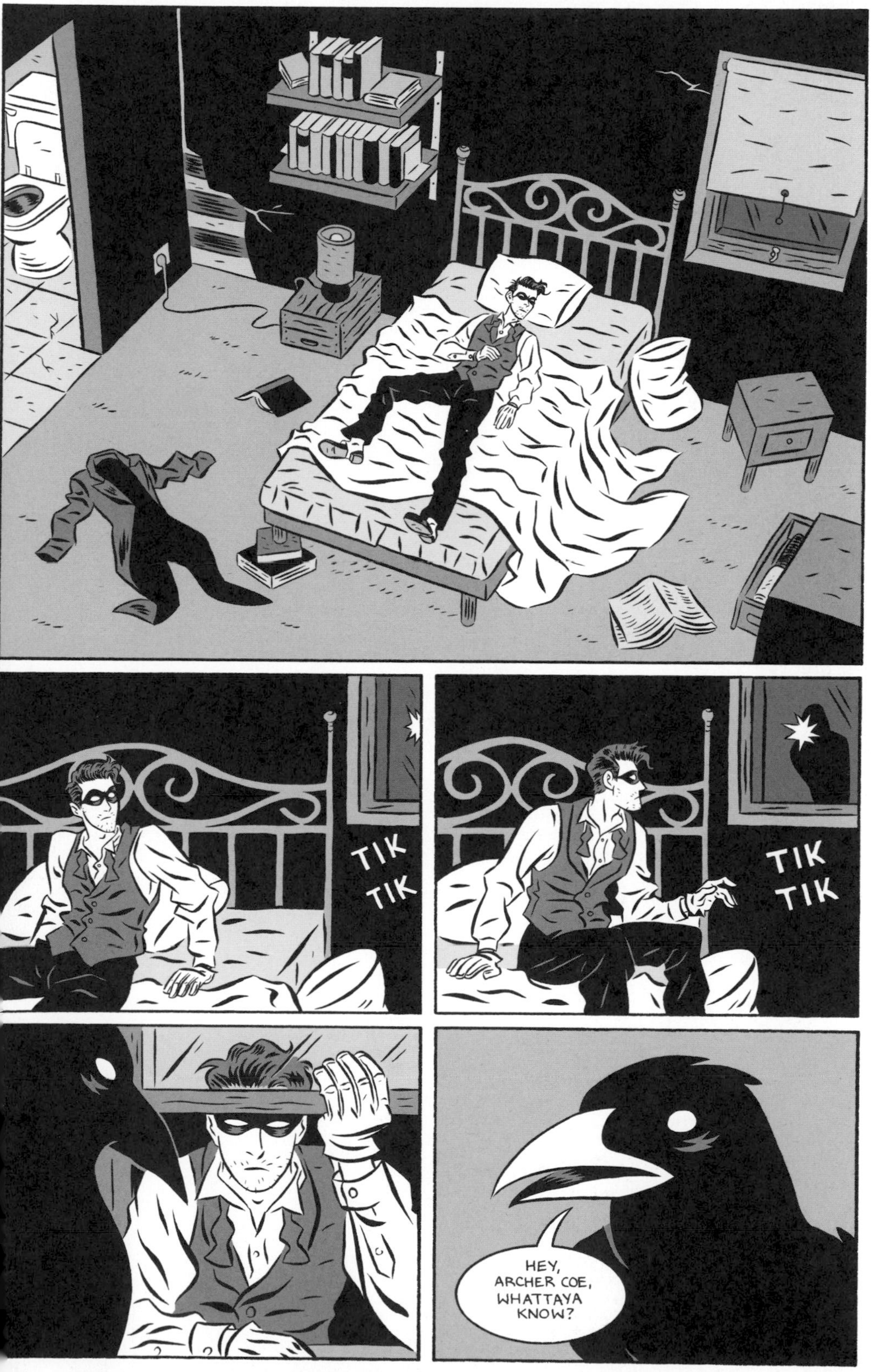
TIK
TIK
TIK
TIK
HEY, ARCHER COE, WHATTAYA KNOW?

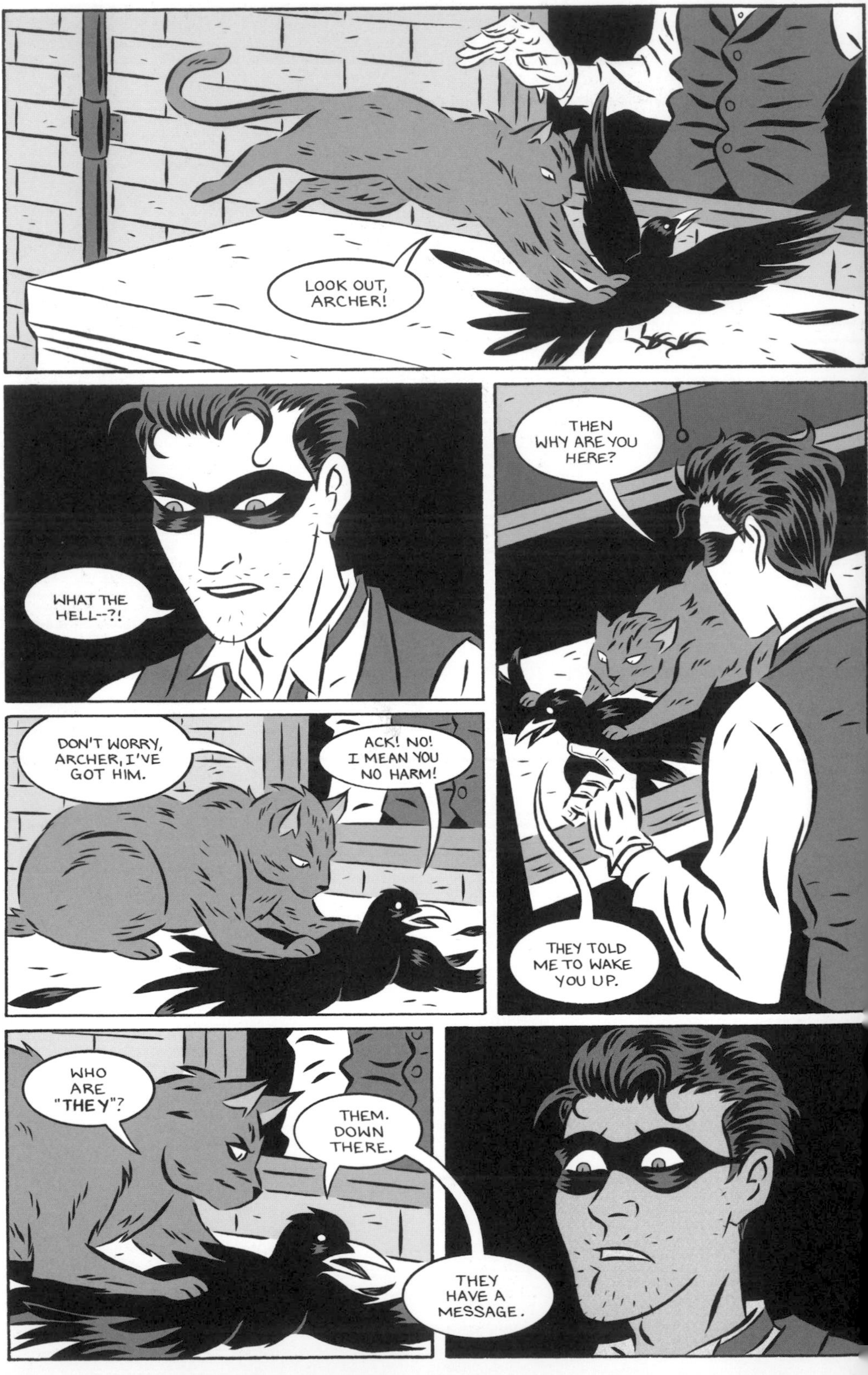
LOOK OUT, ARCHER!
WHAT THE HELL--?!
THEN WHY ARE YOU HERE?
DON'T WORRY, ARCHER, I'VE GOT HIM.
ACK! NO! I MEAN YOU NO HARM!
THEY TOLD ME TO WAKE YOU UP.
WHO ARE "THEY"?
THEM. DOWN THERE.
THEY HAVE A MESSAGE.

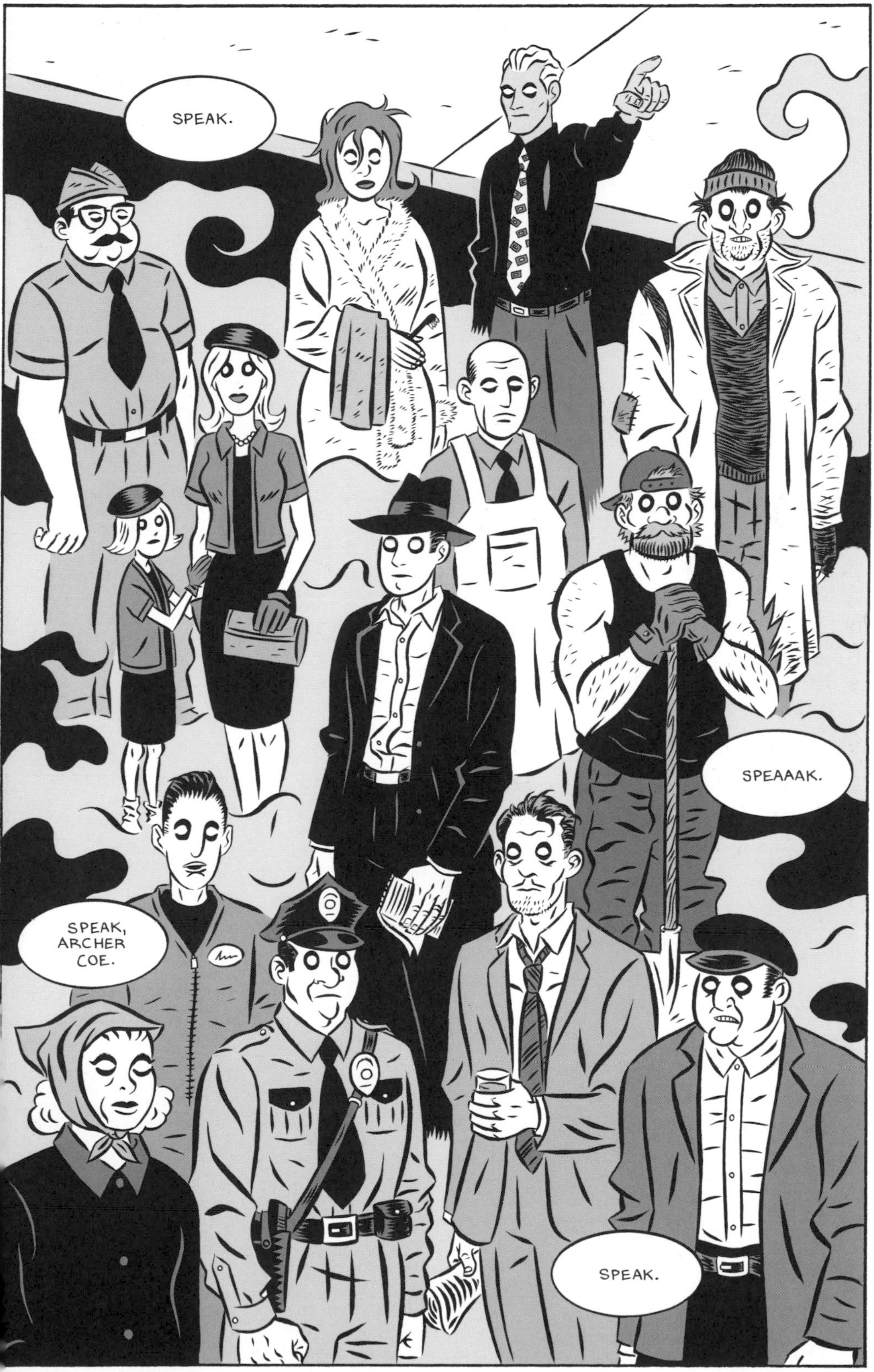
SPEAK.
SPEAAAK.
SPEAK, ARCHER COE.
SPEAK.

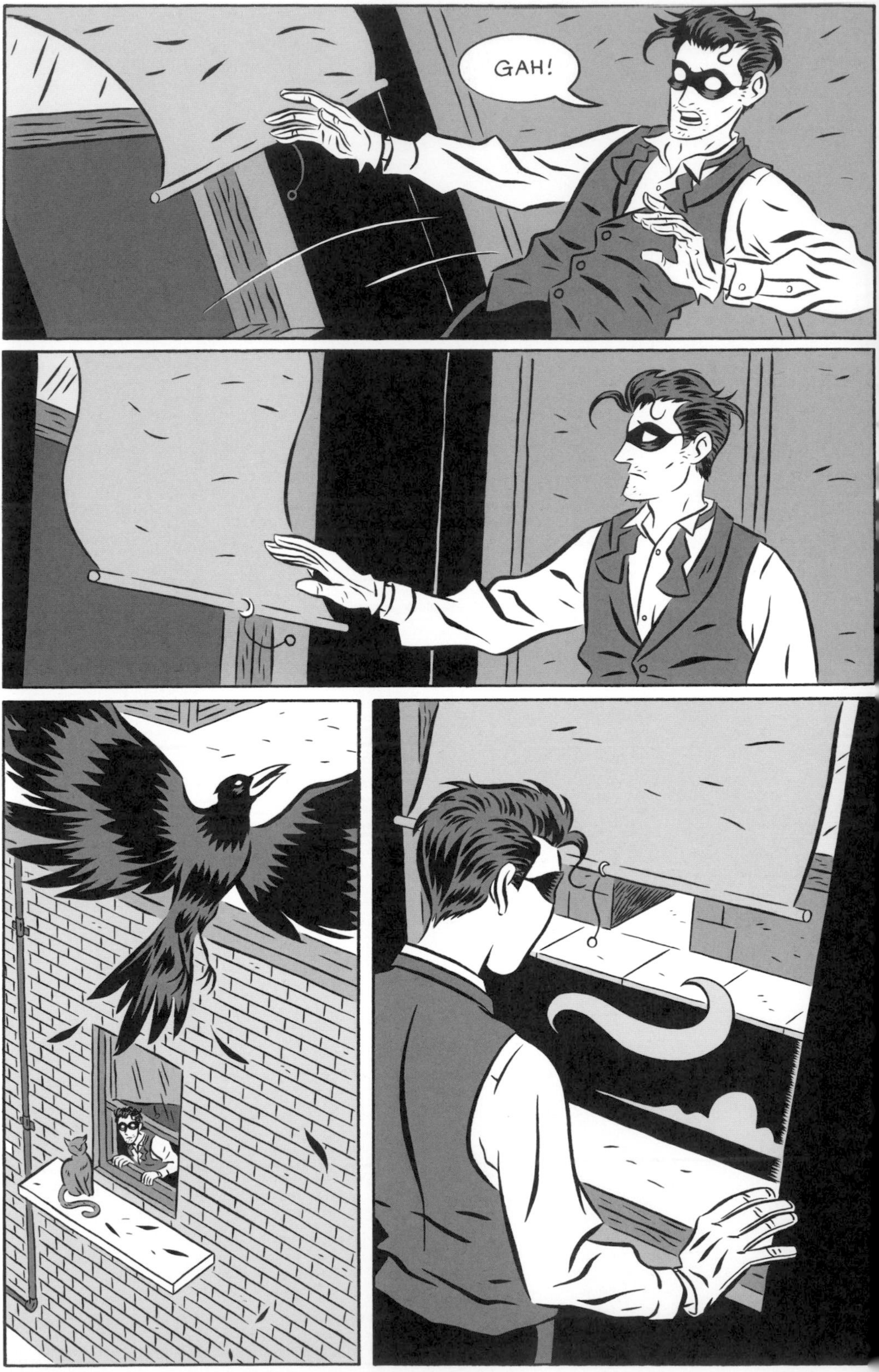
GAH!

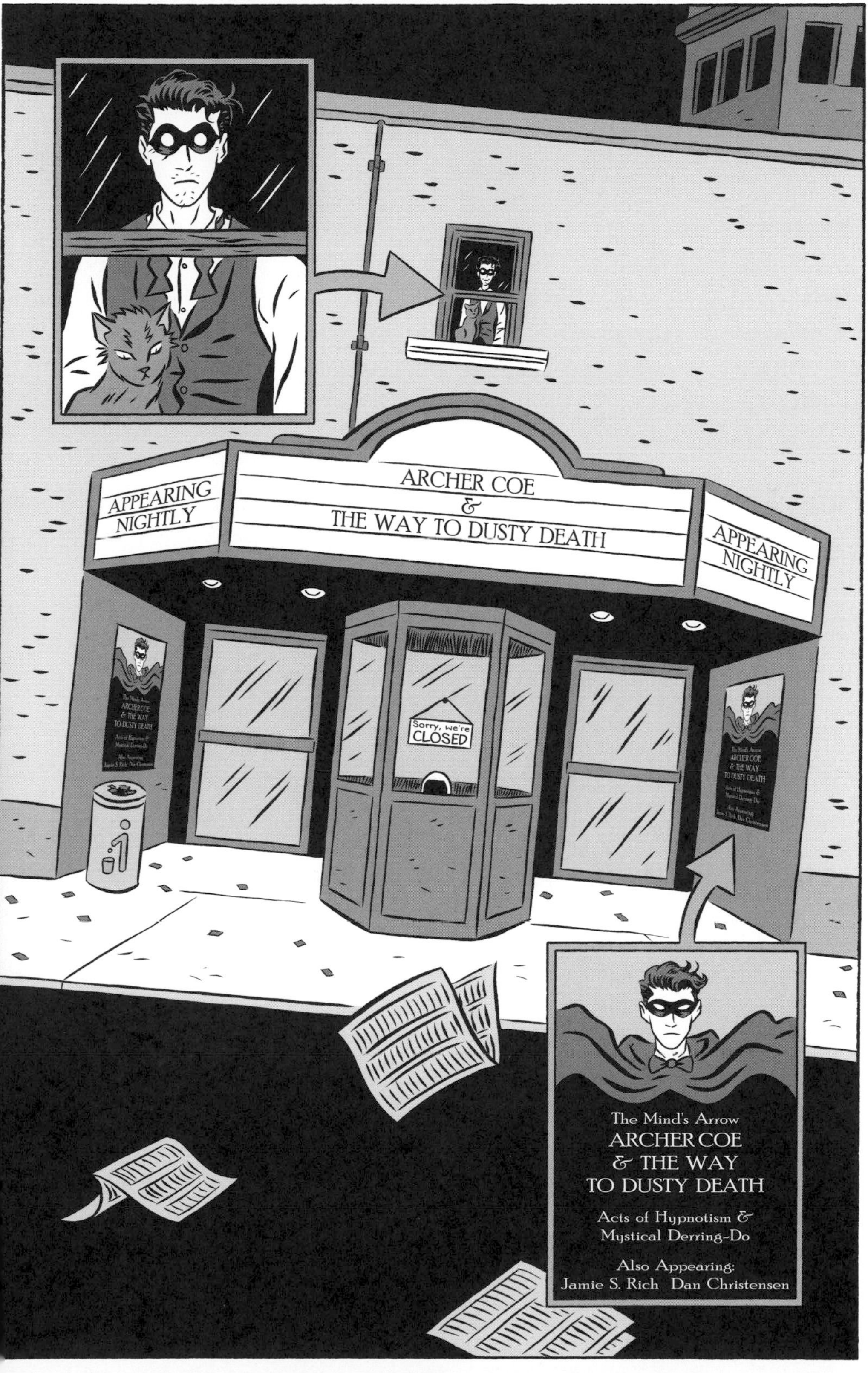
APPEARING NIGHTLY
ARCHER COE
&
THE WAY TO DUSTY DEATH
APPEARING NIGHTLY
Sorry, we're CLOSED
The Mind's Arrow
ARCHER COE
& THE WAY
TO DUSTY DEATH
Acts of Hypnotism &
Mystical Derring-Do
Also Appearing:
Jamie S. Rich Dan Christensen

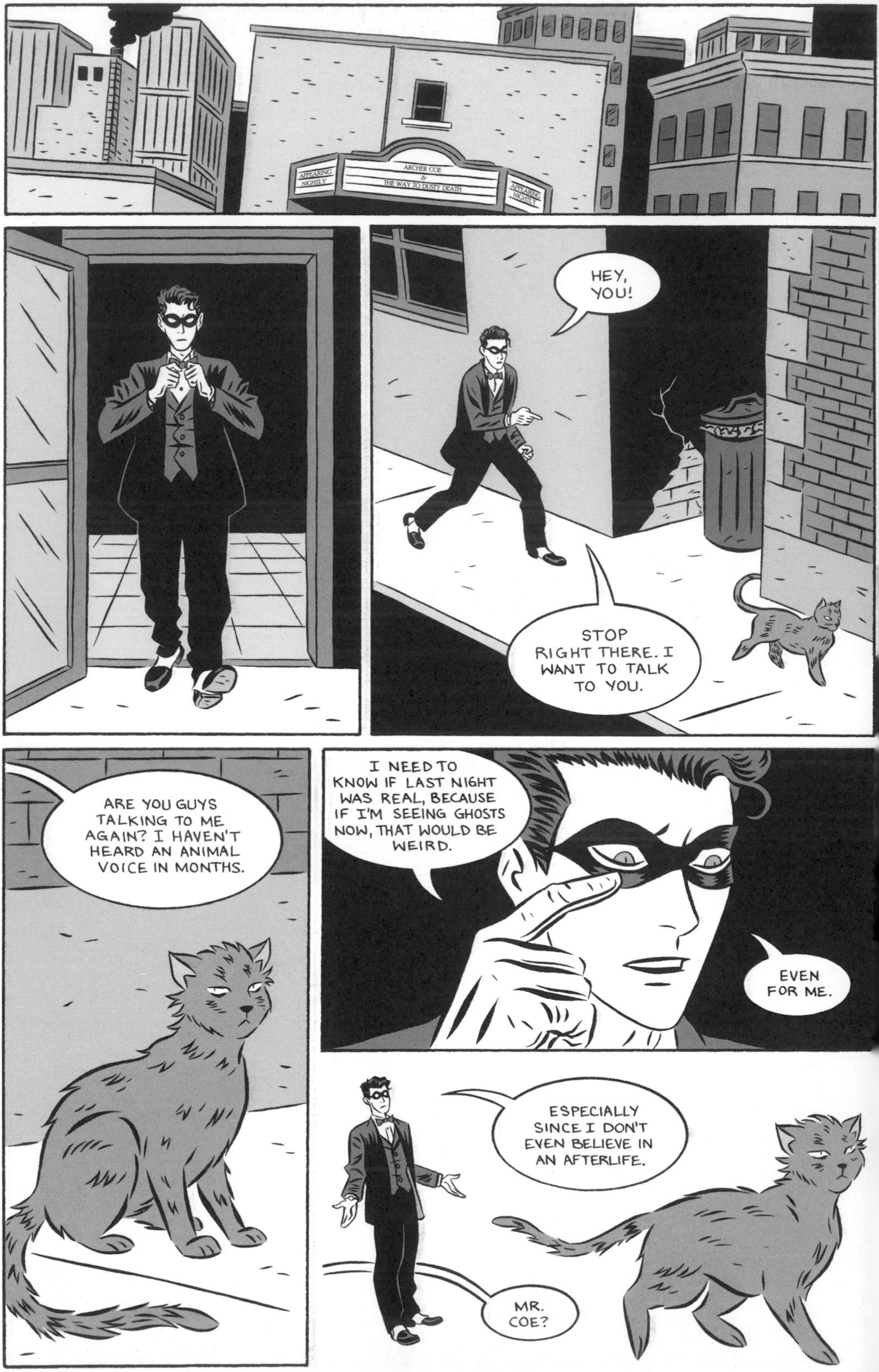
APPEARING NIGHTLY
ARCHER COE & THE WAY TO DUSTY DEATH
APPEARING NIGHTLY
HEY, YOU!
STOP RIGHT THERE. I WANT TO TALK TO YOU.
ARE YOU GUYS TALKING TO ME AGAIN? I HAVEN'T HEARD AN ANIMAL VOICE IN MONTHS.
I NEED TO KNOW IF LAST NIGHT WAS REAL, BECAUSE IF I'M SEEING GHOSTS NOW, THAT WOULD BE WEIRD.
EVEN FOR ME.
ESPECIALLY SINCE I DON'T EVEN BELIEVE IN AN AFTERLIFE.
MR. COE?

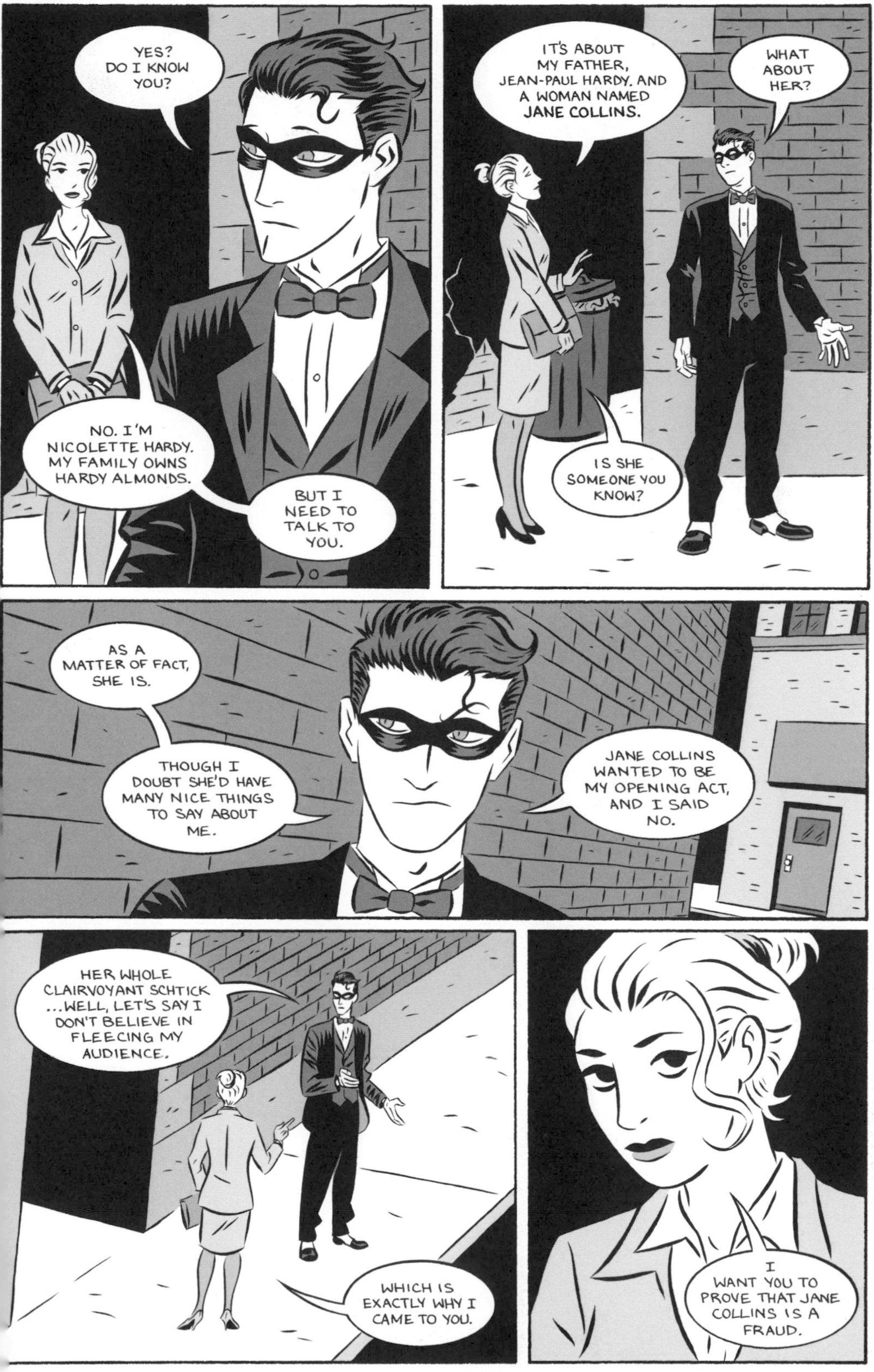
YES? DO I KNOW YOU?
NO. I'M NICOLETTE HARDY. MY FAMILY OWNS HARDY ALMONDS.
BUT I NEED TO TALK TO YOU.
IT'S ABOUT MY FATHER, JEAN-PAUL HARDY. AND A WOMAN NAMED JANE COLLINS.
WHAT ABOUT HER?
IS SHE SOMEONE YOU KNOW?
AS A MATTER OF FACT, SHE IS.
THOUGH I DOUBT SHE'D HAVE MANY NICE THINGS TO SAY ABOUT ME.
JANE COLLINS WANTED TO BE MY OPENING ACT, AND I SAID NO.
HER WHOLE CLAIRVOYANT SCHTICK ...WELL, LET'S SAY I DON'T BELIEVE IN FLEECING MY AUDIENCE.
WHICH IS EXACTLY WHY I CAME TO YOU.
I WANT YOU TO PROVE THAT JANE COLLINS IS A FRAUD.

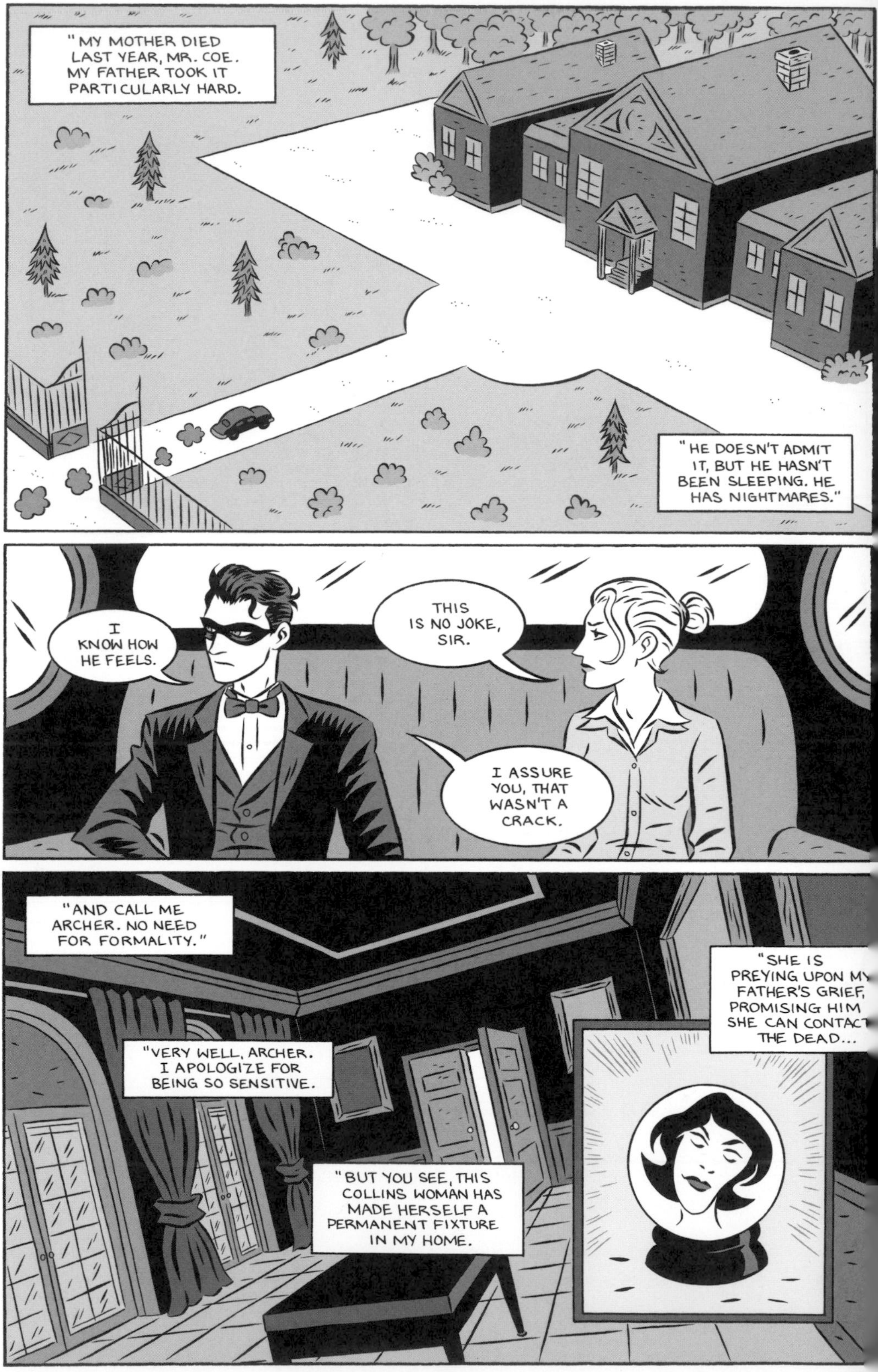
"MY MOTHER DIED LAST YEAR, MR. COE. MY FATHER TOOK IT PARTICULARLY HARD.
"HE DOESN'T ADMIT IT, BUT HE HASN'T BEEN SLEEPING. HE HAS NIGHTMARES."
I KNOW HOW HE FEELS.
THIS IS NO JOKE, SIR.
I ASSURE YOU, THAT WASN'T A CRACK.
"AND CALL ME ARCHER. NO NEED FOR FORMALITY."
"VERY WELL, ARCHER. I APOLOGIZE FOR BEING SO SENSITIVE.
"BUT YOU SEE, THIS COLLINS WOMAN HAS MADE HERSELF A PERMANENT FIXTURE IN MY HOME.
"SHE IS PREYING UPON MY FATHER'S GRIEF, PROMISING HIM SHE CAN CONTACT THE DEAD...

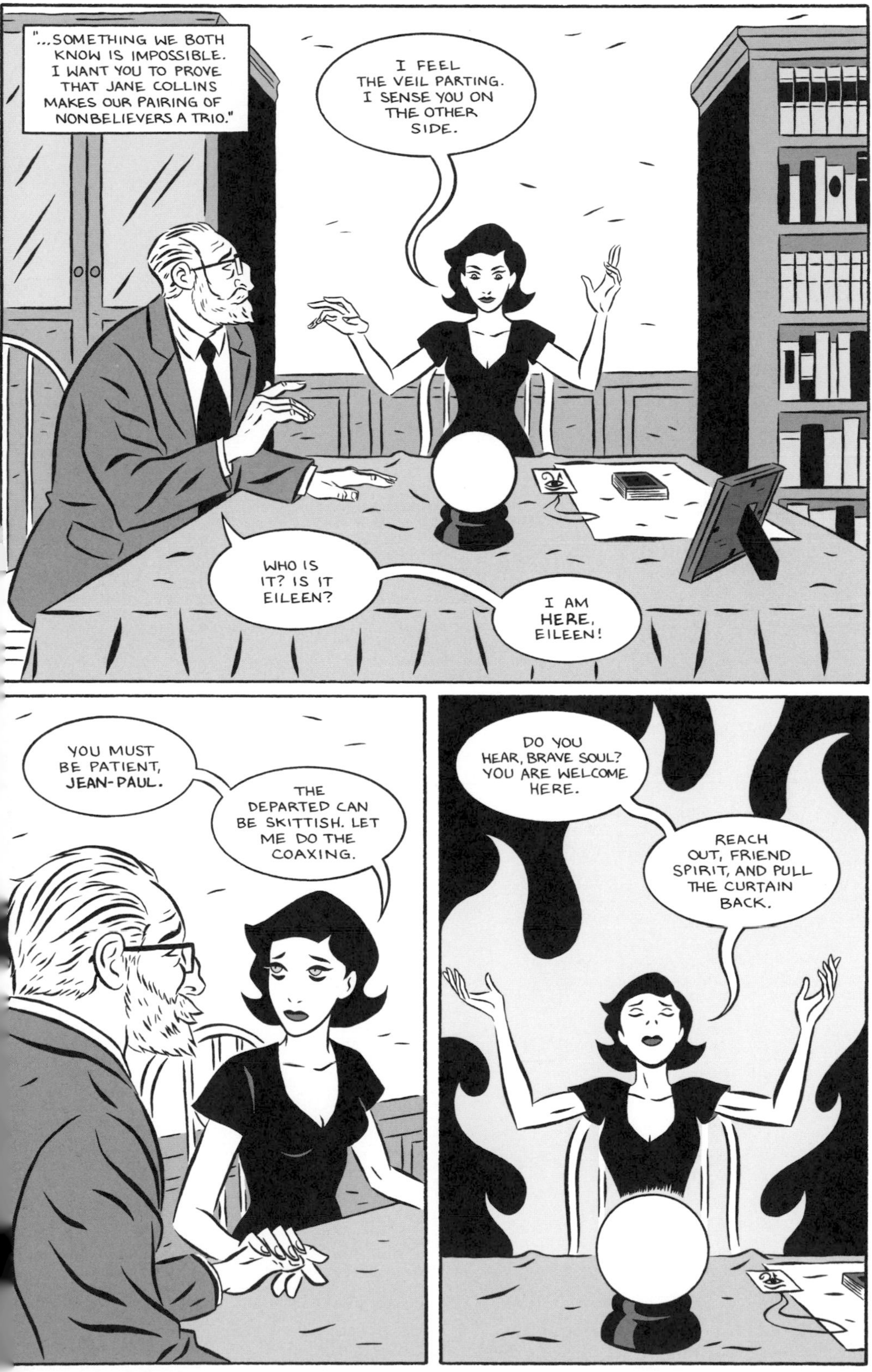
"...SOMETHING WE BOTH KNOW IS IMPOSSIBLE. I WANT YOU TO PROVE THAT JANE COLLINS MAKES OUR PAIRING OF NONBELIEVERS A TRIO."
I FEEL THE VEIL PARTING. I SENSE YOU ON THE OTHER SIDE.
WHO IS IT? IS IT EILEEN?
I AM **HERE**, EILEEN!
YOU MUST BE PATIENT, **JEAN-PAUL.**
THE DEPARTED CAN BE SKITTISH. LET ME DO THE COAXING.
DO YOU HEAR, BRAVE SOUL? YOU ARE WELCOME HERE.
REACH OUT, FRIEND SPIRIT, AND PULL THE CURTAIN BACK.

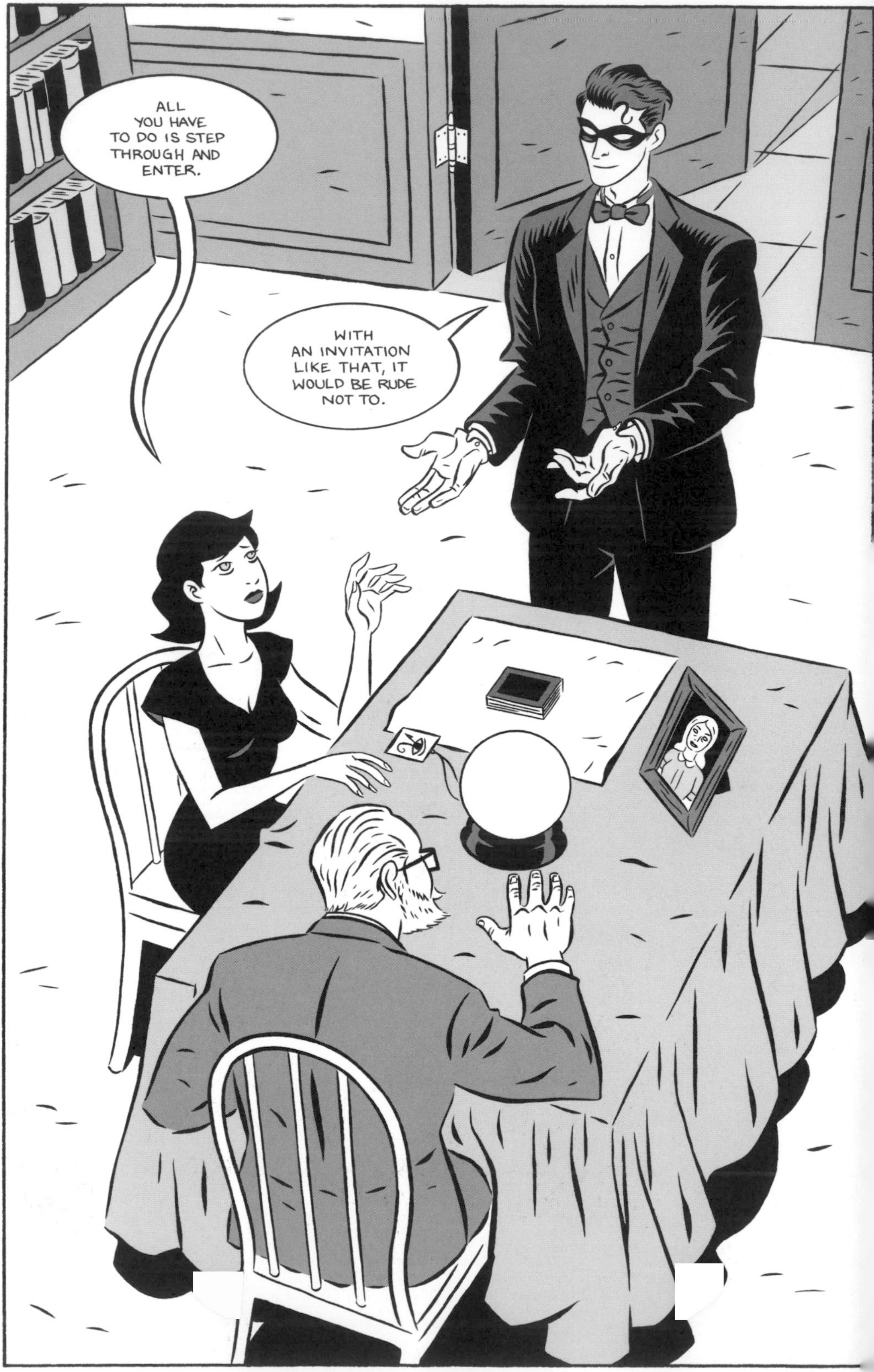
ALL YOU HAVE TO DO IS STEP THROUGH AND ENTER.
WITH AN INVITATION LIKE THAT, IT WOULD BE RUDE NOT TO.

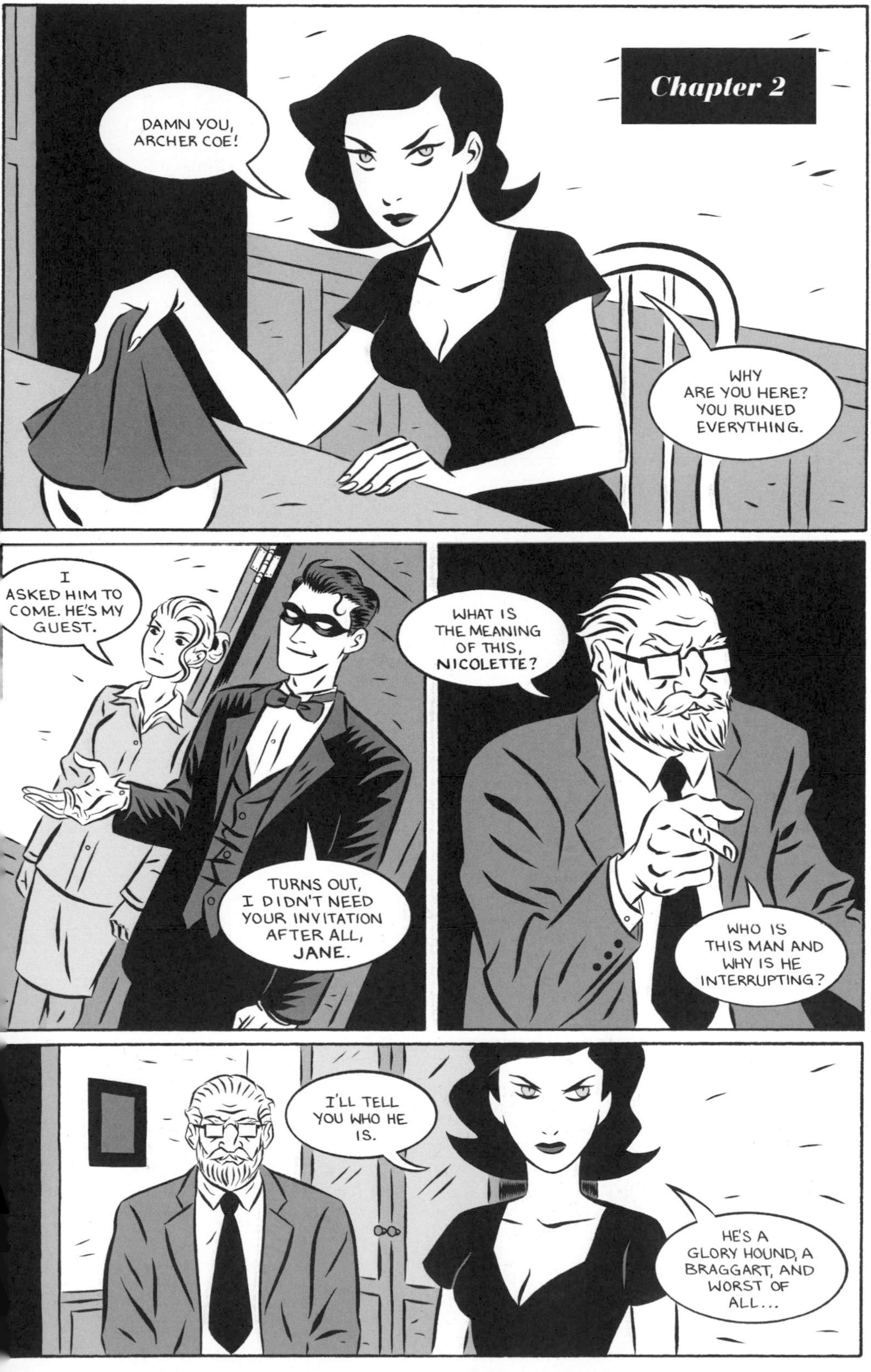
Chapter 2
DAMN YOU, ARCHER COE!
WHY ARE YOU HERE? YOU RUINED EVERYTHING.
I ASKED HIM TO COME. HE'S MY GUEST.
TURNS OUT, I DIDN'T NEED YOUR INVITATION AFTER ALL, JANE.
WHAT IS THE MEANING OF THIS, NICOLETTE?
WHO IS THIS MAN AND WHY IS HE INTERRUPTING?
I'LL TELL YOU WHO HE IS.
HE'S A GLORY HOUND, A BRAGGART, AND WORST OF ALL...

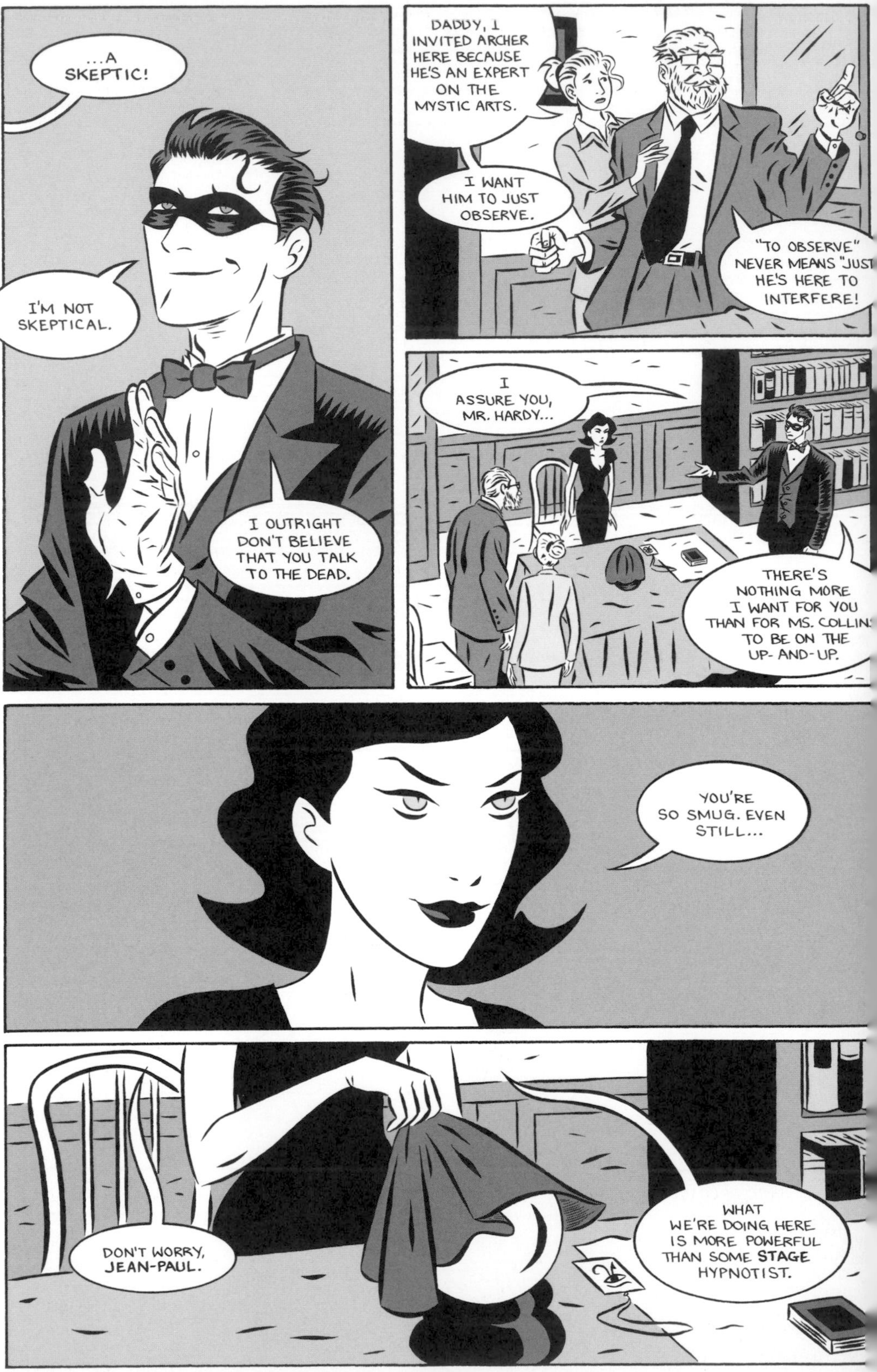
...A SKEPTIC!
I'M NOT SKEPTICAL.
I OUTRIGHT DON'T BELIEVE THAT YOU TALK TO THE DEAD.
DADDY, I INVITED ARCHER HERE BECAUSE HE'S AN EXPERT ON THE MYSTIC ARTS.
I WANT HIM TO JUST OBSERVE.
"TO OBSERVE" NEVER MEANS "JUST HE'S HERE TO INTERFERE!
I ASSURE YOU, MR. HARDY...
THERE'S NOTHING MORE I WANT FOR YOU THAN FOR MS. COLLINS TO BE ON THE UP-AND-UP.
YOU'RE SO SMUG. EVEN STILL...
DON'T WORRY, JEAN-PAUL.
WHAT WE'RE DOING HERE IS MORE POWERFUL THAN SOME STAGE HYPNOTIST.

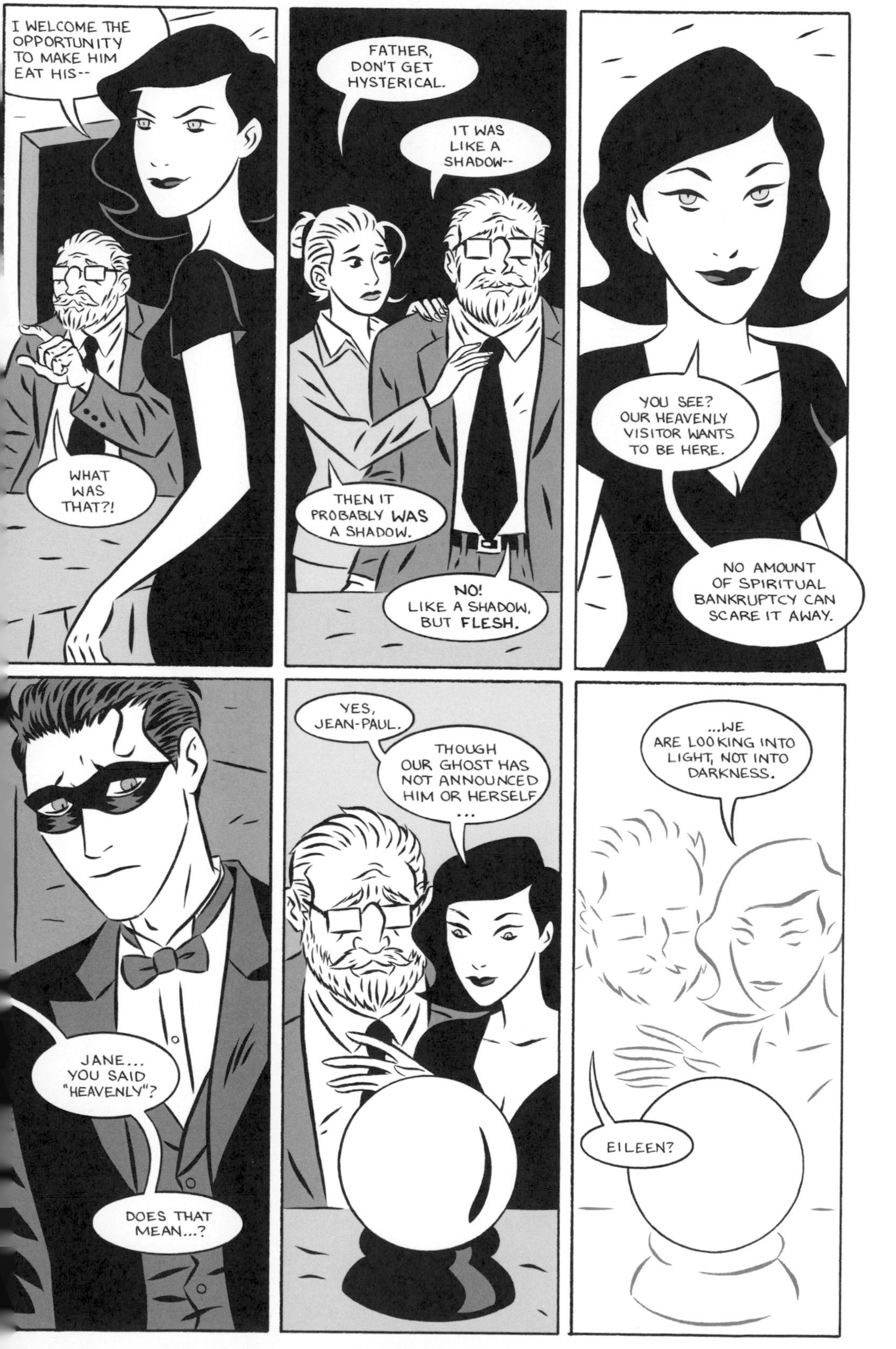
I WELCOME THE OPPORTUNITY TO MAKE HIM EAT HIS--
WHAT WAS THAT?!
FATHER, DON'T GET HYSTERICAL.
IT WAS LIKE A SHADOW--
THEN IT PROBABLY WAS A SHADOW.
NO! LIKE A SHADOW, BUT FLESH.
YOU SEE? OUR HEAVENLY VISITOR WANTS TO BE HERE.
NO AMOUNT OF SPIRITUAL BANKRUPTCY CAN SCARE IT AWAY.
JANE... YOU SAID "HEAVENLY"?
DOES THAT MEAN...?
YES, JEAN-PAUL.
THOUGH OUR GHOST HAS NOT ANNOUNCED HIM OR HERSELF ...
...WE ARE LOOKING INTO LIGHT, NOT INTO DARKNESS.
EILEEN?

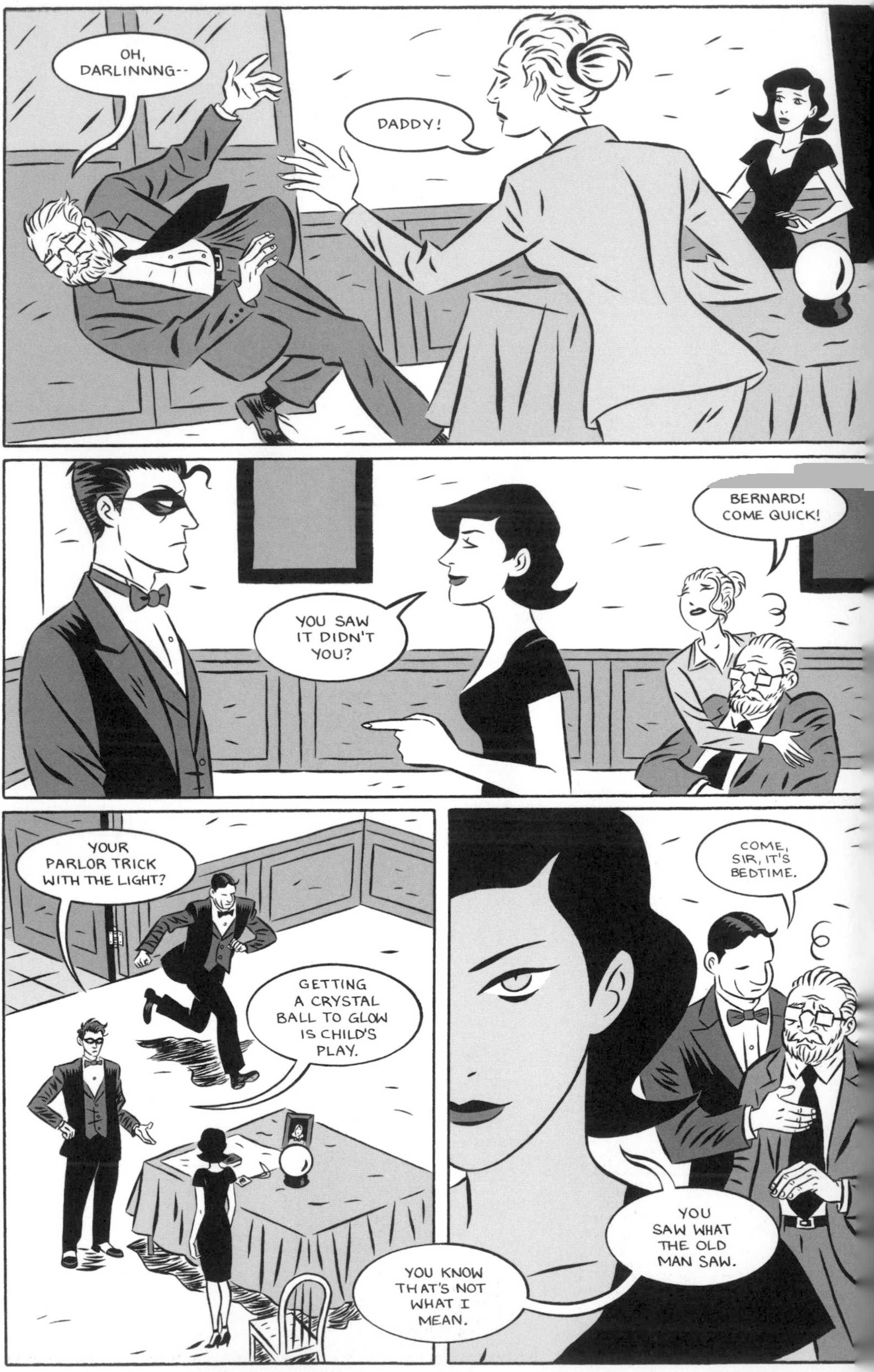
OH, DARLINNNG--
DADDY!
YOU SAW IT DIDN'T YOU?
BERNARD! COME QUICK!
YOUR PARLOR TRICK WITH THE LIGHT?
GETTING A CRYSTAL BALL TO GLOW IS CHILD'S PLAY.
COME, SIR, IT'S BEDTIME.
YOU SAW WHAT THE OLD MAN SAW.
YOU KNOW THAT'S NOT WHAT I MEAN.

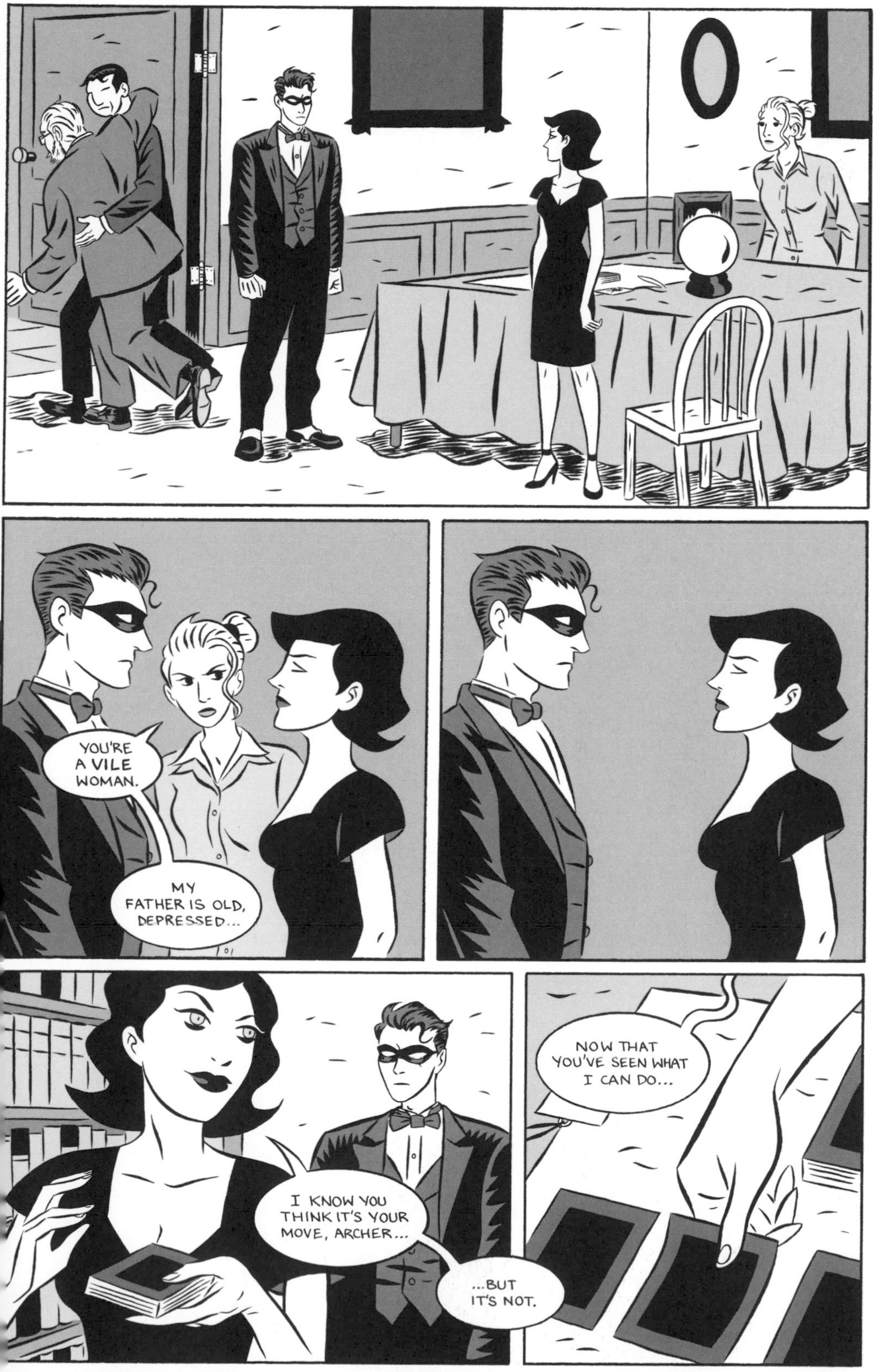
YOU'RE A VILE WOMAN.
MY FATHER IS OLD, DEPRESSED...
I KNOW YOU THINK IT'S YOUR MOVE, ARCHER...
...BUT IT'S NOT.
NOW THAT YOU'VE SEEN WHAT I CAN DO...

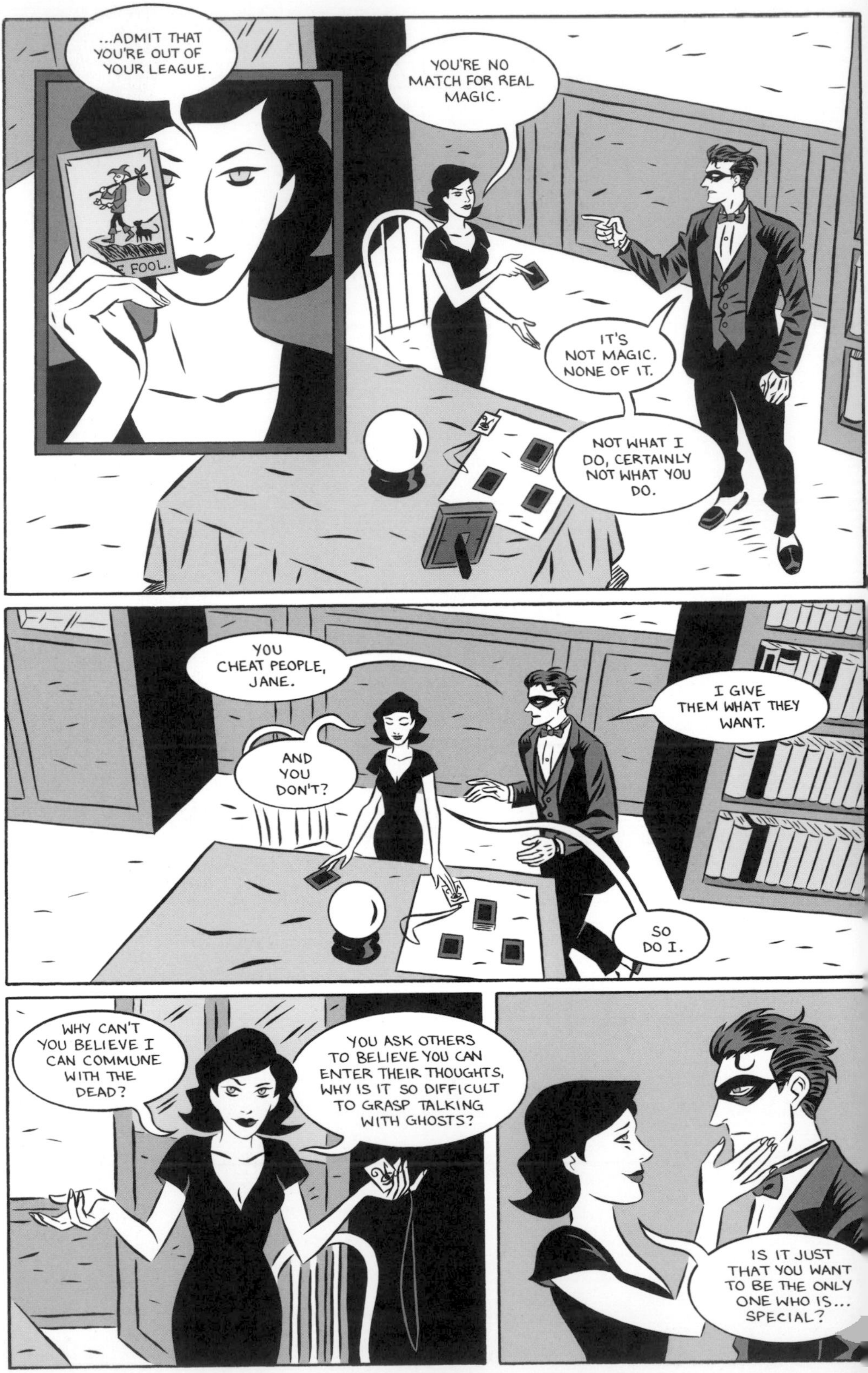
...ADMIT THAT YOU'RE OUT OF YOUR LEAGUE.
E FOOL.
YOU'RE NO MATCH FOR REAL MAGIC.
IT'S NOT MAGIC. NONE OF IT.
NOT WHAT I DO, CERTAINLY NOT WHAT YOU DO.
YOU CHEAT PEOPLE, JANE.
I GIVE THEM WHAT THEY WANT.
AND YOU DON'T?
SO DO I.
WHY CAN'T YOU BELIEVE I CAN COMMUNE WITH THE DEAD?
YOU ASK OTHERS TO BELIEVE YOU CAN ENTER THEIR THOUGHTS, WHY IS IT SO DIFFICULT TO GRASP TALKING WITH GHOSTS?
IS IT JUST THAT YOU WANT TO BE THE ONLY ONE WHO IS... SPECIAL?

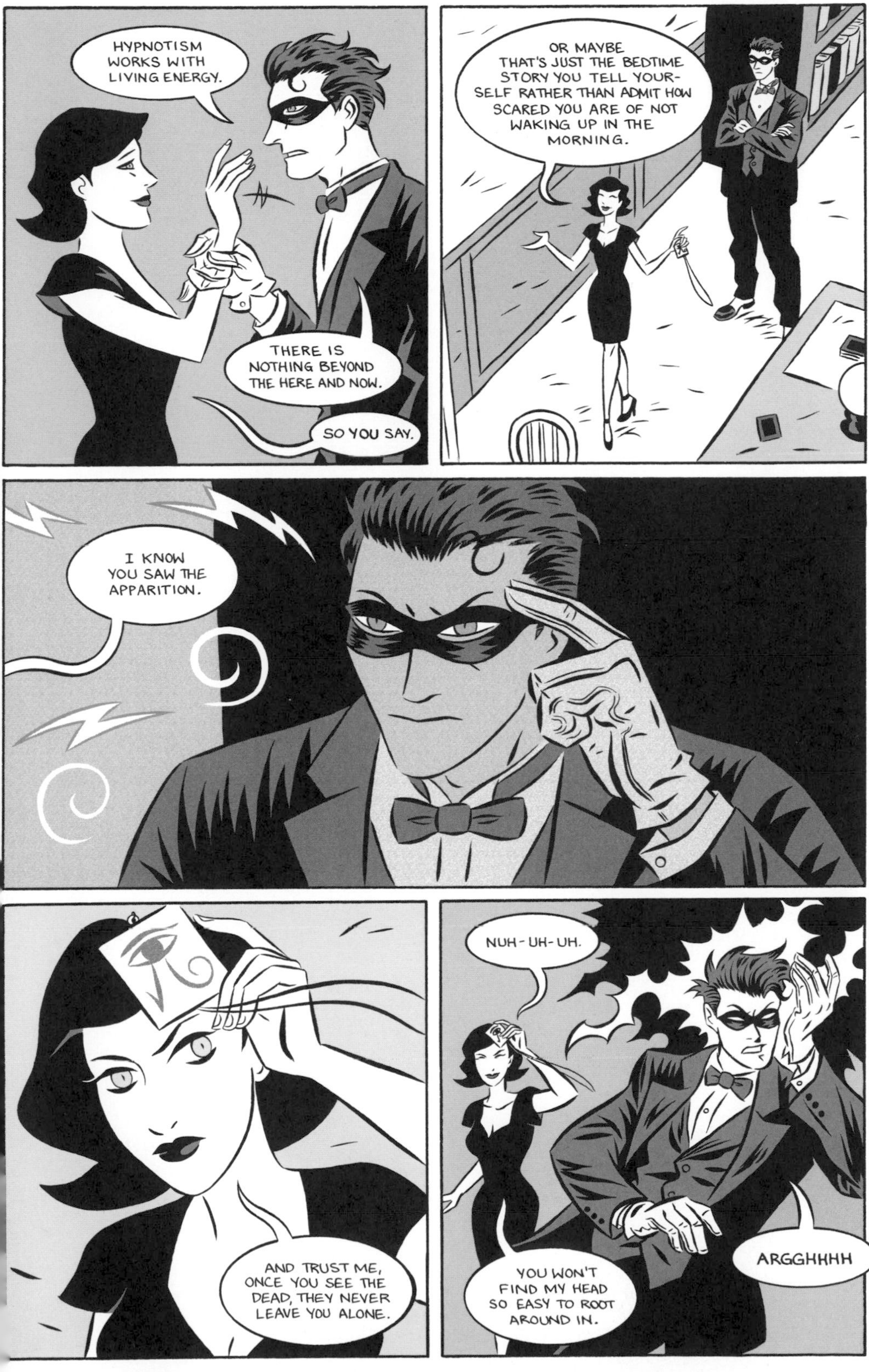
HYPNOTISM WORKS WITH LIVING ENERGY.
THERE IS NOTHING BEYOND THE HERE AND NOW.
SO YOU SAY.
OR MAYBE THAT'S JUST THE BEDTIME STORY YOU TELL YOURSELF RATHER THAN ADMIT HOW SCARED YOU ARE OF NOT WAKING UP IN THE MORNING.
I KNOW YOU SAW THE APPARITION.
AND TRUST ME, ONCE YOU SEE THE DEAD, THEY NEVER LEAVE YOU ALONE.
NUH-UH-UH.
YOU WON'T FIND MY HEAD SO EASY TO ROOT AROUND IN.
ARGGHHHH

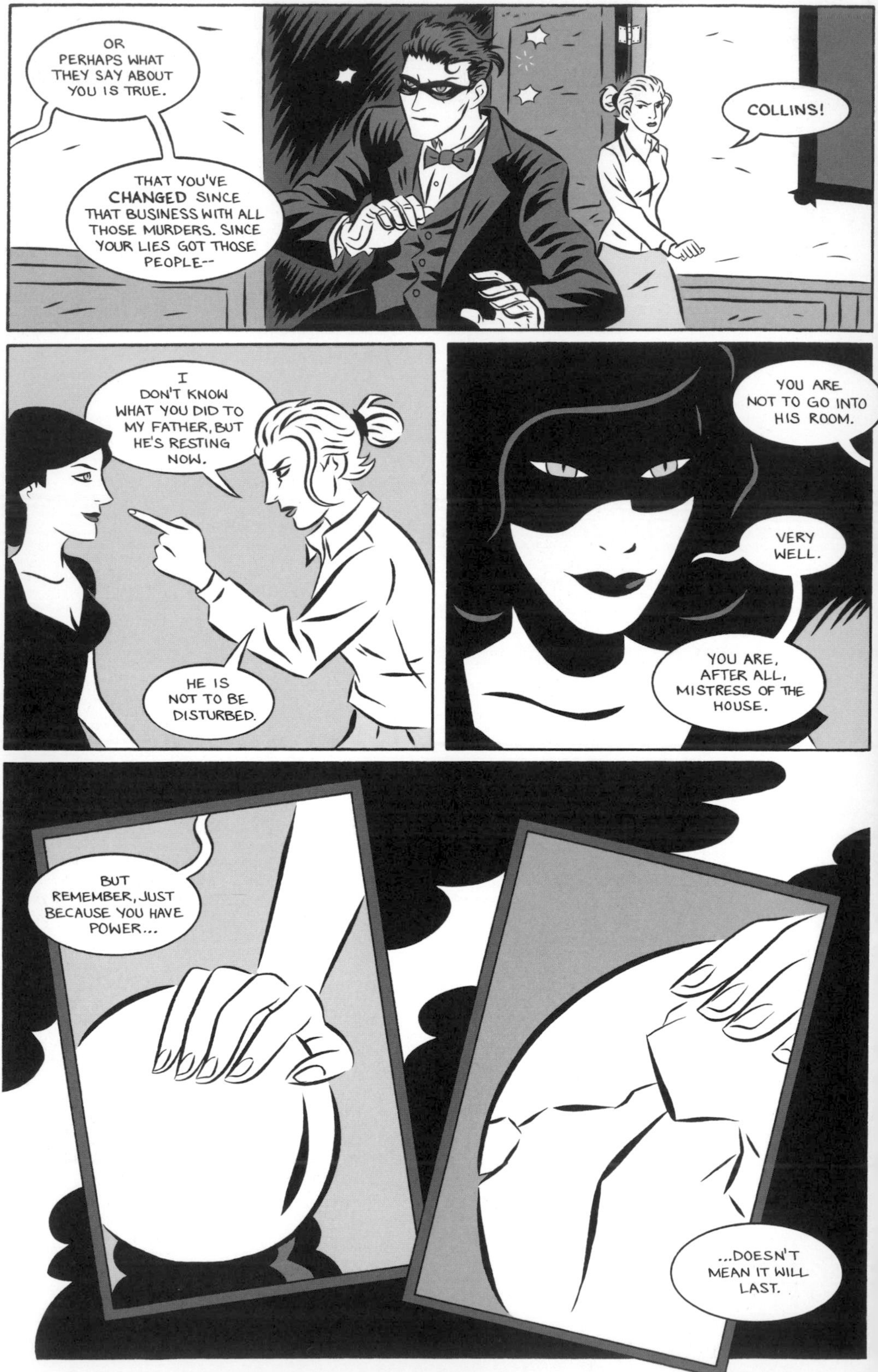
OR PERHAPS WHAT THEY SAY ABOUT YOU IS TRUE.
THAT YOU'VE CHANGED SINCE THAT BUSINESS WITH ALL THOSE MURDERS. SINCE YOUR LIES GOT THOSE PEOPLE--
COLLINS!
I DON'T KNOW WHAT YOU DID TO MY FATHER, BUT HE'S RESTING NOW.
HE IS NOT TO BE DISTURBED.
YOU ARE NOT TO GO INTO HIS ROOM.
VERY WELL.
YOU ARE, AFTER ALL, MISTRESS OF THE HOUSE.
BUT REMEMBER, JUST BECAUSE YOU HAVE POWER...
...DOESN'T MEAN IT WILL LAST.

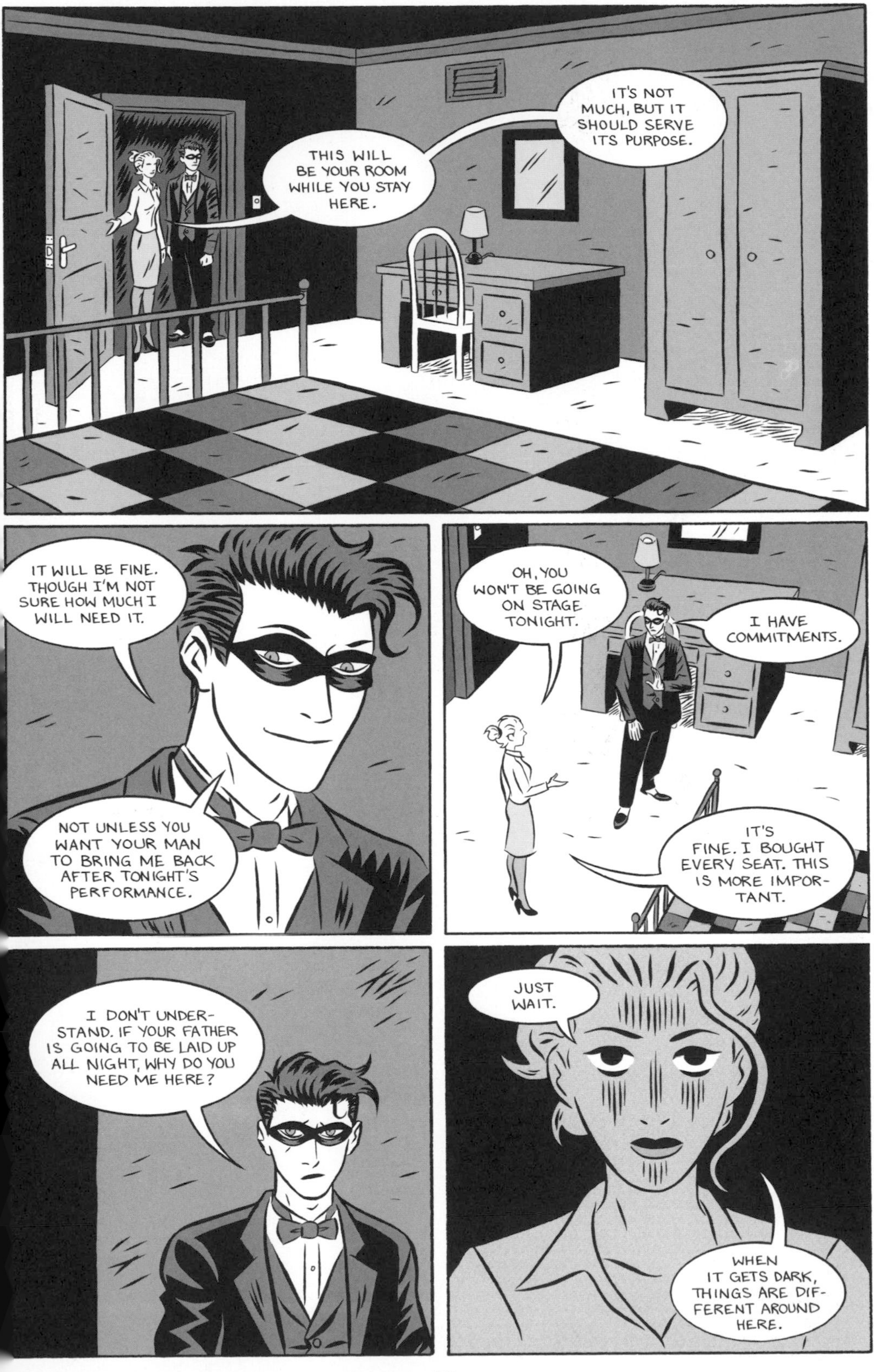

THIS WILL BE YOUR ROOM WHILE YOU STAY HERE.
IT'S NOT MUCH, BUT IT SHOULD SERVE ITS PURPOSE.
IT WILL BE FINE. THOUGH I'M NOT SURE HOW MUCH I WILL NEED IT.
NOT UNLESS YOU WANT YOUR MAN TO BRING ME BACK AFTER TONIGHT'S PERFORMANCE.
OH, YOU WON'T BE GOING ON STAGE TONIGHT.
I HAVE COMMITMENTS.
IT'S FINE. I BOUGHT EVERY SEAT. THIS IS MORE IMPOR-TANT.
I DON'T UNDER-STAND. IF YOUR FATHER IS GOING TO BE LAID UP ALL NIGHT, WHY DO YOU NEED ME HERE?
JUST WAIT.
WHEN IT GETS DARK, THINGS ARE DIF-FERENT AROUND HERE.

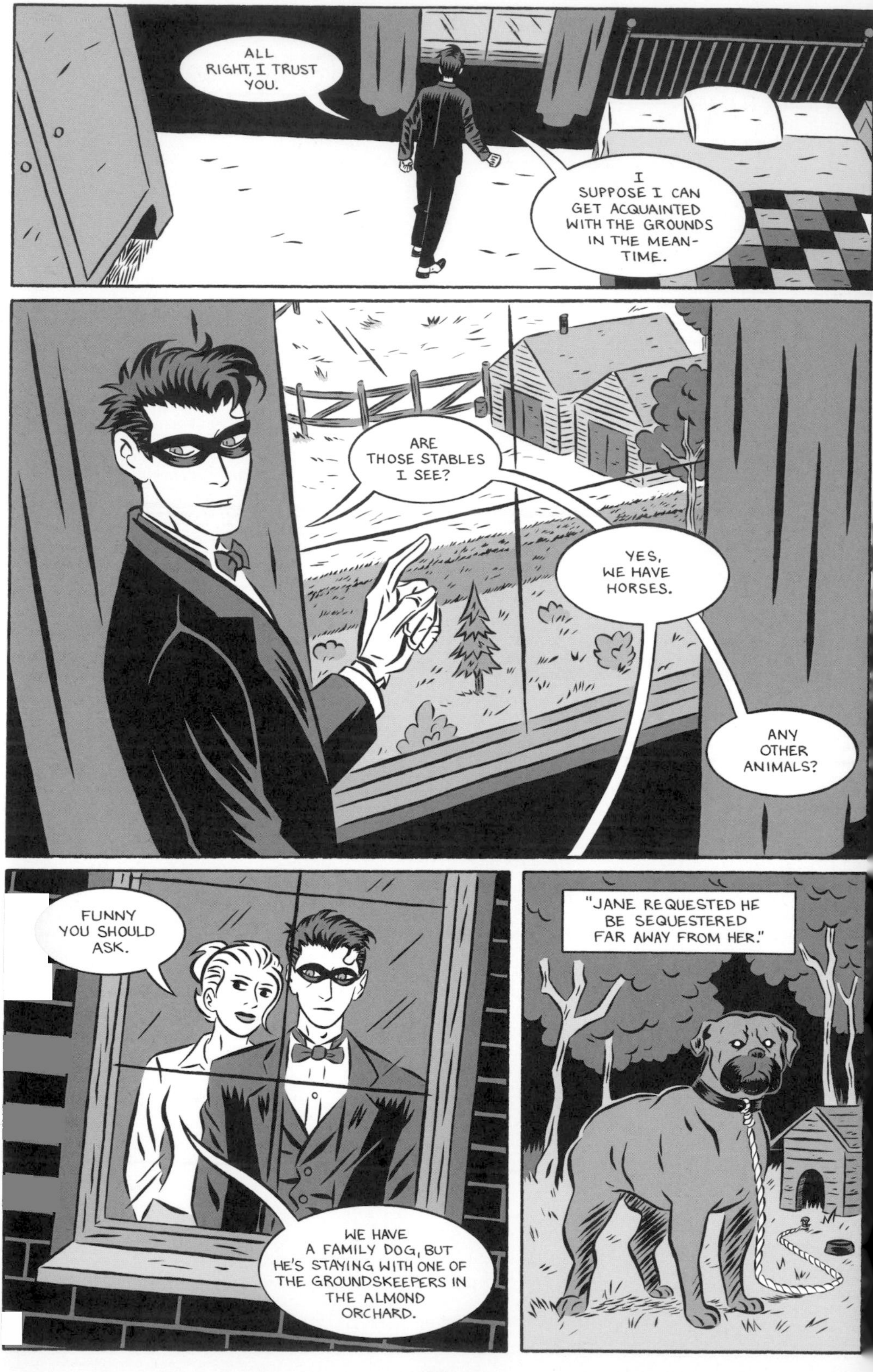
ALL RIGHT, I TRUST YOU.
I SUPPOSE I CAN GET ACQUAINTED WITH THE GROUNDS IN THE MEAN-TIME.
ARE THOSE STABLES I SEE?
YES, WE HAVE HORSES.
ANY OTHER ANIMALS?
FUNNY YOU SHOULD ASK.
WE HAVE A FAMILY DOG, BUT HE'S STAYING WITH ONE OF THE GROUNDSKEEPERS IN THE ALMOND ORCHARD.
"JANE REQUESTED HE BE SEQUESTERED FAR AWAY FROM HER."

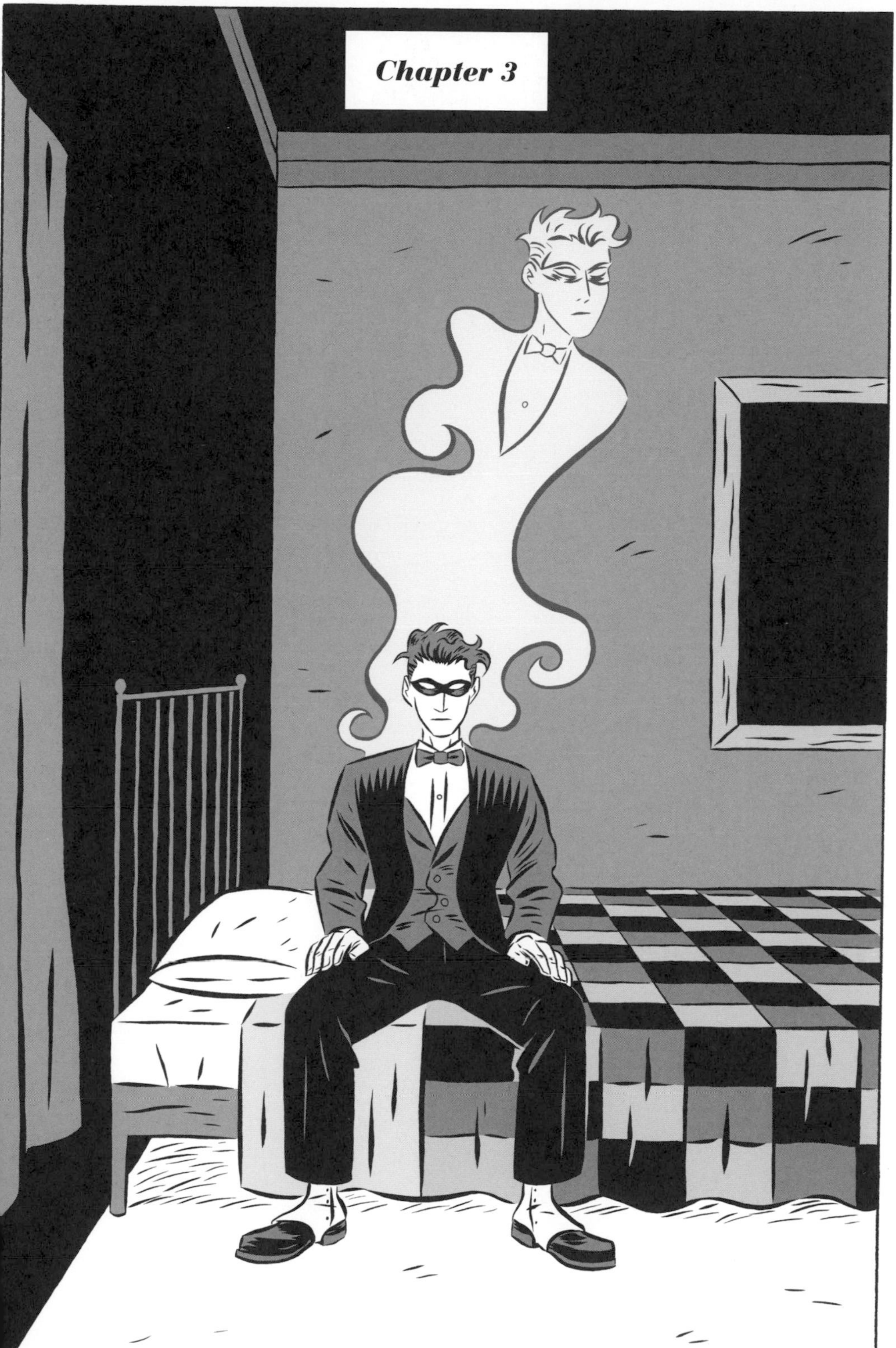
Chapter 3

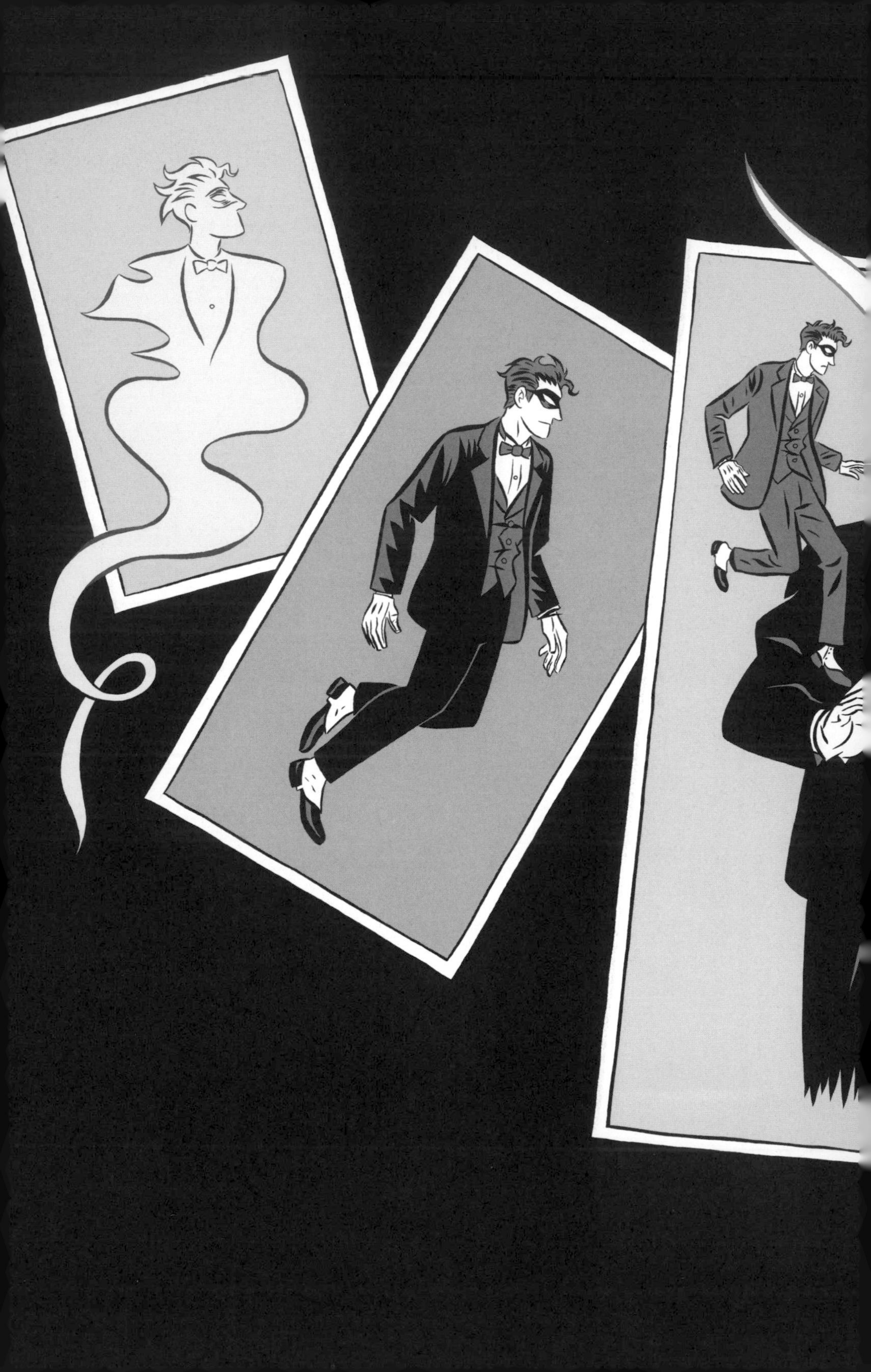

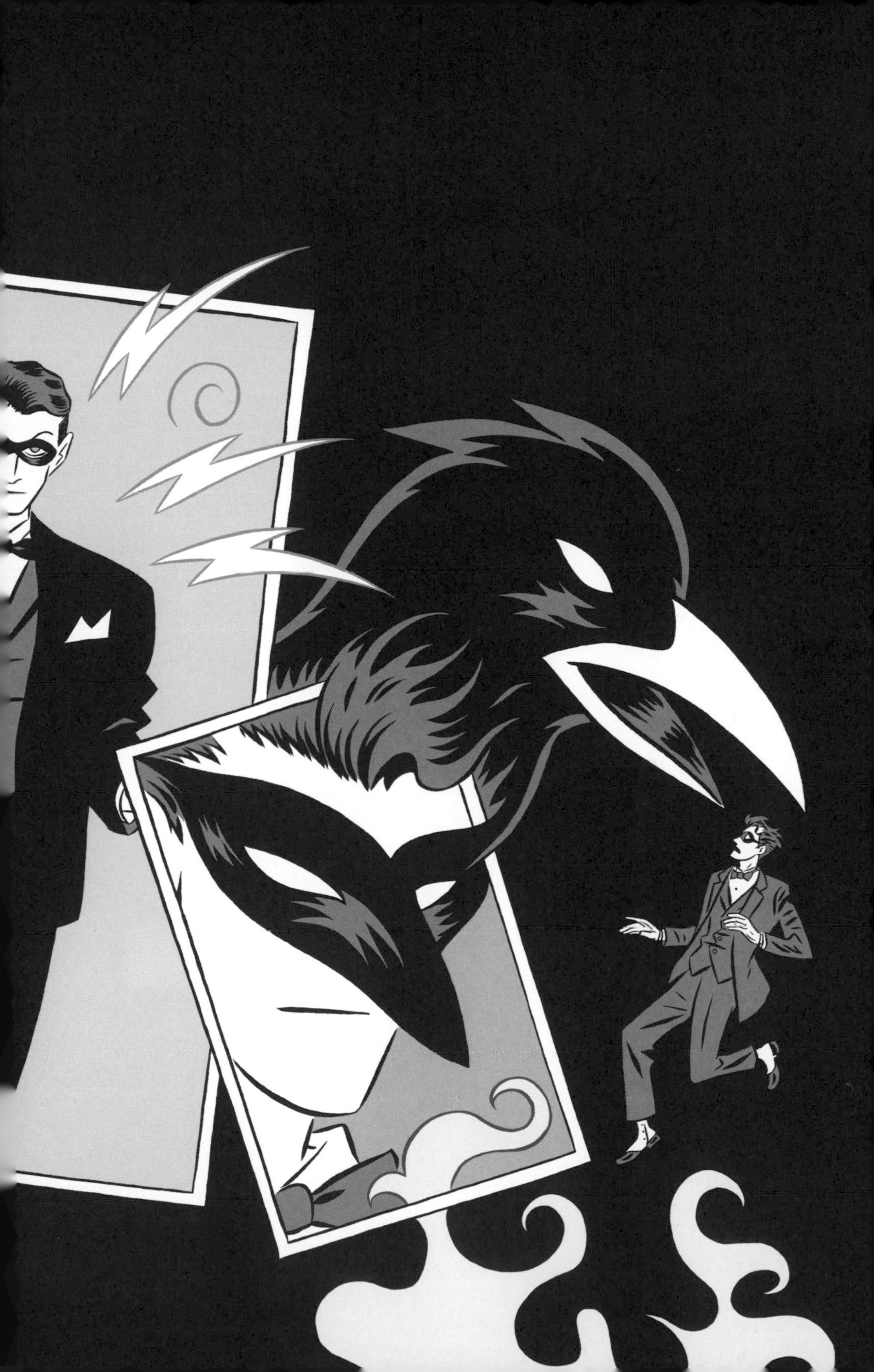

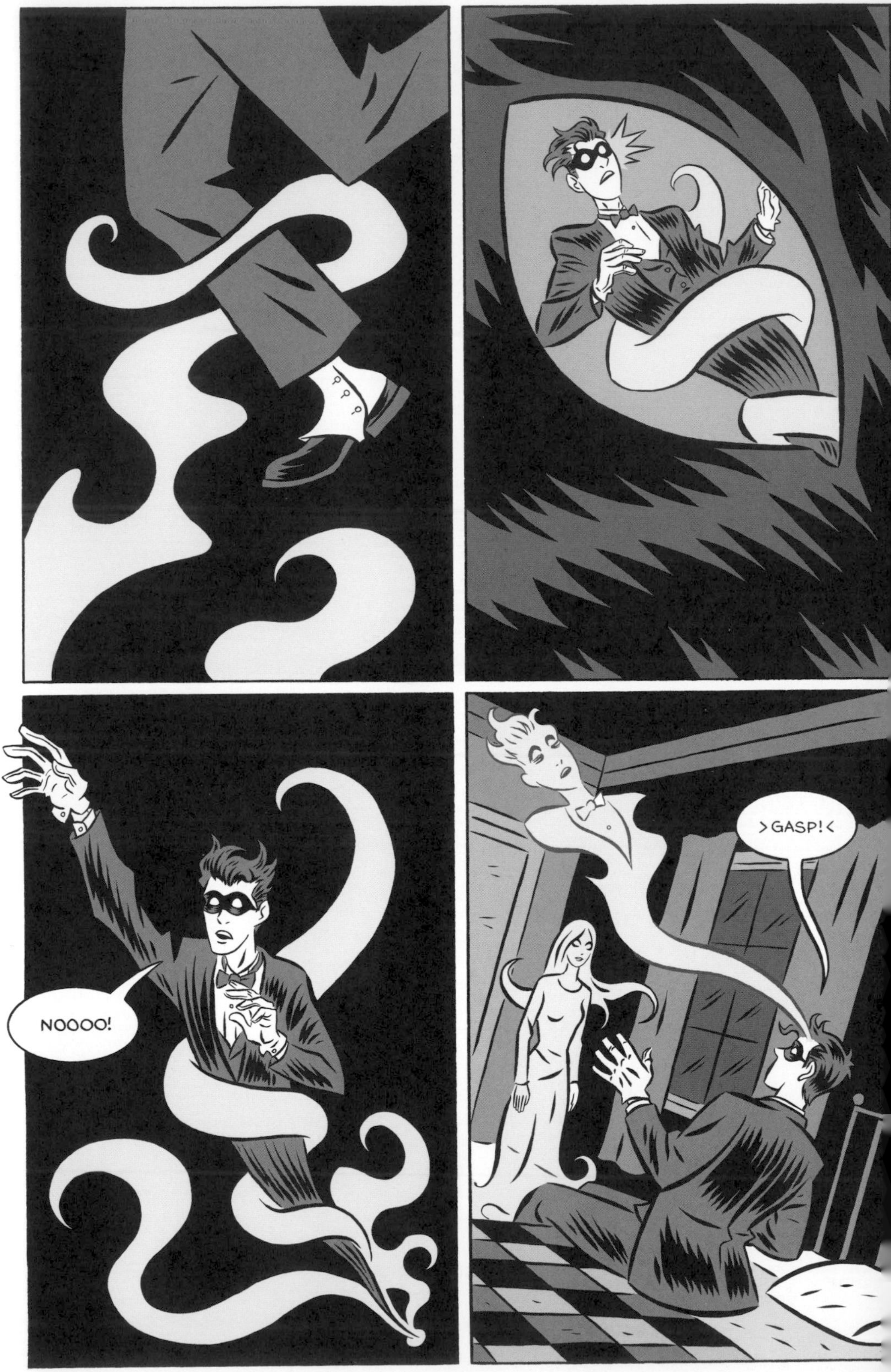
NOOOO!
>GASP!<

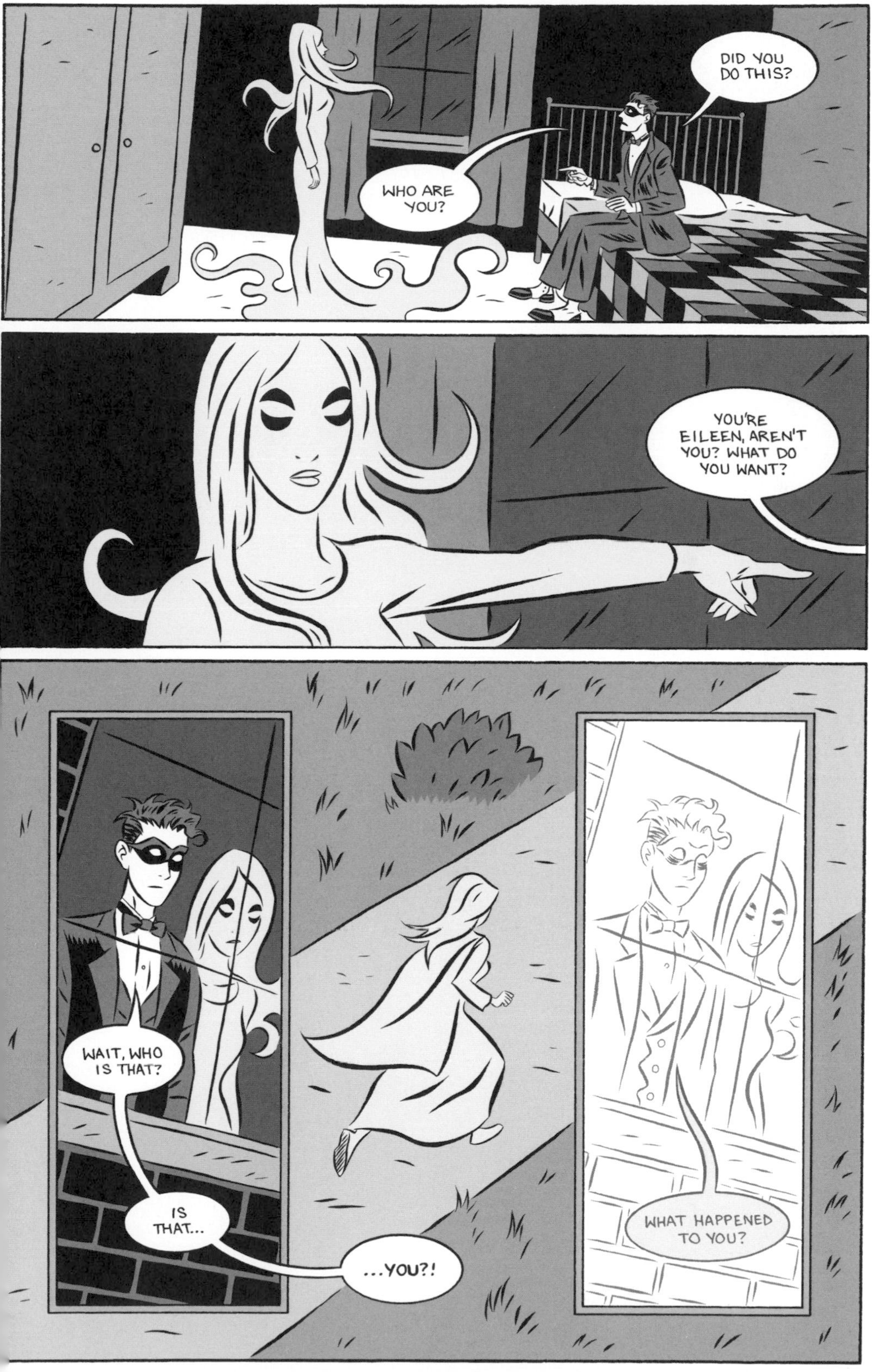
DID YOU DO THIS?
WHO ARE YOU?
YOU'RE EILEEN, AREN'T YOU? WHAT DO YOU WANT?
WAIT, WHO IS THAT?
IS THAT...
...YOU?!
WHAT HAPPENED TO YOU?

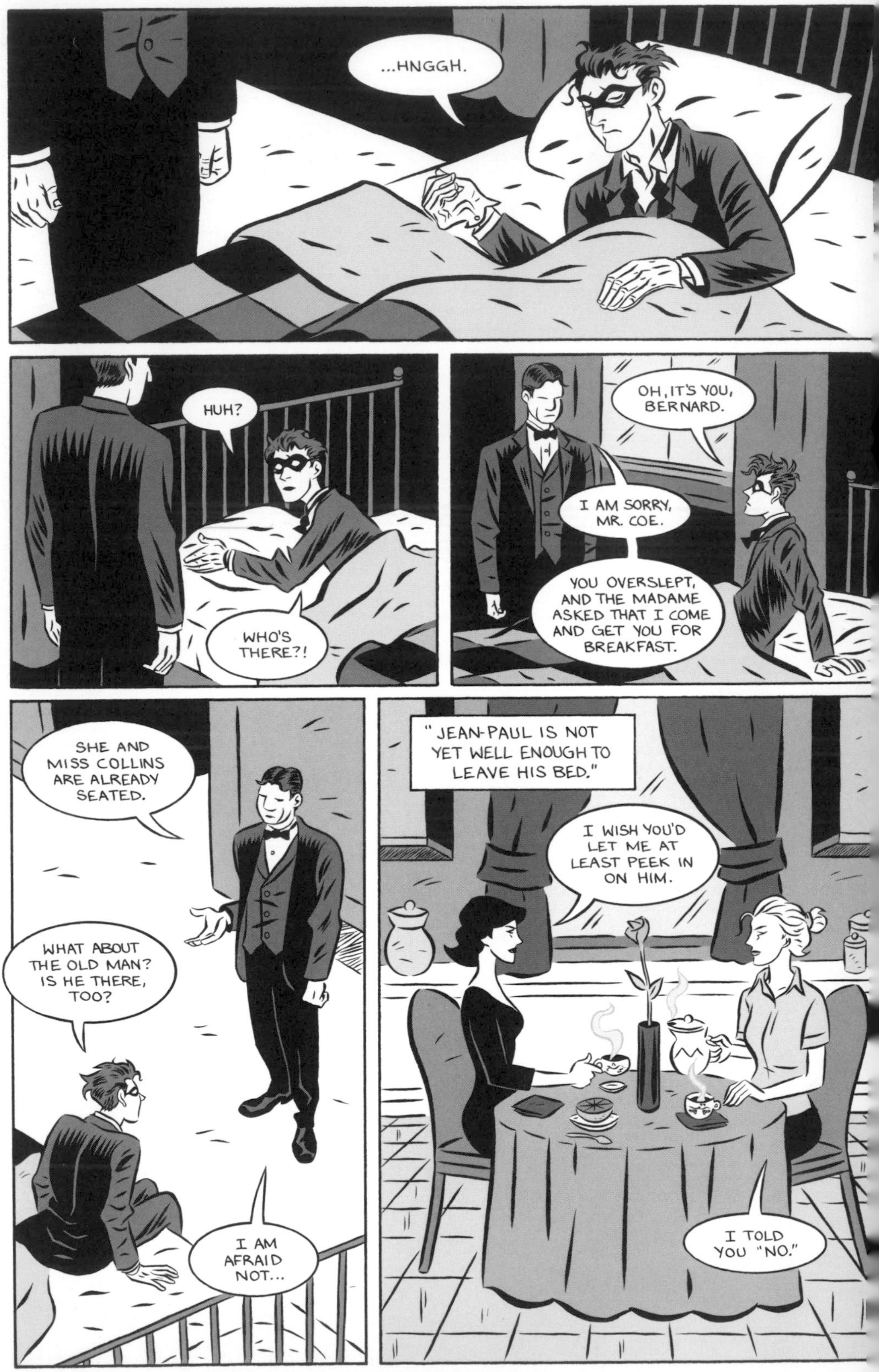
...HNGGH.
HUH?
WHO'S THERE?!
OH, IT'S YOU, BERNARD.
I AM SORRY, MR. COE.
YOU OVERSLEPT, AND THE MADAME ASKED THAT I COME AND GET YOU FOR BREAKFAST.
SHE AND MISS COLLINS ARE ALREADY SEATED.
WHAT ABOUT THE OLD MAN? IS HE THERE, TOO?
I AM AFRAID NOT...
"JEAN-PAUL IS NOT YET WELL ENOUGH TO LEAVE HIS BED."
I WISH YOU'D LET ME AT LEAST PEEK IN ON HIM.
I TOLD YOU "NO."

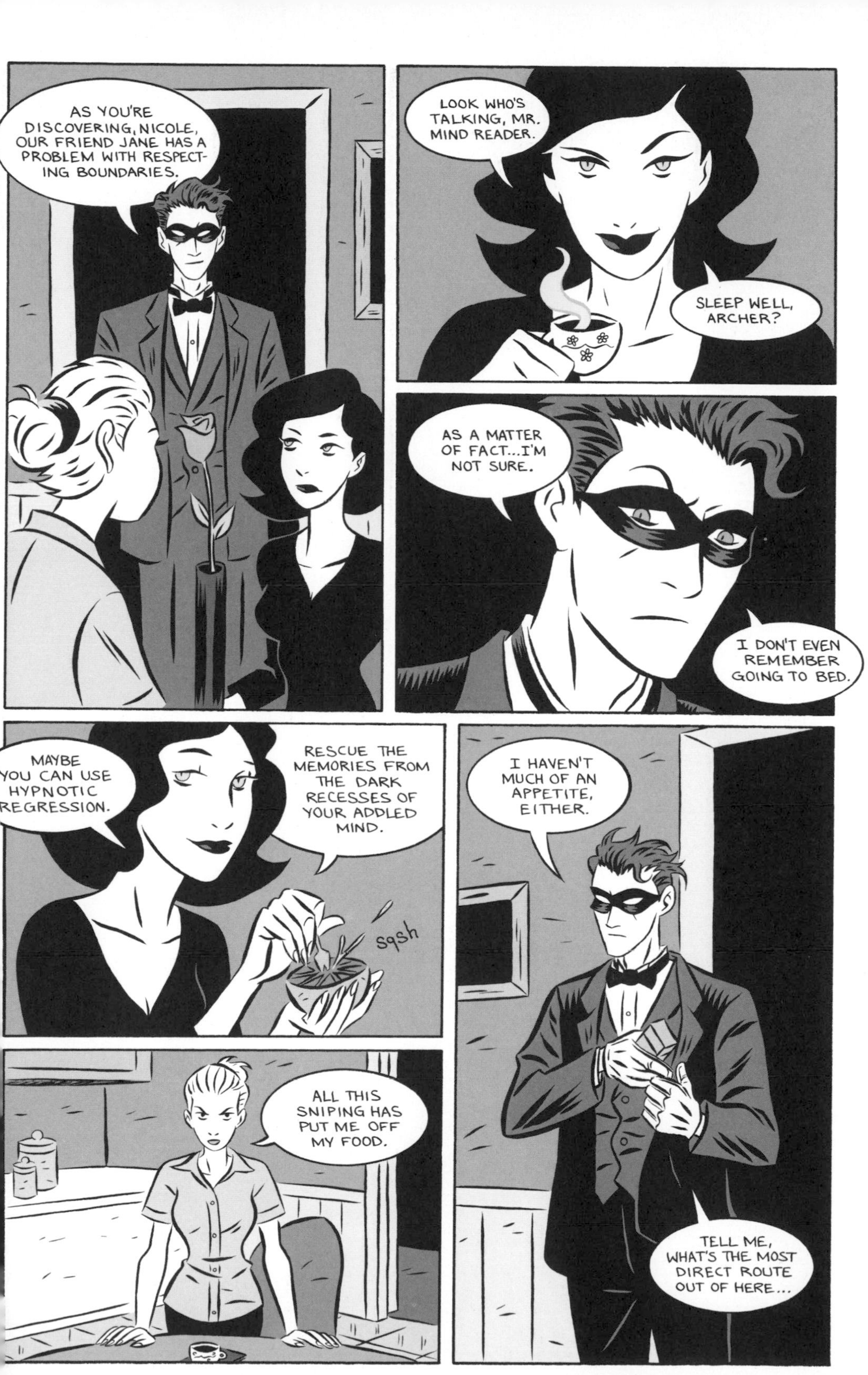
AS YOU'RE DISCOVERING, NICOLE, OUR FRIEND JANE HAS A PROBLEM WITH RESPECT-ING BOUNDARIES.
LOOK WHO'S TALKING, MR. MIND READER.
SLEEP WELL, ARCHER?
AS A MATTER OF FACT...I'M NOT SURE.
I DON'T EVEN REMEMBER GOING TO BED.
MAYBE YOU CAN USE HYPNOTIC REGRESSION.
RESCUE THE MEMORIES FROM THE DARK RECESSES OF YOUR ADDLED MIND.
sqsh
ALL THIS SNIPING HAS PUT ME OFF MY FOOD.
I HAVEN'T MUCH OF AN APPETITE, EITHER.
TELL ME, WHAT'S THE MOST DIRECT ROUTE OUT OF HERE...

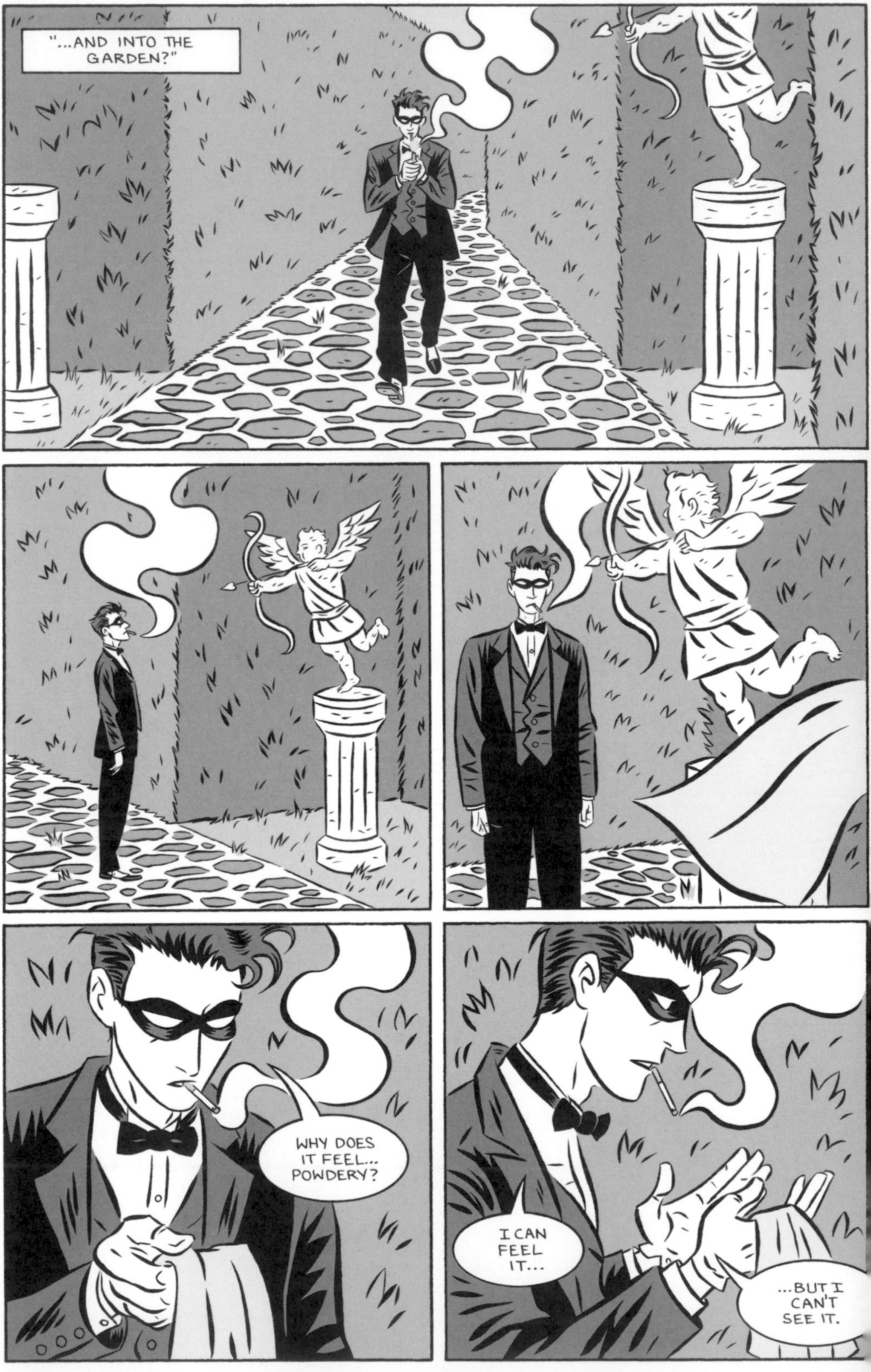
"...AND INTO THE GARDEN?"
WHY DOES IT FEEL... POWDERY?
I CAN FEEL IT...
...BUT I CAN'T SEE IT.

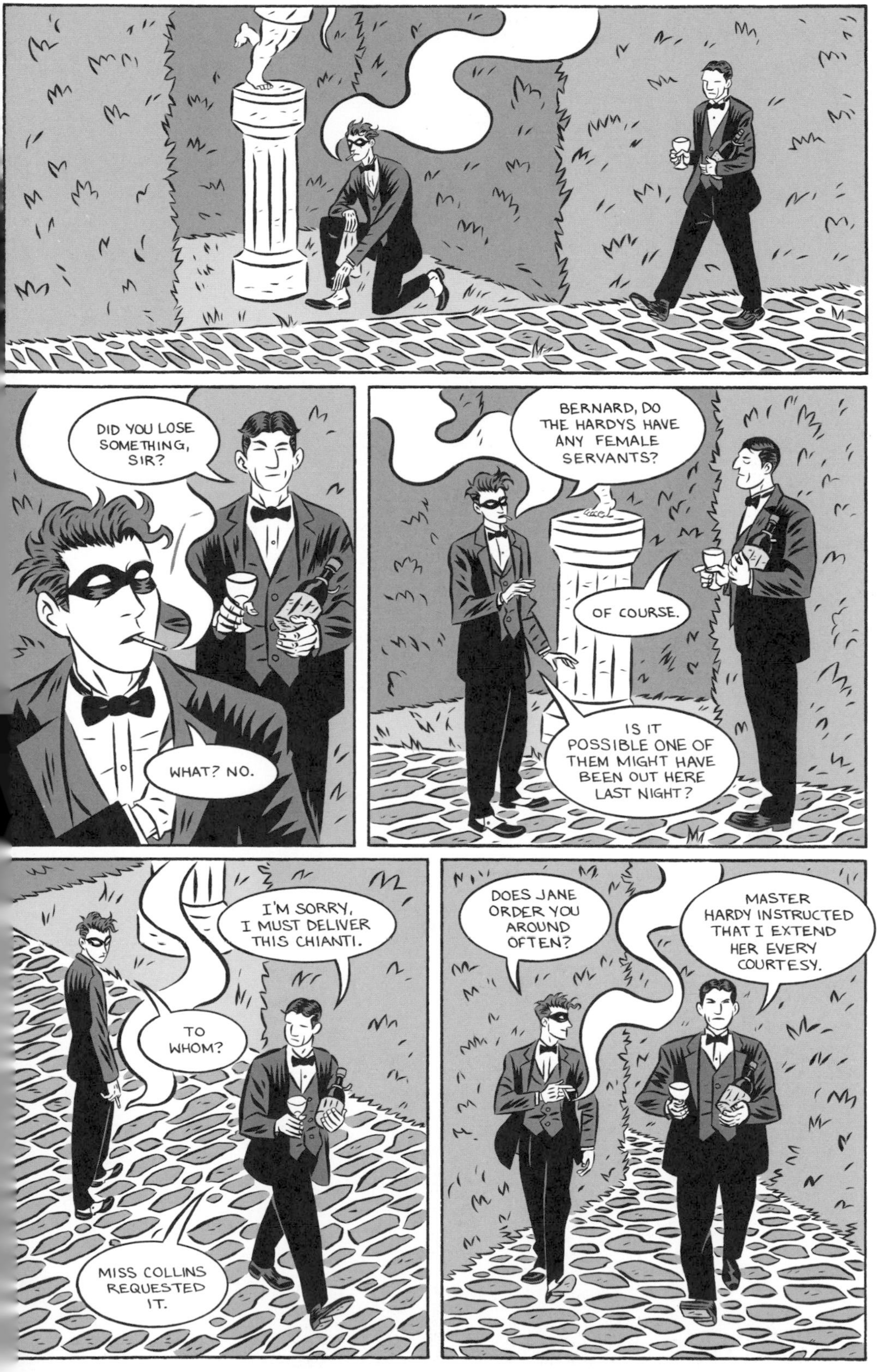
DID YOU LOSE SOMETHING, SIR?
WHAT? NO.
BERNARD, DO THE HARDYS HAVE ANY FEMALE SERVANTS?
OF COURSE.
IS IT POSSIBLE ONE OF THEM MIGHT HAVE BEEN OUT HERE LAST NIGHT?
I'M SORRY, I MUST DELIVER THIS CHIANTI.
TO WHOM?
MISS COLLINS REQUESTED IT.
DOES JANE ORDER YOU AROUND OFTEN?
MASTER HARDY INSTRUCTED THAT I EXTEND HER EVERY COURTESY.

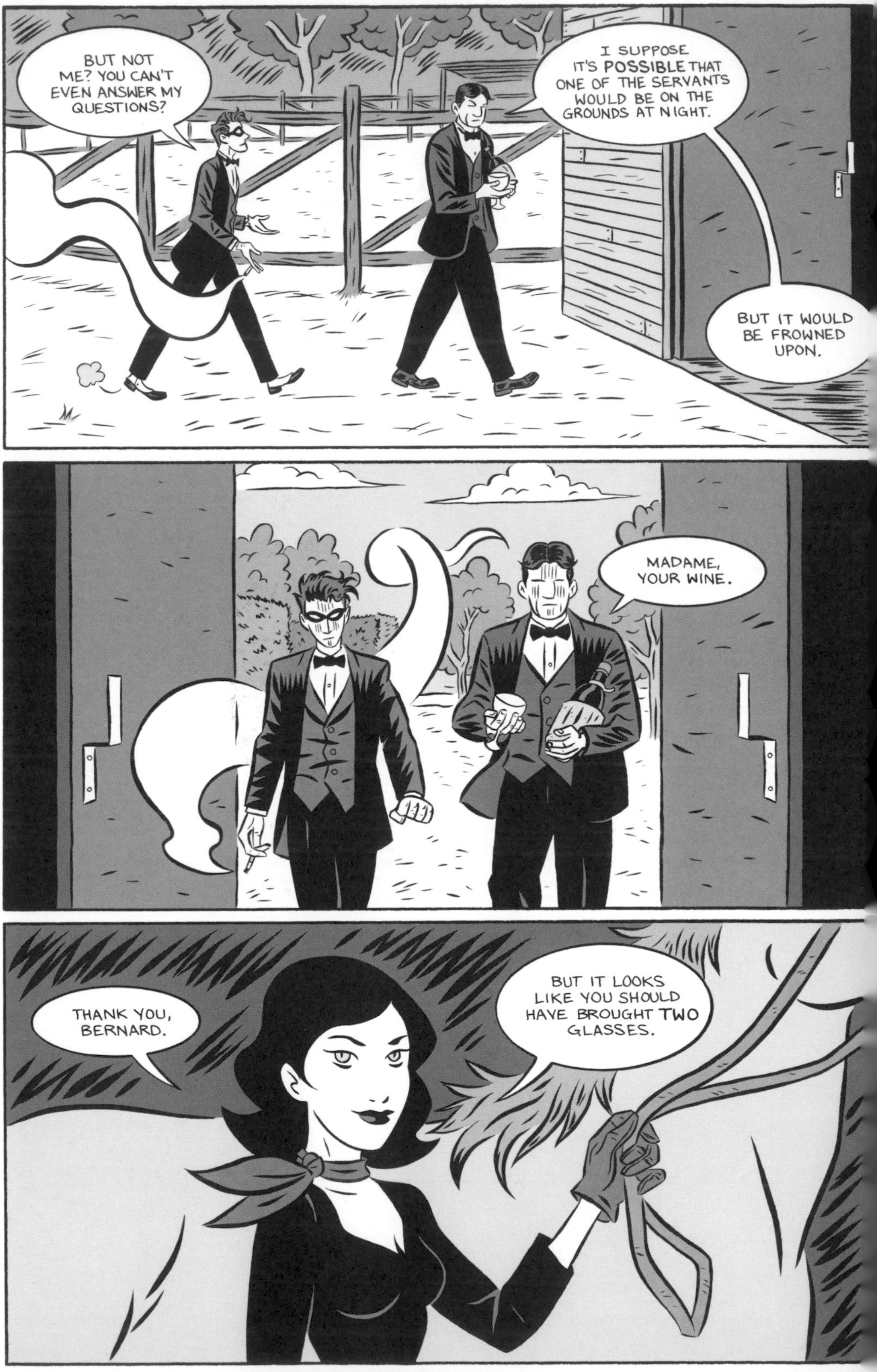
BUT NOT ME? YOU CAN'T EVEN ANSWER MY QUESTIONS?
I SUPPOSE IT'S POSSIBLE THAT ONE OF THE SERVANTS WOULD BE ON THE GROUNDS AT NIGHT.
BUT IT WOULD BE FROWNED UPON.
MADAME, YOUR WINE.
THANK YOU, BERNARD.
BUT IT LOOKS LIKE YOU SHOULD HAVE BROUGHT TWO GLASSES.

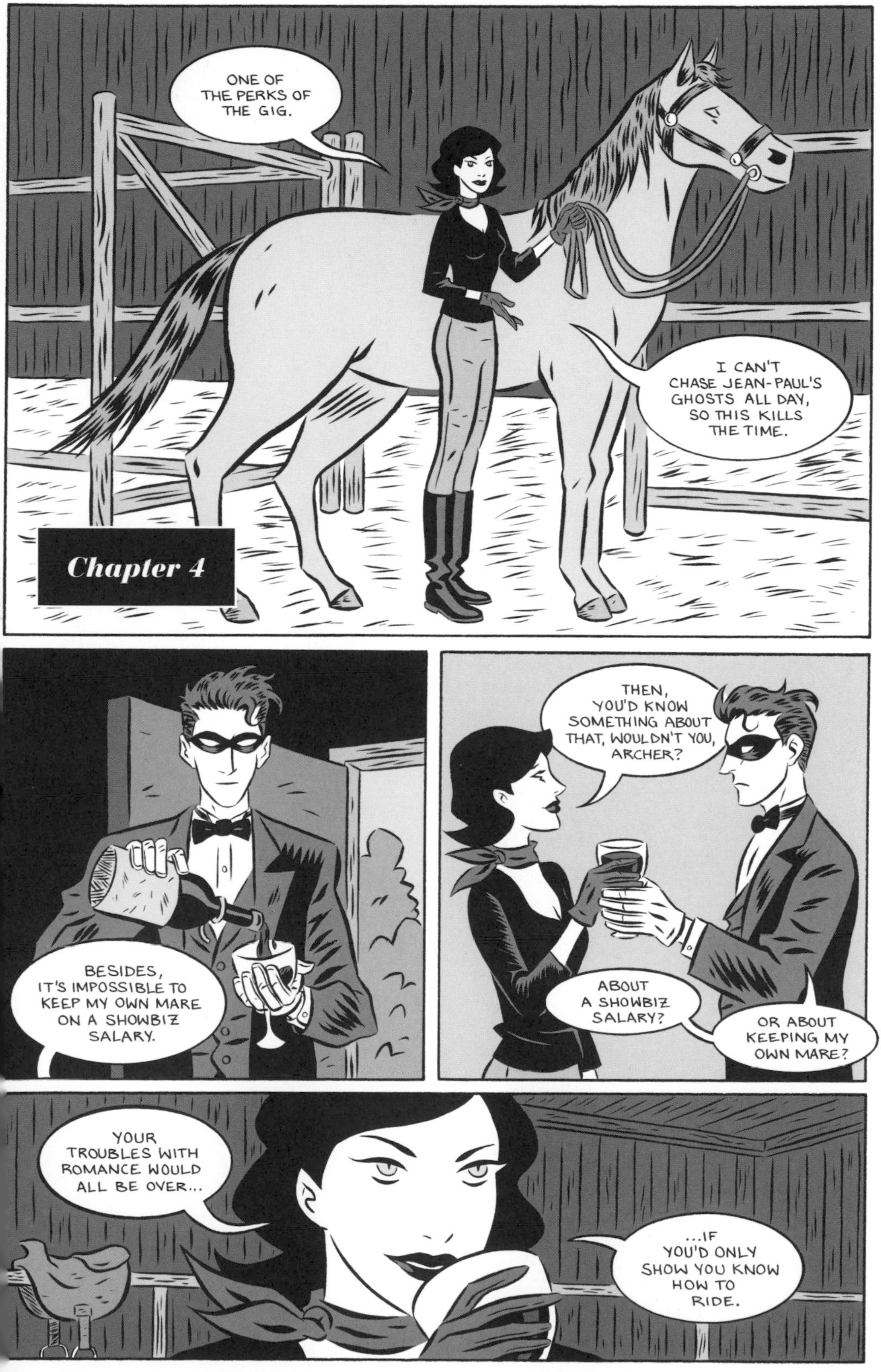
ONE OF THE PERKS OF THE GIG.
I CAN'T CHASE JEAN-PAUL'S GHOSTS ALL DAY, SO THIS KILLS THE TIME.
Chapter 4
BESIDES, IT'S IMPOSSIBLE TO KEEP MY OWN MARE ON A SHOWBIZ SALARY.
THEN, YOU'D KNOW SOMETHING ABOUT THAT, WOULDN'T YOU, ARCHER?
ABOUT A SHOWBIZ SALARY?
OR ABOUT KEEPING MY OWN MARE?
YOUR TROUBLES WITH ROMANCE WOULD ALL BE OVER...
...IF YOU'D ONLY SHOW YOU KNOW HOW TO RIDE.

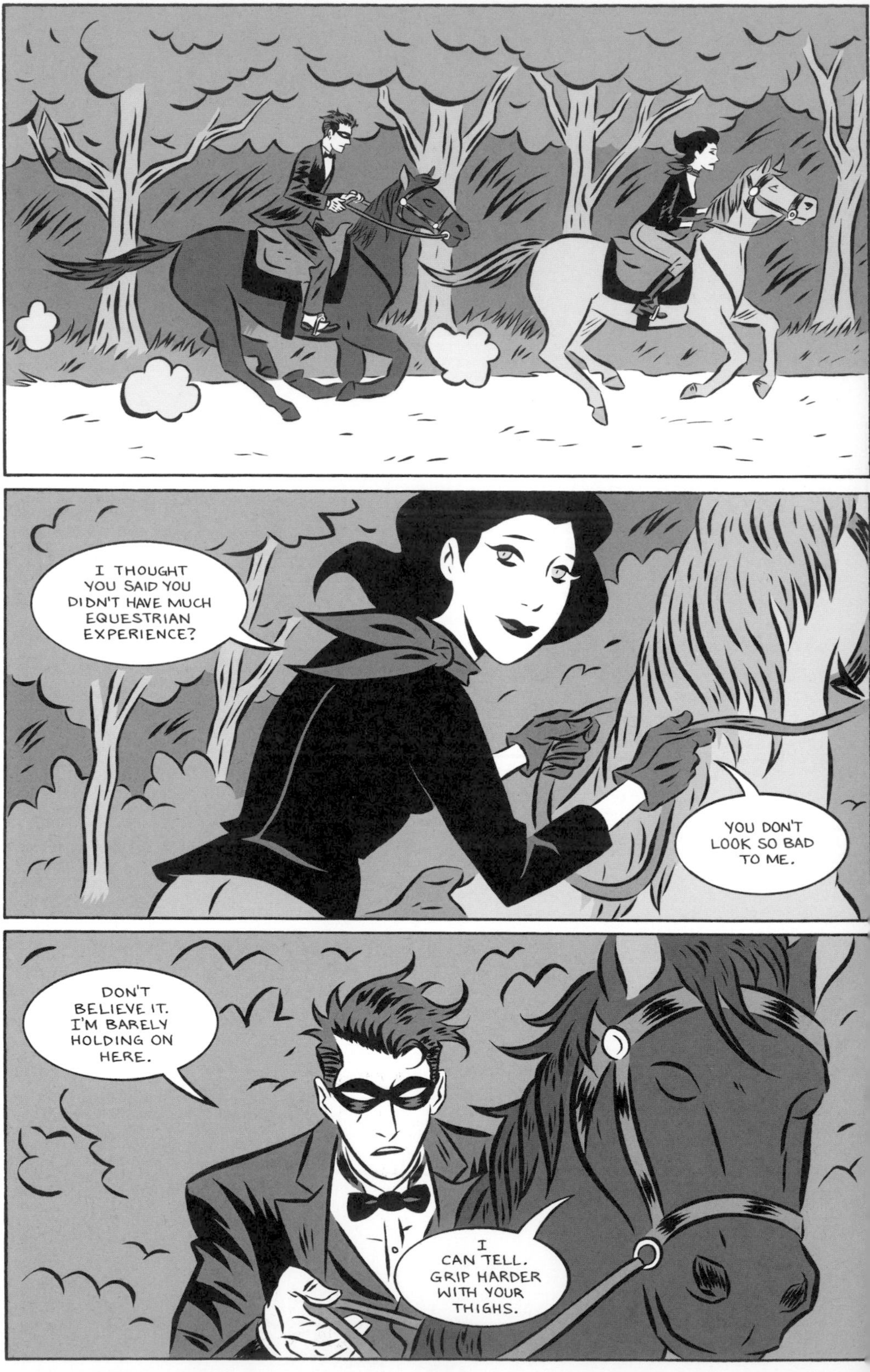
I THOUGHT YOU SAID YOU DIDN'T HAVE MUCH EQUESTRIAN EXPERIENCE?
YOU DON'T LOOK SO BAD TO ME.
DON'T BELIEVE IT. I'M BARELY HOLDING ON HERE.
I CAN TELL. GRIP HARDER WITH YOUR THIGHS.

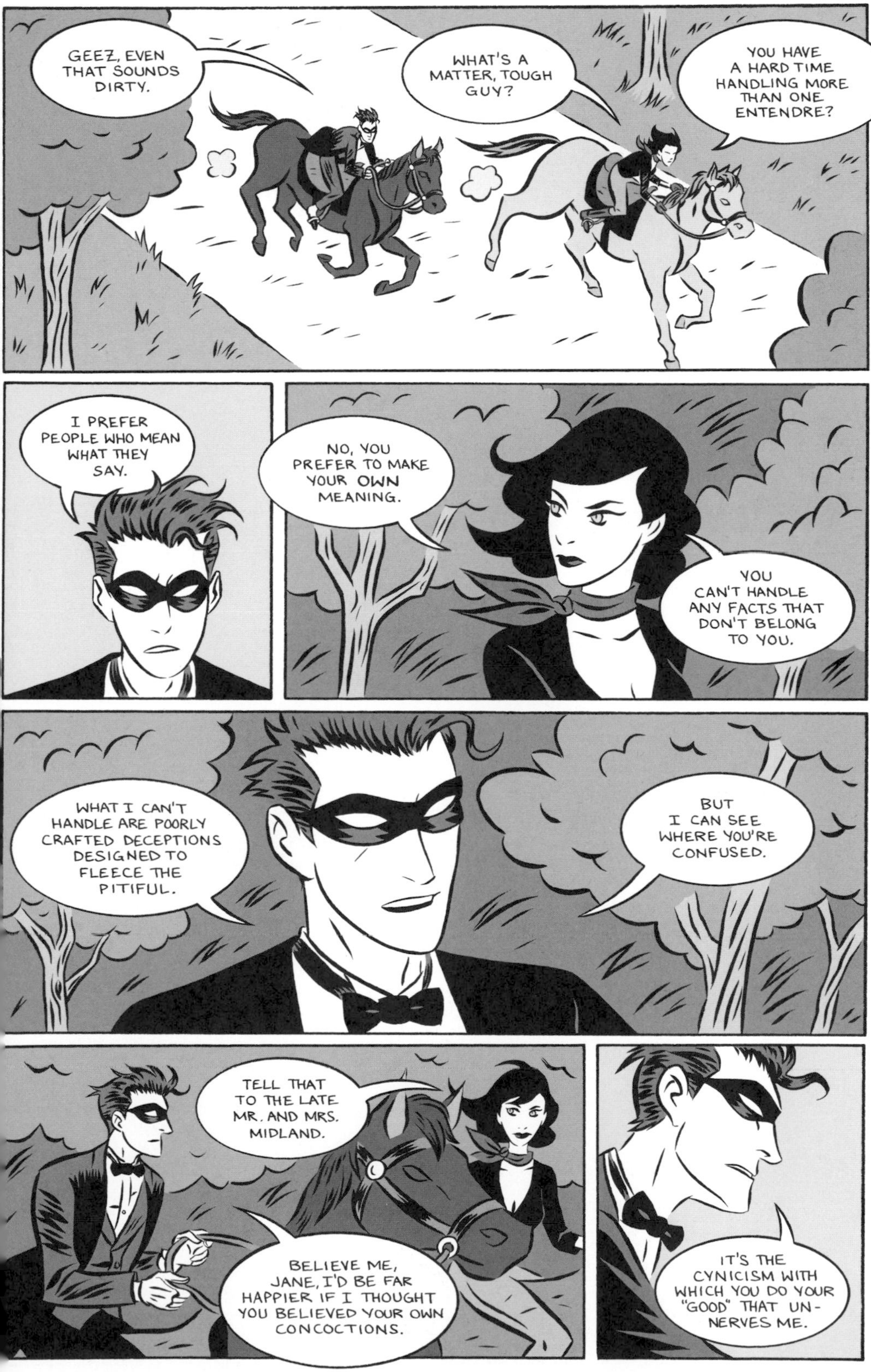
GEEZ, EVEN THAT SOUNDS DIRTY.
WHAT'S A MATTER, TOUGH GUY?
YOU HAVE A HARD TIME HANDLING MORE THAN ONE ENTENDRE?
I PREFER PEOPLE WHO MEAN WHAT THEY SAY.
NO, YOU PREFER TO MAKE YOUR OWN MEANING.
YOU CAN'T HANDLE ANY FACTS THAT DON'T BELONG TO YOU.
WHAT I CAN'T HANDLE ARE POORLY CRAFTED DECEPTIONS DESIGNED TO FLEECE THE PITIFUL.
BUT I CAN SEE WHERE YOU'RE CONFUSED.
TELL THAT TO THE LATE MR. AND MRS. MIDLAND.
BELIEVE ME, JANE, I'D BE FAR HAPPIER IF I THOUGHT YOU BELIEVED YOUR OWN CONCOCTIONS.
IT'S THE CYNICISM WITH WHICH YOU DO YOUR "GOOD" THAT UN-NERVES ME.

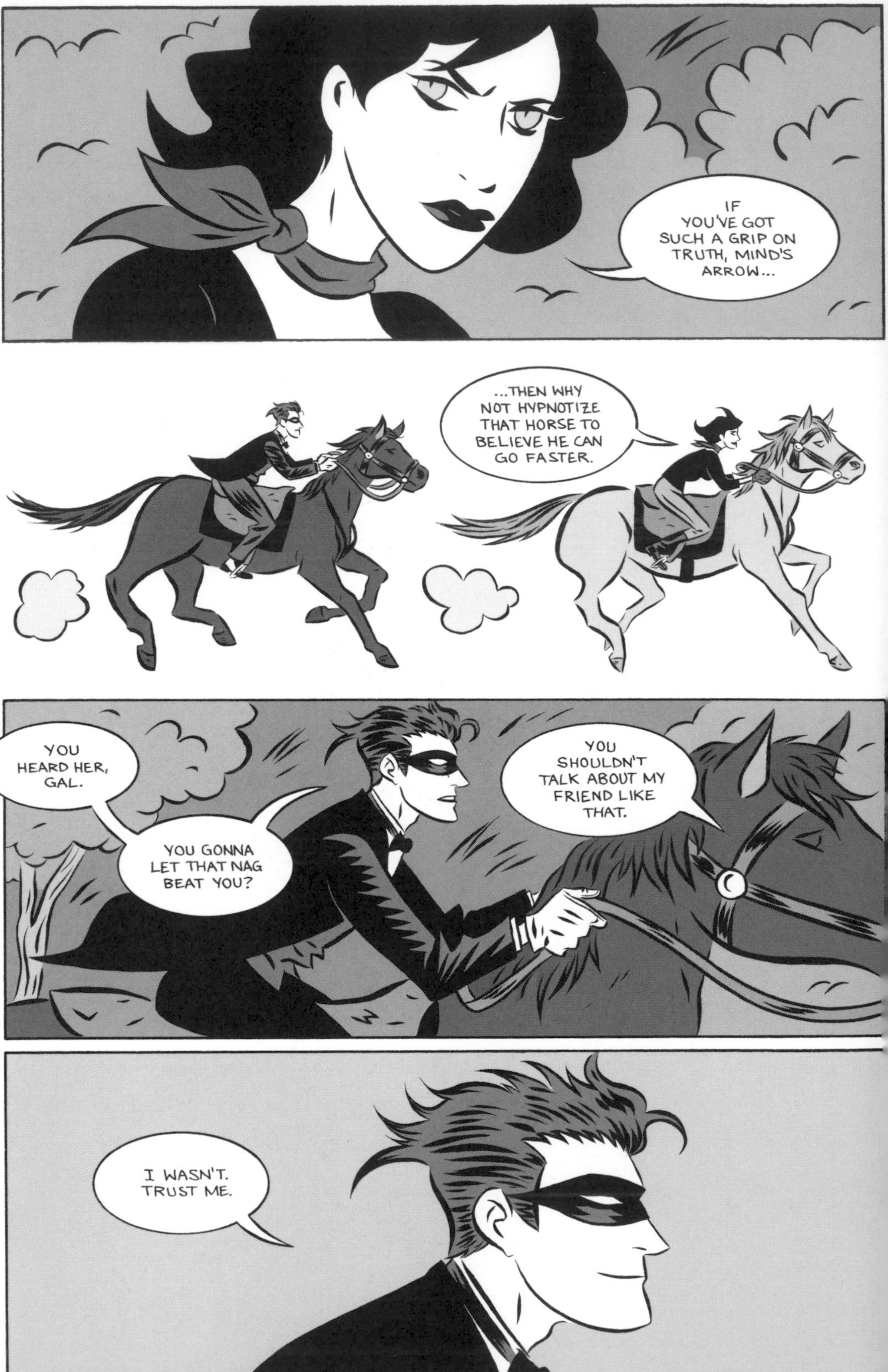
IF YOU'VE GOT SUCH A GRIP ON TRUTH, MIND'S ARROW...
...THEN WHY NOT HYPNOTIZE THAT HORSE TO BELIEVE HE CAN GO FASTER.
YOU HEARD HER, GAL.
YOU GONNA LET THAT NAG BEAT YOU?
YOU SHOULDN'T TALK ABOUT MY FRIEND LIKE THAT.
I WASN'T. TRUST ME.

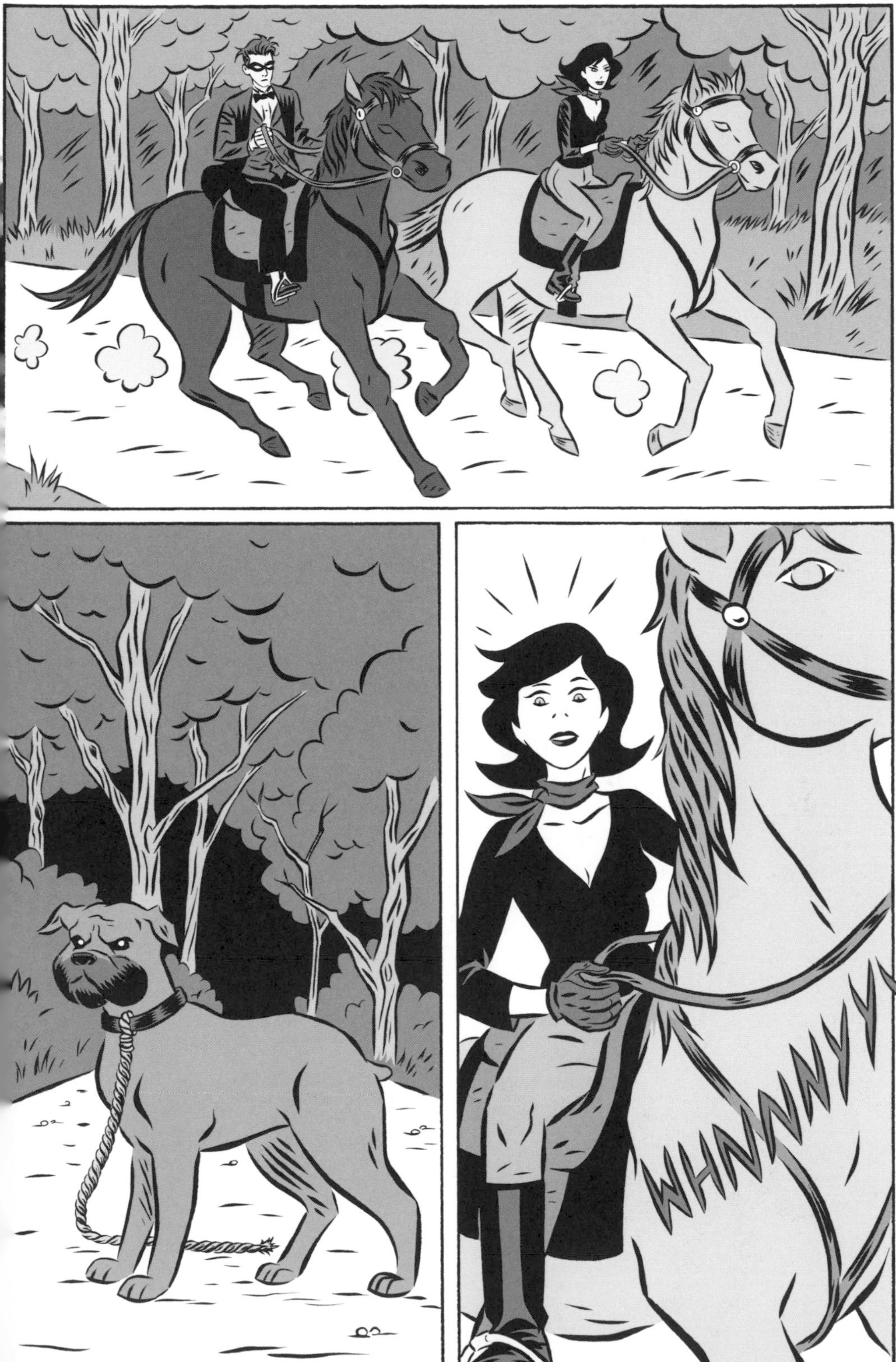
WHNNNYYY

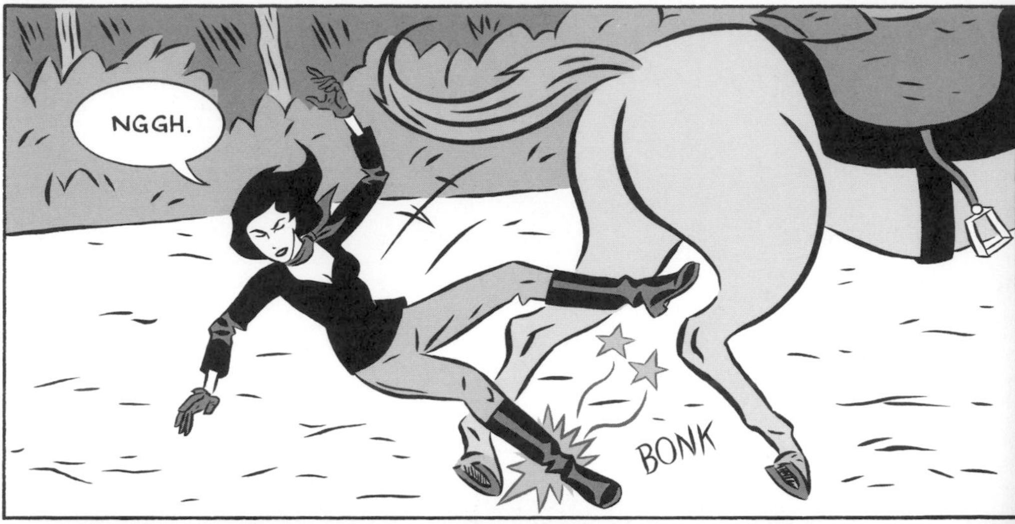
NGGH.
BONK

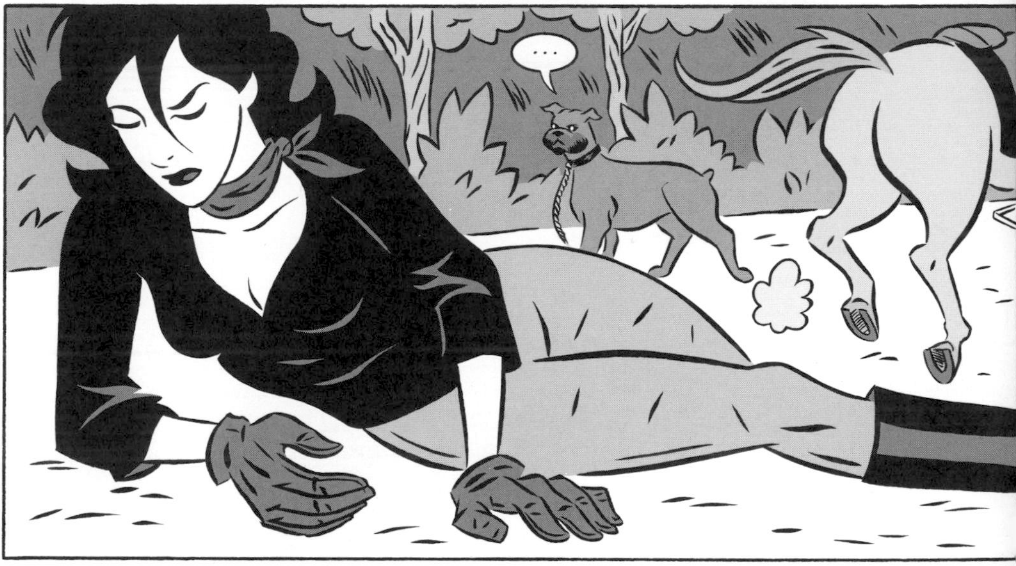
...

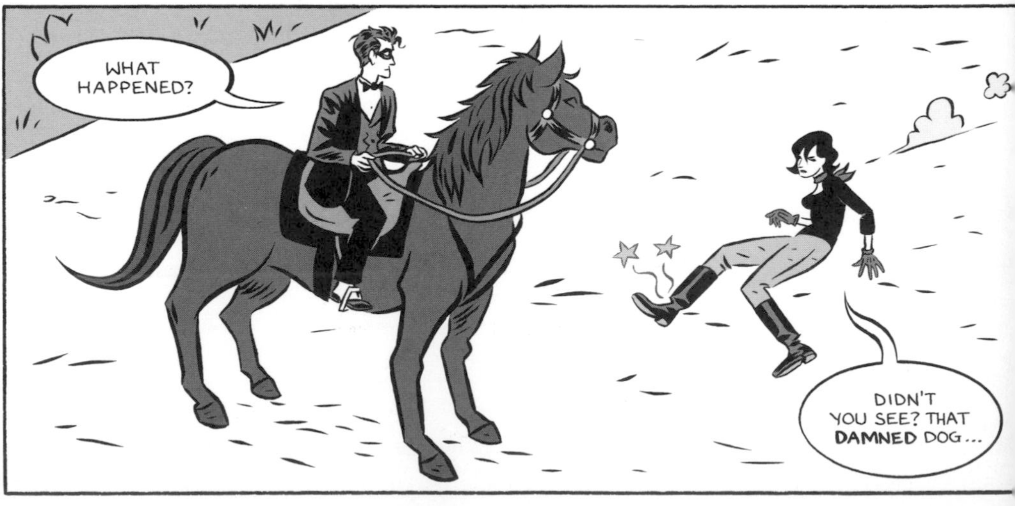
WHAT HAPPENED?
DIDN'T YOU SEE? THAT **DAMNED** DOG...

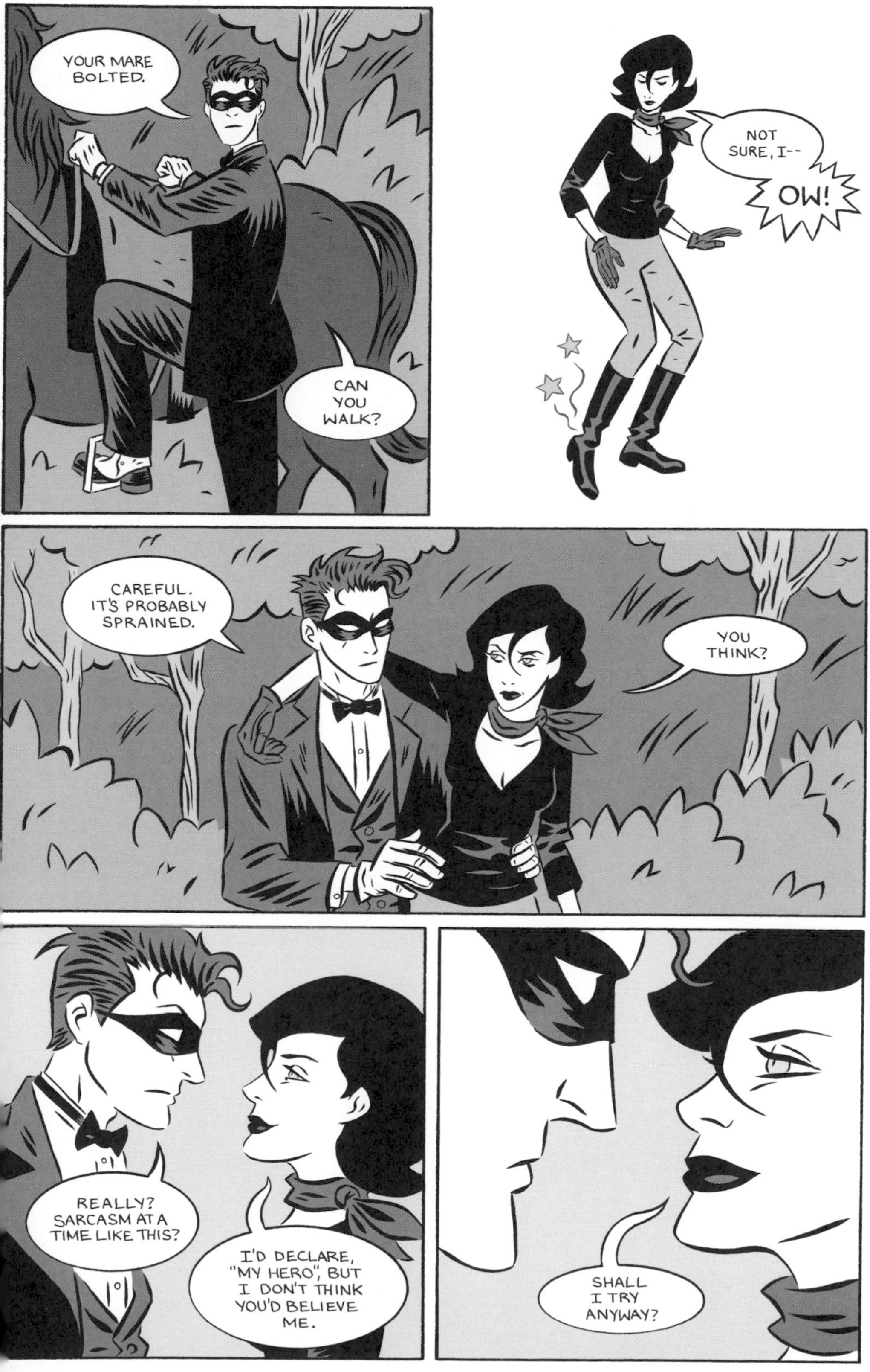
YOUR MARE BOLTED.
CAN YOU WALK?
NOT SURE, I--
OW!
CAREFUL. IT'S PROBABLY SPRAINED.
YOU THINK?
REALLY? SARCASM AT A TIME LIKE THIS?
I'D DECLARE, "MY HERO", BUT I DON'T THINK YOU'D BELIEVE ME.
SHALL I TRY ANYWAY?

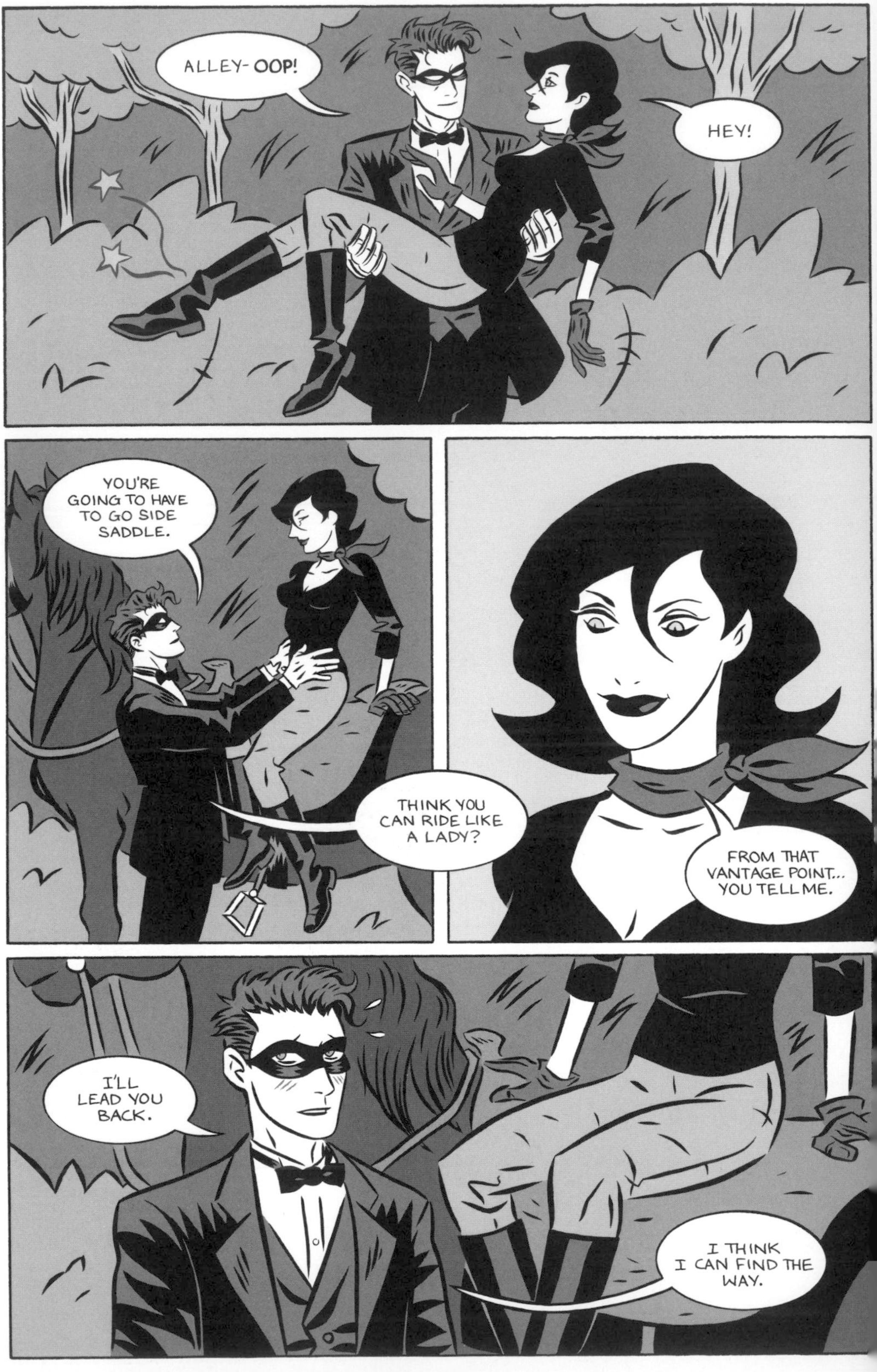
ALLEY-OOP!
HEY!
YOU'RE GOING TO HAVE TO GO SIDE SADDLE.
THINK YOU CAN RIDE LIKE A LADY?
FROM THAT VANTAGE POINT... YOU TELL ME.
I'LL LEAD YOU BACK.
I THINK I CAN FIND THE WAY.

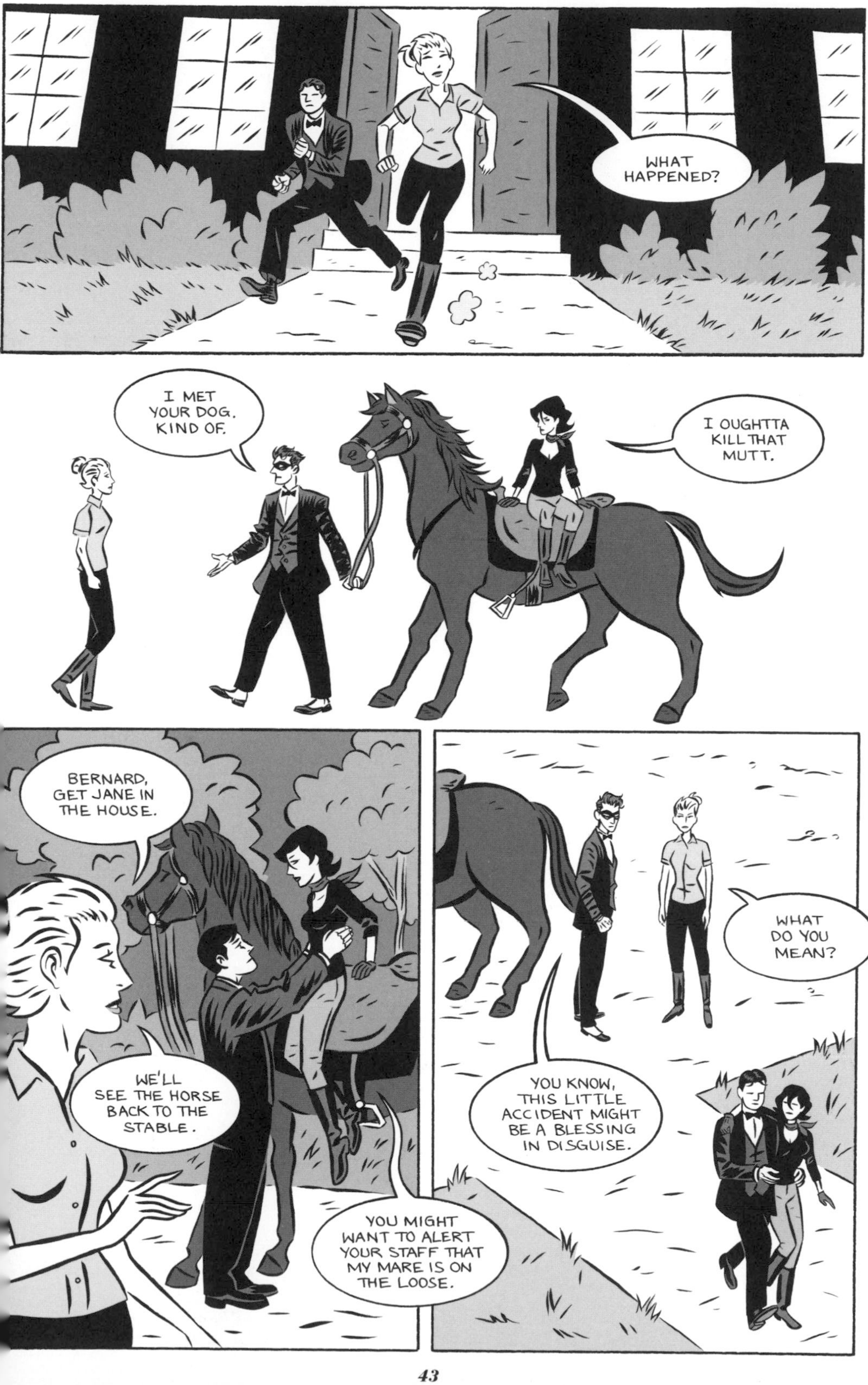
WHAT HAPPENED?
I MET YOUR DOG. KIND OF.
I OUGHTTA KILL THAT MUTT.
BERNARD, GET JANE IN THE HOUSE.
WE'LL SEE THE HORSE BACK TO THE STABLE.
YOU MIGHT WANT TO ALERT YOUR STAFF THAT MY MARE IS ON THE LOOSE.
WHAT DO YOU MEAN?
YOU KNOW, THIS LITTLE ACCIDENT MIGHT BE A BLESSING IN DISGUISE.

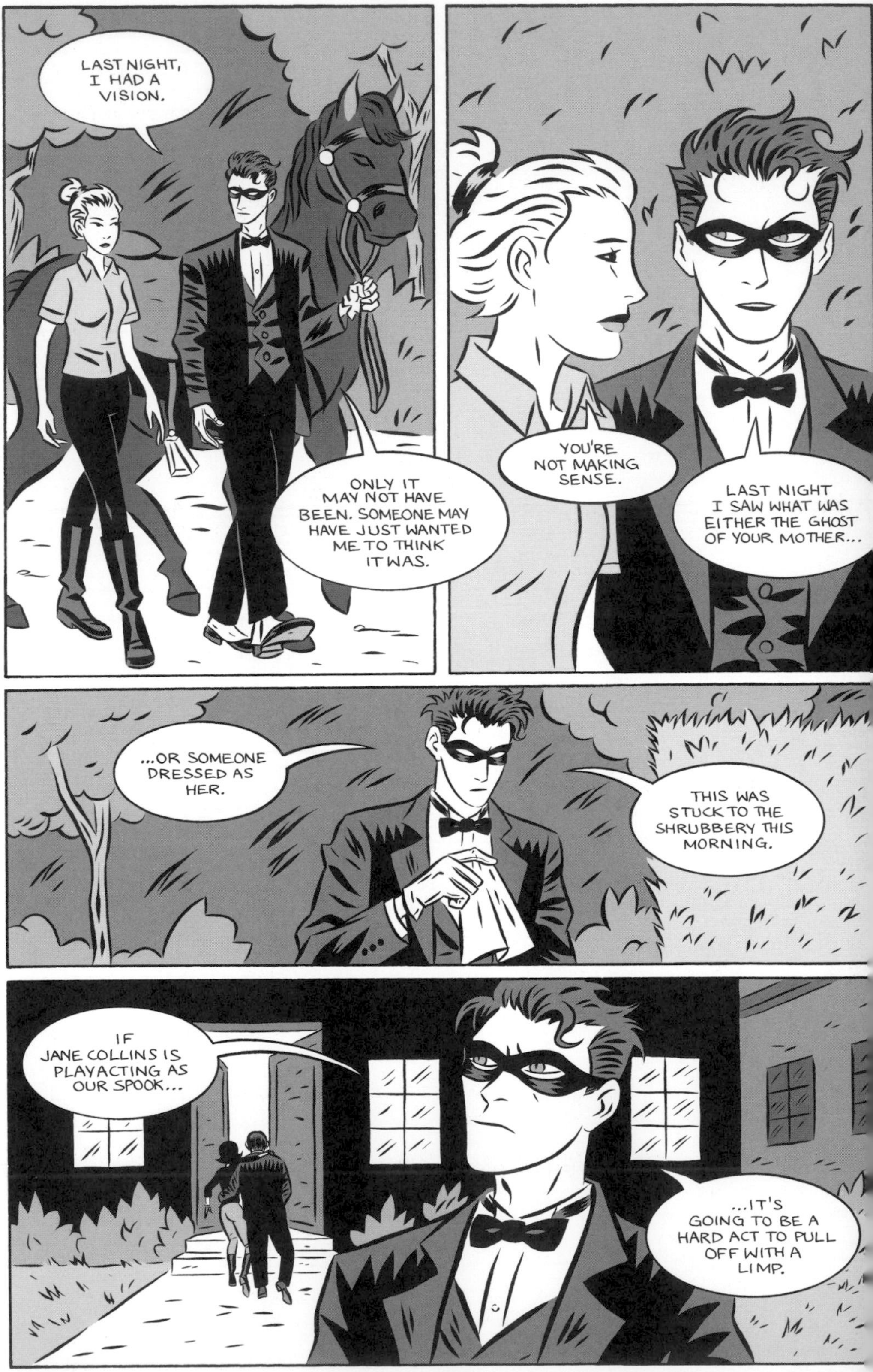
LAST NIGHT, I HAD A VISION.
ONLY IT MAY NOT HAVE BEEN. SOMEONE MAY HAVE JUST WANTED ME TO THINK IT WAS.
YOU'RE NOT MAKING SENSE.
LAST NIGHT I SAW WHAT WAS EITHER THE GHOST OF YOUR MOTHER...
...OR SOMEONE DRESSED AS HER.
THIS WAS STUCK TO THE SHRUBBERY THIS MORNING.
IF JANE COLLINS IS PLAYACTING AS OUR SPOOK...
...IT'S GOING TO BE A HARD ACT TO PULL OFF WITH A LIMP.

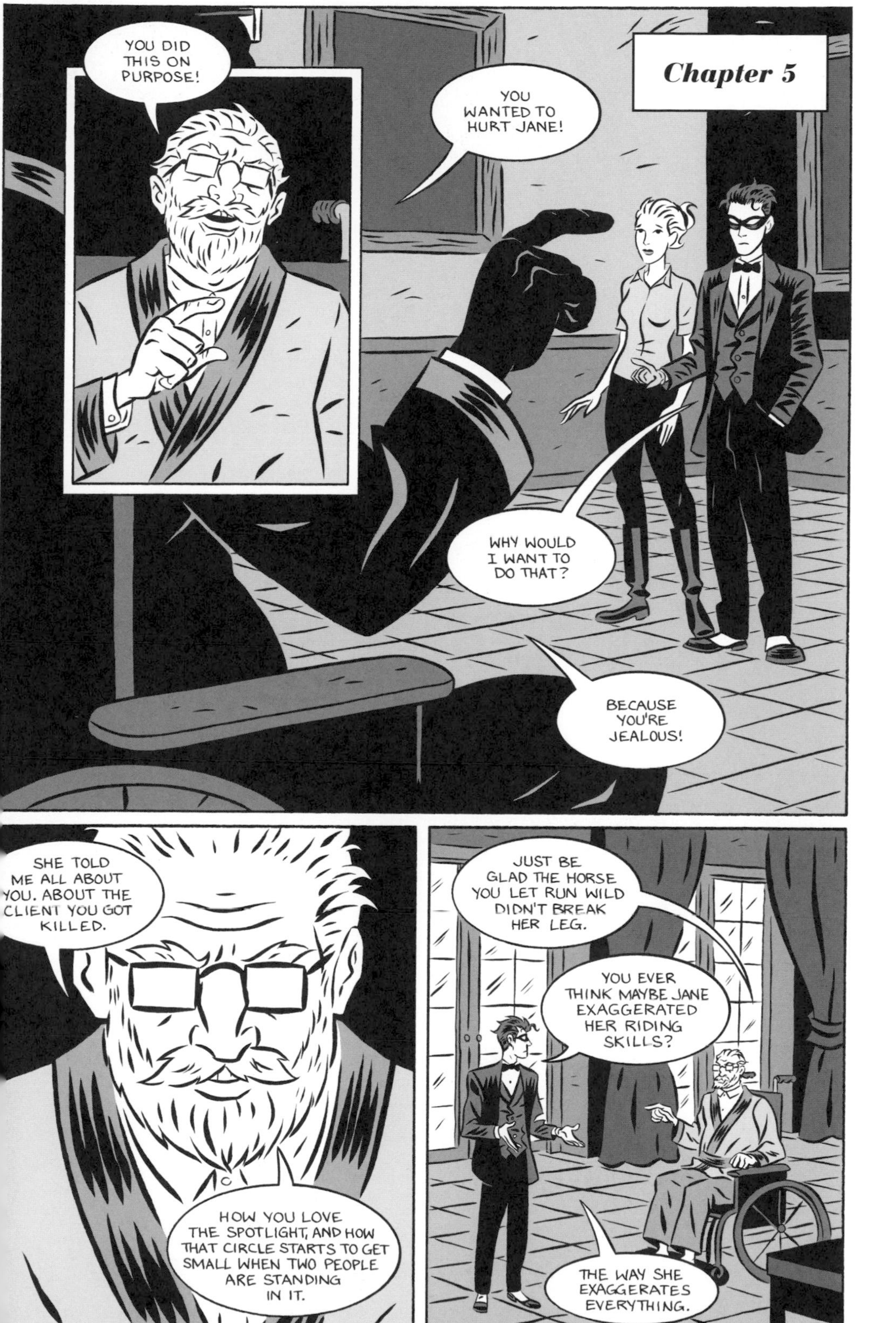
Chapter 5
YOU DID THIS ON PURPOSE!
YOU WANTED TO HURT JANE!
WHY WOULD I WANT TO DO THAT?
BECAUSE YOU'RE JEALOUS!
SHE TOLD ME ALL ABOUT YOU. ABOUT THE CLIENT YOU GOT KILLED.
HOW YOU LOVE THE SPOTLIGHT, AND HOW THAT CIRCLE STARTS TO GET SMALL WHEN TWO PEOPLE ARE STANDING IN IT.
JUST BE GLAD THE HORSE YOU LET RUN WILD DIDN'T BREAK HER LEG.
YOU EVER THINK MAYBE JANE EXAGGERATED HER RIDING SKILLS?
THE WAY SHE EXAGGERATES EVERYTHING.

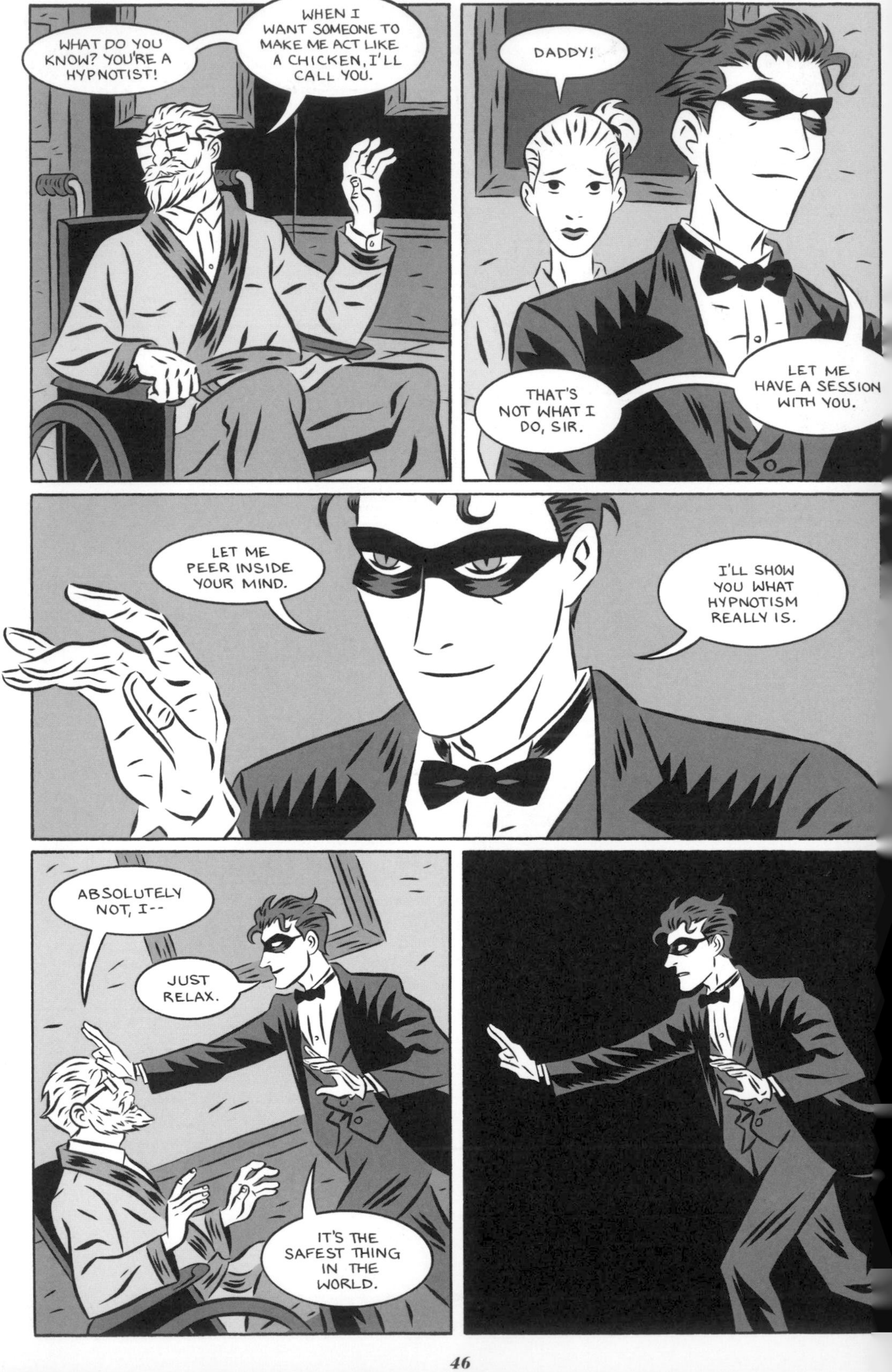
WHAT DO YOU KNOW? YOU'RE A HYPNOTIST!
WHEN I WANT SOMEONE TO MAKE ME ACT LIKE A CHICKEN, I'LL CALL YOU.
DADDY!
THAT'S NOT WHAT I DO, SIR.
LET ME HAVE A SESSION WITH YOU.
LET ME PEER INSIDE YOUR MIND.
I'LL SHOW YOU WHAT HYPNOTISM REALLY IS.
ABSOLUTELY NOT, I--
JUST RELAX.
IT'S THE SAFEST THING IN THE WORLD.

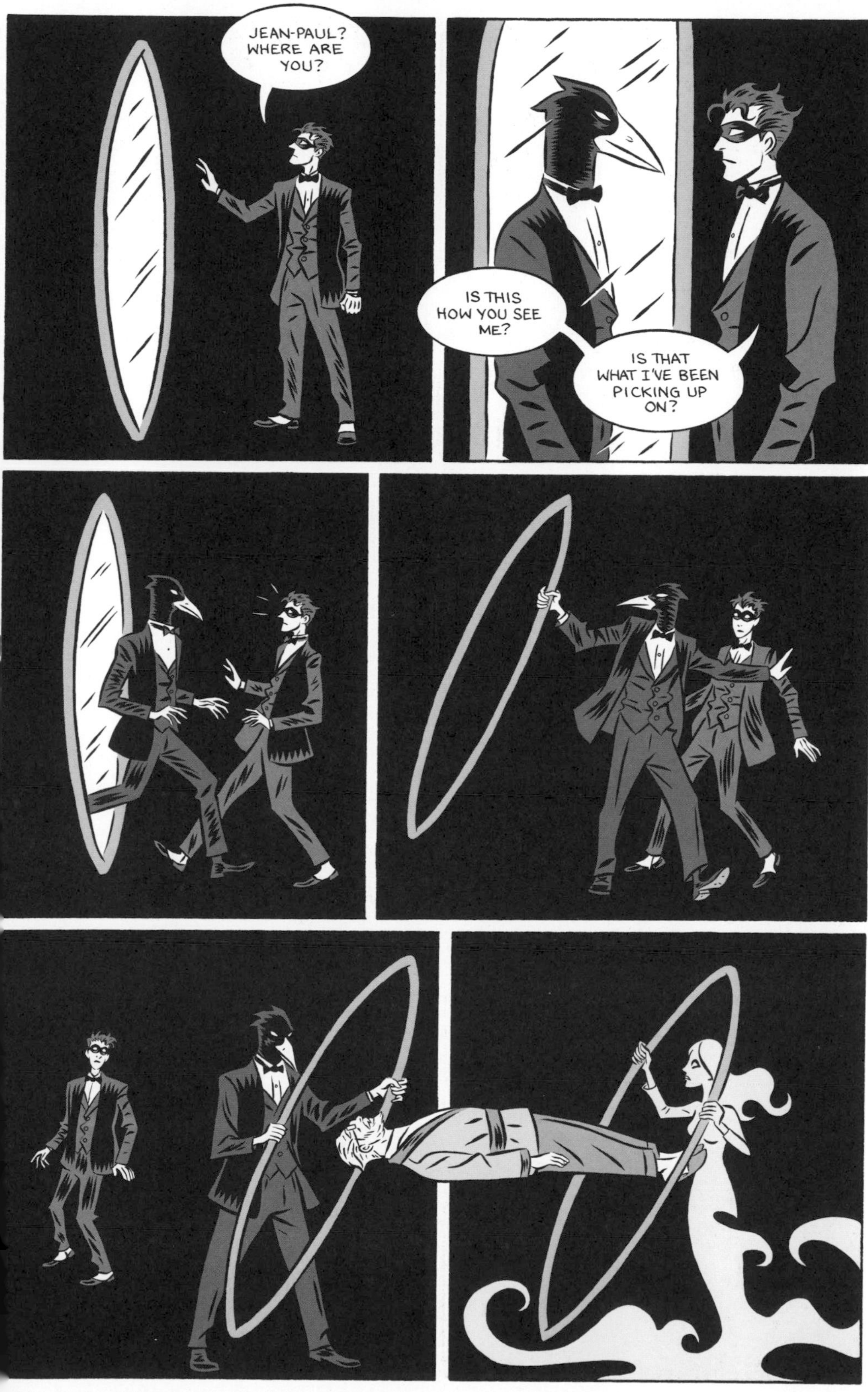
JEAN-PAUL? WHERE ARE YOU?
IS THIS HOW YOU SEE ME?
IS THAT WHAT I'VE BEEN PICKING UP ON?

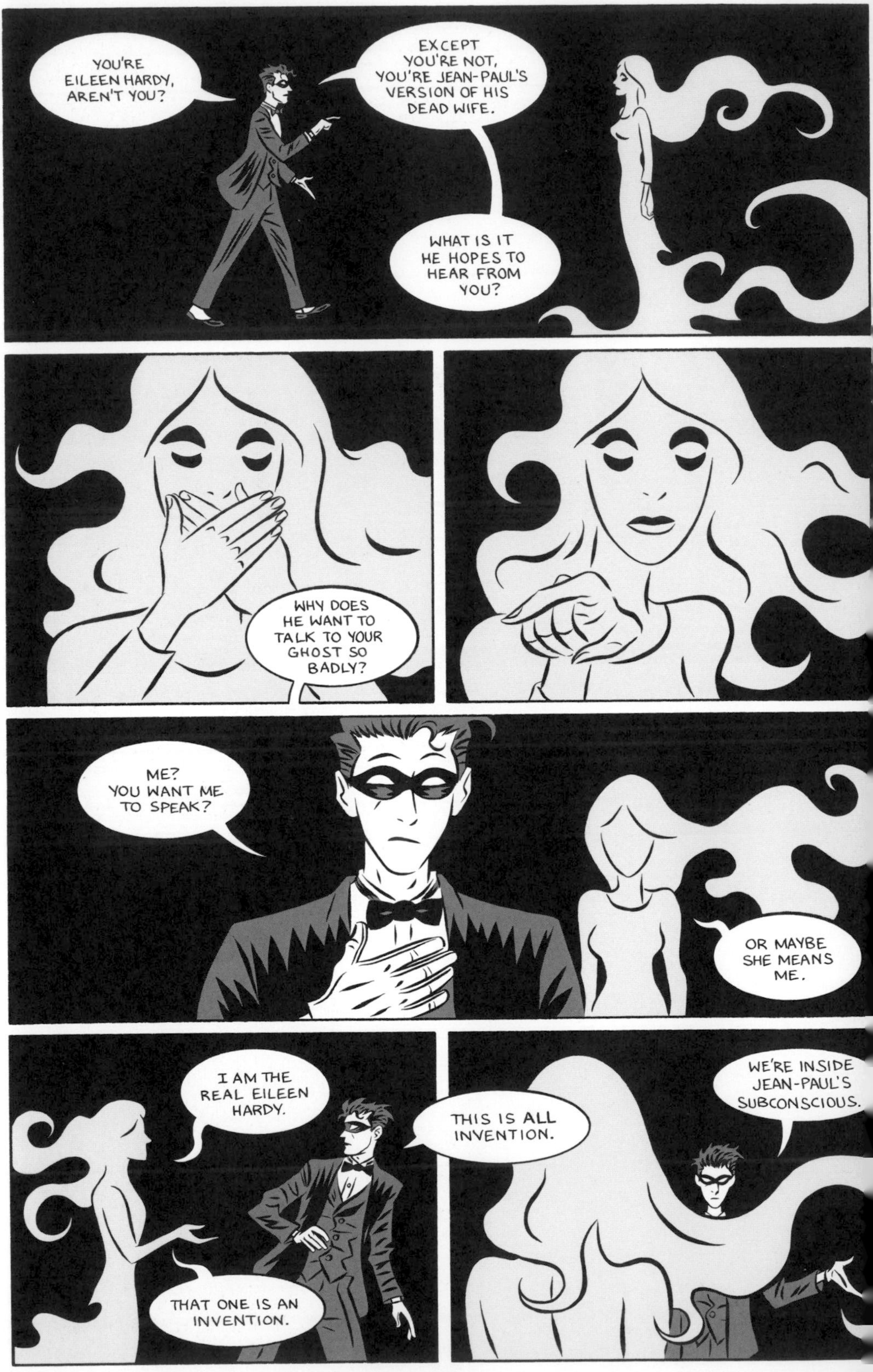
YOU'RE EILEEN HARDY, AREN'T YOU?
EXCEPT YOU'RE NOT, YOU'RE JEAN-PAUL'S VERSION OF HIS DEAD WIFE.
WHAT IS IT HE HOPES TO HEAR FROM YOU?
WHY DOES HE WANT TO TALK TO YOUR GHOST SO BADLY?
ME? YOU WANT ME TO SPEAK?
OR MAYBE SHE MEANS ME.
I AM THE REAL EILEEN HARDY.
THAT ONE IS AN INVENTION.
THIS IS ALL INVENTION.
WE'RE INSIDE JEAN-PAUL'S SUBCONSCIOUS.

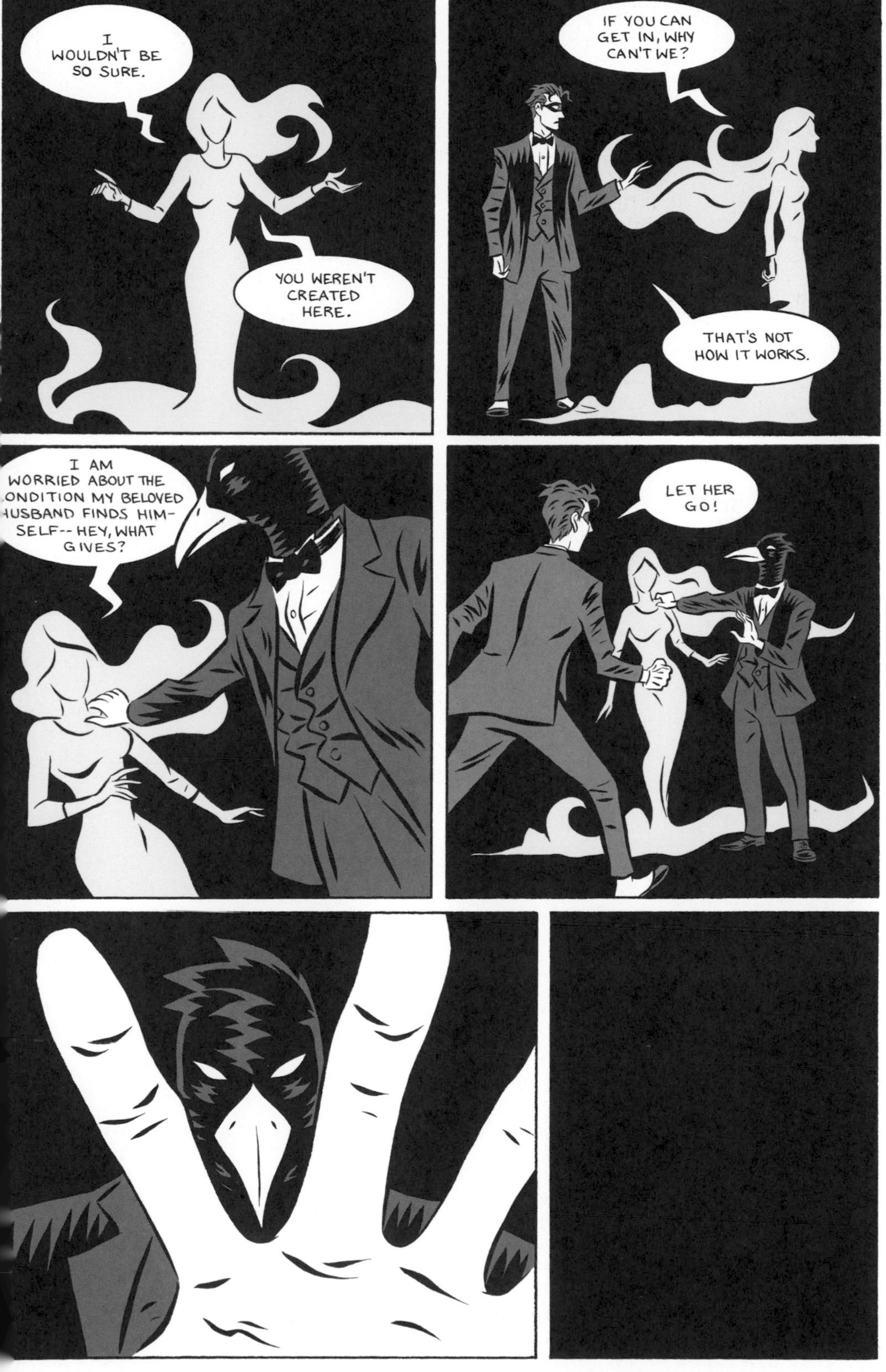
I WOULDN'T BE SO SURE.
YOU WEREN'T CREATED HERE.
IF YOU CAN GET IN, WHY CAN'T WE?
THAT'S NOT HOW IT WORKS.
I AM WORRIED ABOUT THE CONDITION MY BELOVED HUSBAND FINDS HIM-SELF-- HEY, WHAT GIVES?
LET HER GO!

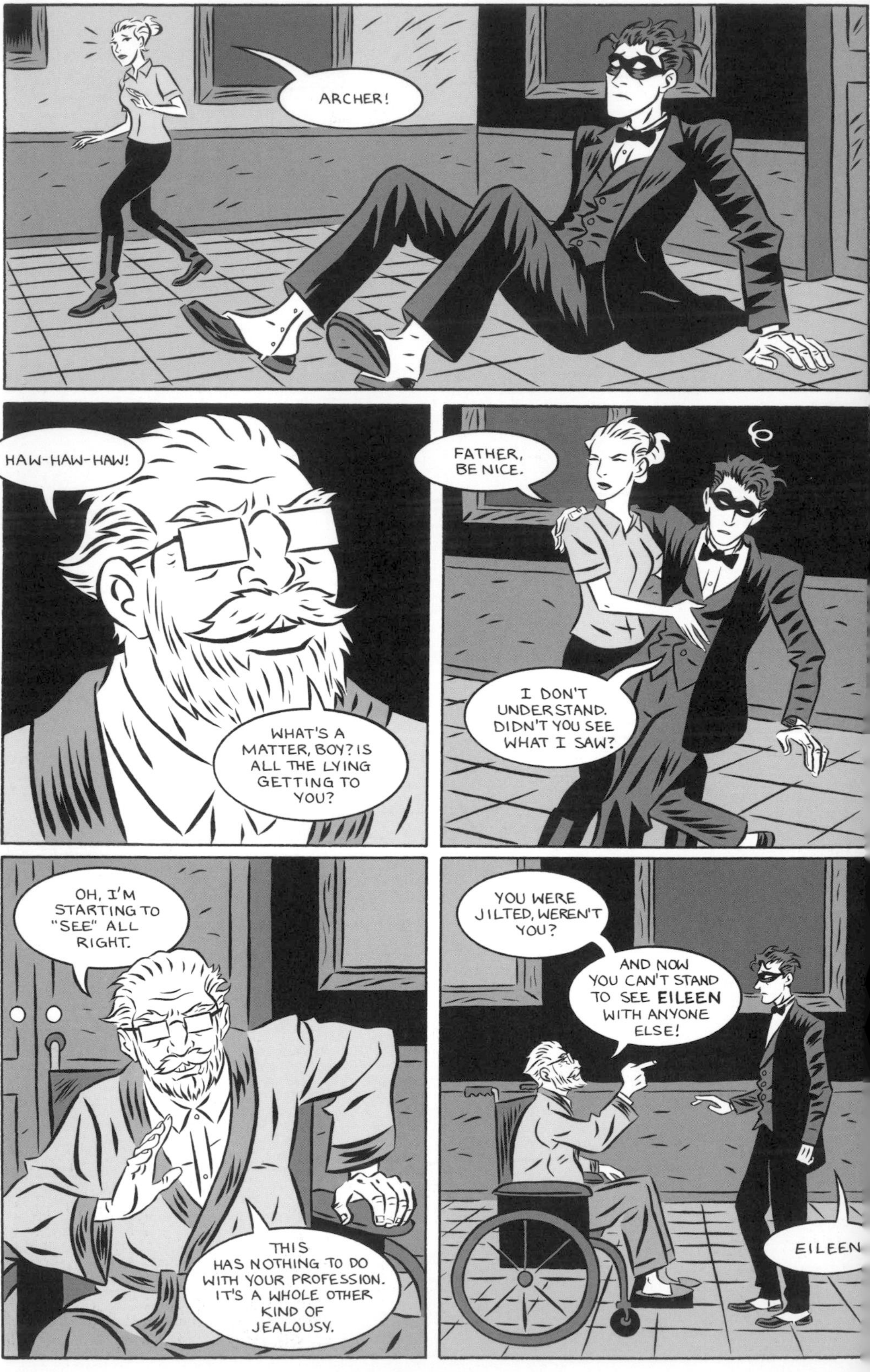
ARCHER!
HAW-HAW-HAW!
WHAT'S A MATTER, BOY? IS ALL THE LYING GETTING TO YOU?
FATHER, BE NICE.
I DON'T UNDERSTAND. DIDN'T YOU SEE WHAT I SAW?
OH, I'M STARTING TO "SEE" ALL RIGHT.
THIS HAS NOTHING TO DO WITH YOUR PROFESSION. IT'S A WHOLE OTHER KIND OF JEALOUSY.
YOU WERE JILTED, WEREN'T YOU?
AND NOW YOU CAN'T STAND TO SEE EILEEN WITH ANYONE ELSE!
EILEEN

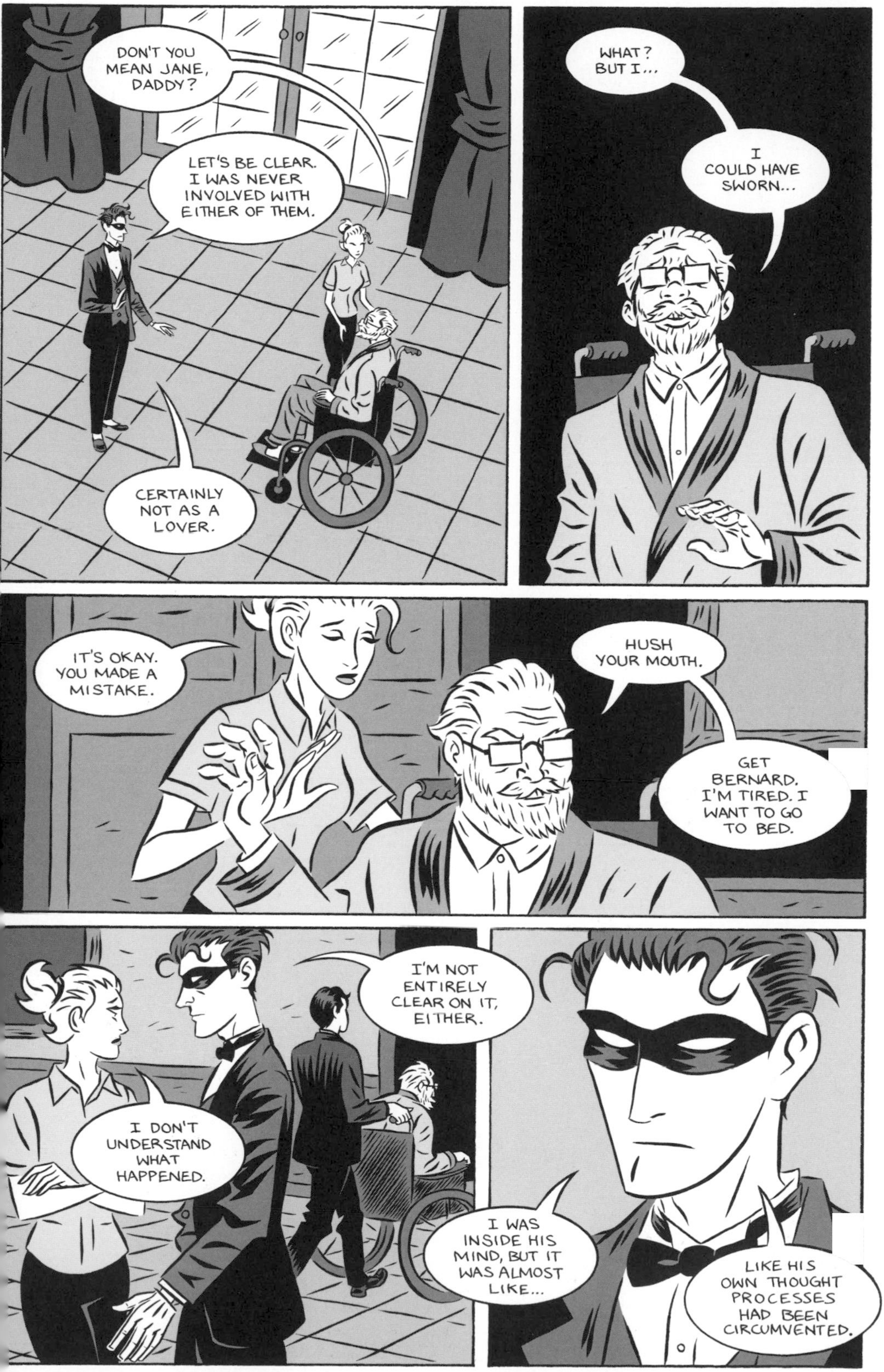
DON'T YOU MEAN JANE, DADDY?
LET'S BE CLEAR. I WAS NEVER INVOLVED WITH EITHER OF THEM.
CERTAINLY NOT AS A LOVER.
WHAT? BUT I...
I COULD HAVE SWORN...
IT'S OKAY. YOU MADE A MISTAKE.
HUSH YOUR MOUTH.
GET BERNARD. I'M TIRED. I WANT TO GO TO BED.
I'M NOT ENTIRELY CLEAR ON IT, EITHER.
I DON'T UNDERSTAND WHAT HAPPENED.
I WAS INSIDE HIS MIND, BUT IT WAS ALMOST LIKE...
LIKE HIS OWN THOUGHT PROCESSES HAD BEEN CIRCUMVENTED.

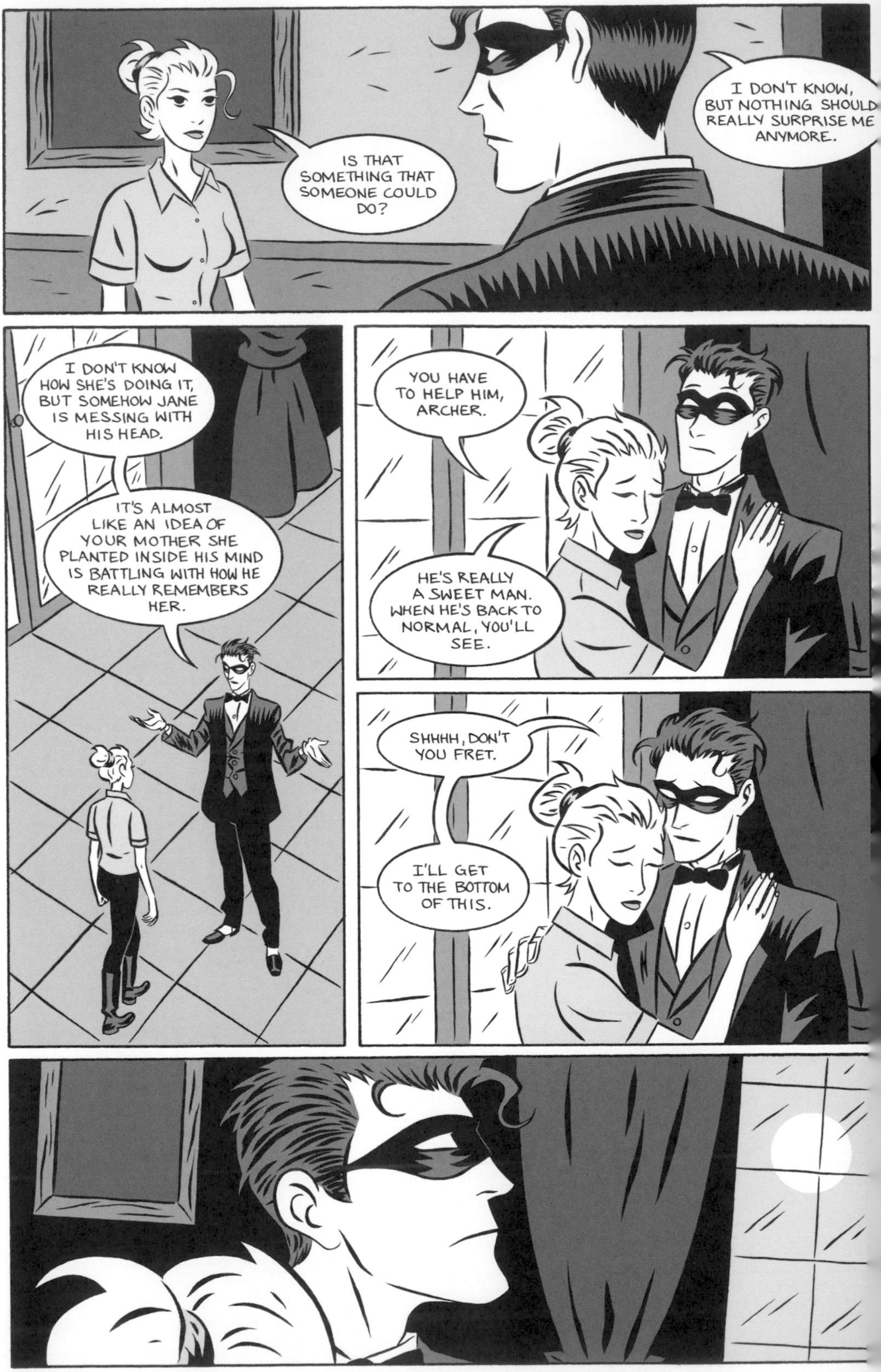
IS THAT SOMETHING THAT SOMEONE COULD DO?
I DON'T KNOW, BUT NOTHING SHOULD REALLY SURPRISE ME ANYMORE.
I DON'T KNOW HOW SHE'S DOING IT, BUT SOMEHOW JANE IS MESSING WITH HIS HEAD.
IT'S ALMOST LIKE AN IDEA OF YOUR MOTHER SHE PLANTED INSIDE HIS MIND IS BATTLING WITH HOW HE REALLY REMEMBERS HER.
YOU HAVE TO HELP HIM, ARCHER.
HE'S REALLY A SWEET MAN. WHEN HE'S BACK TO NORMAL, YOU'LL SEE.
SHHHH, DON'T YOU FRET.
I'LL GET TO THE BOTTOM OF THIS.

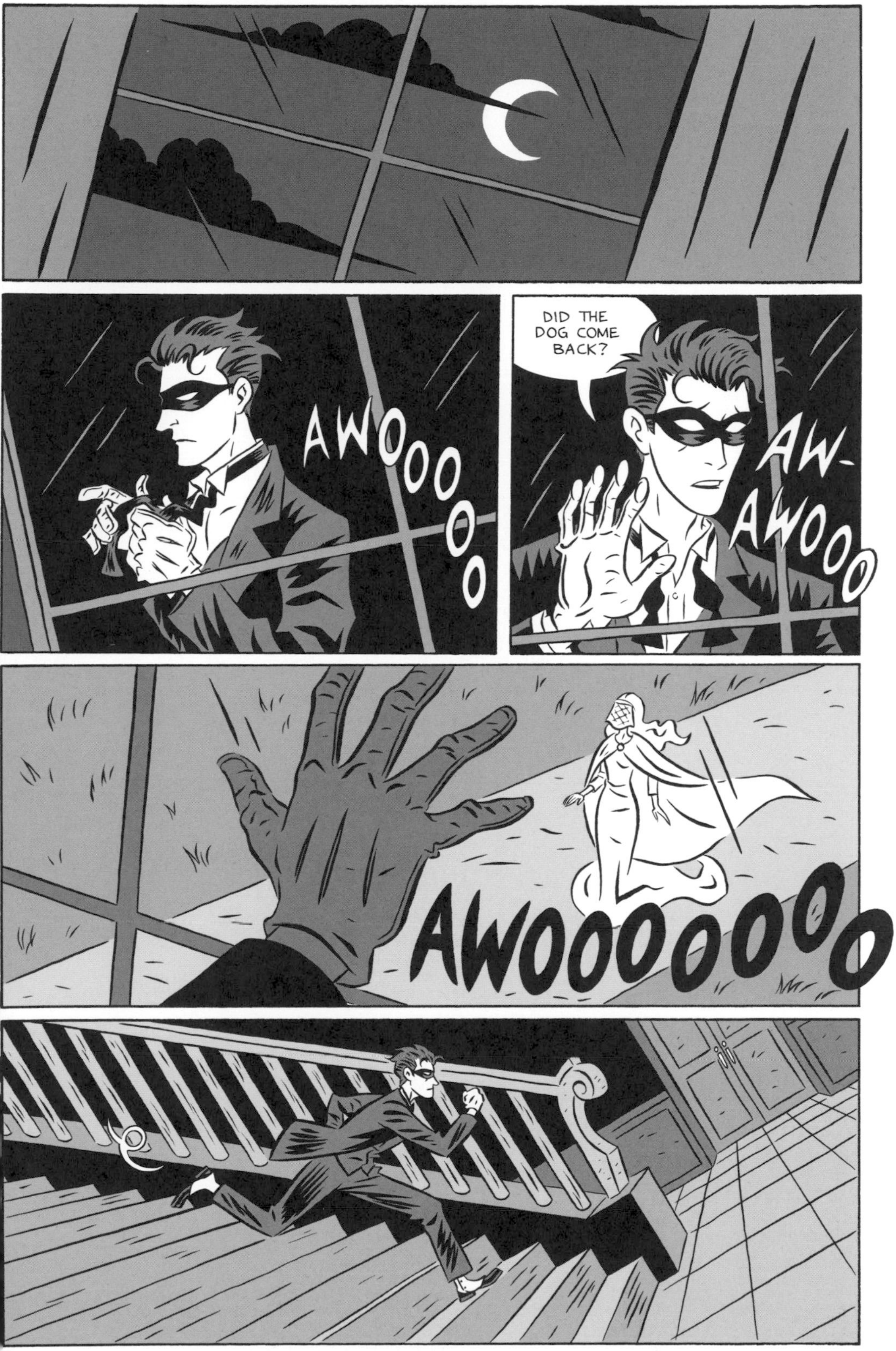
AWOOOOO
DID THE DOG COME BACK?
AW-AWOOO
AWOOOOOOO

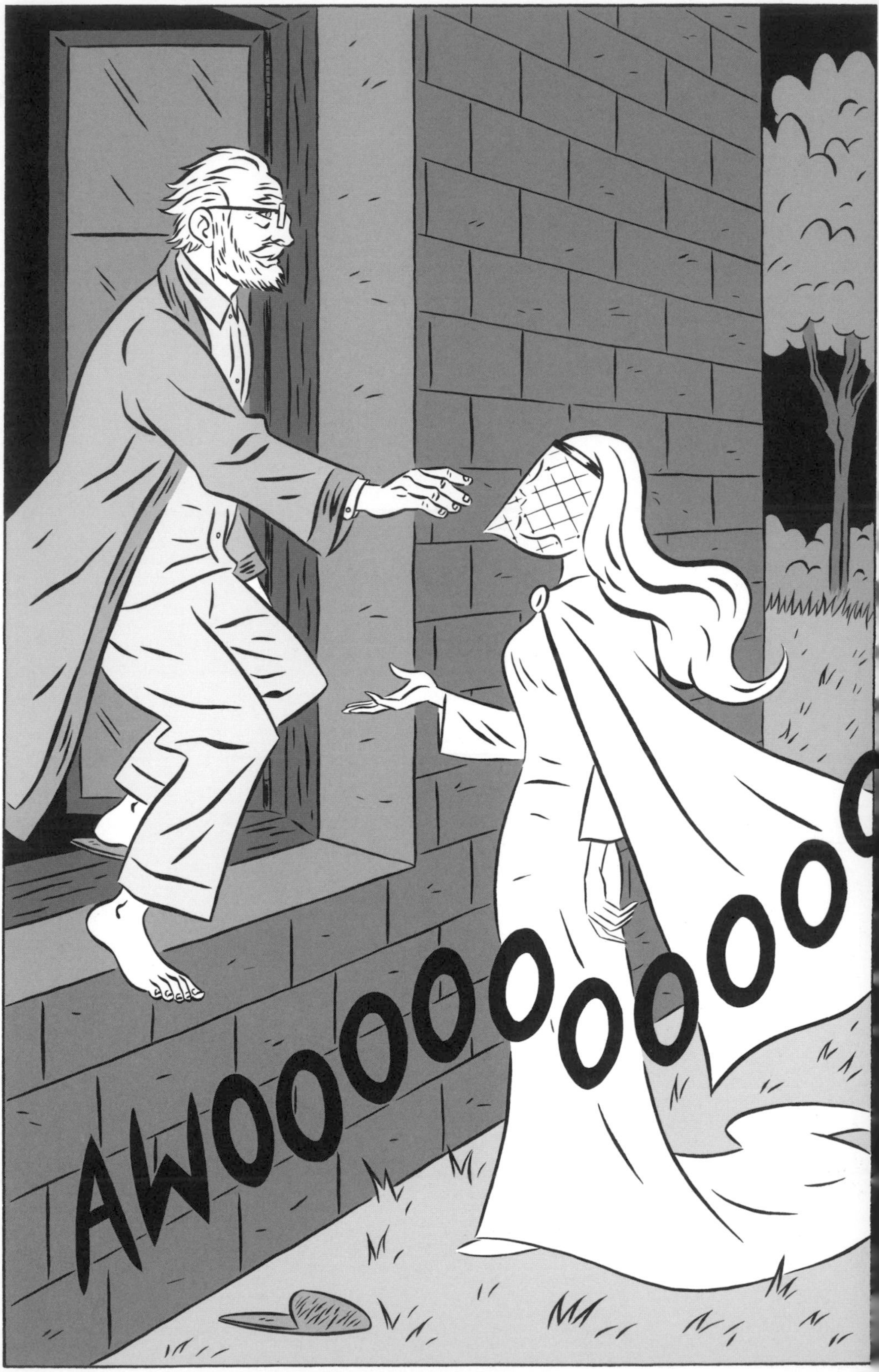
AWOOOOOOOOOOOOO

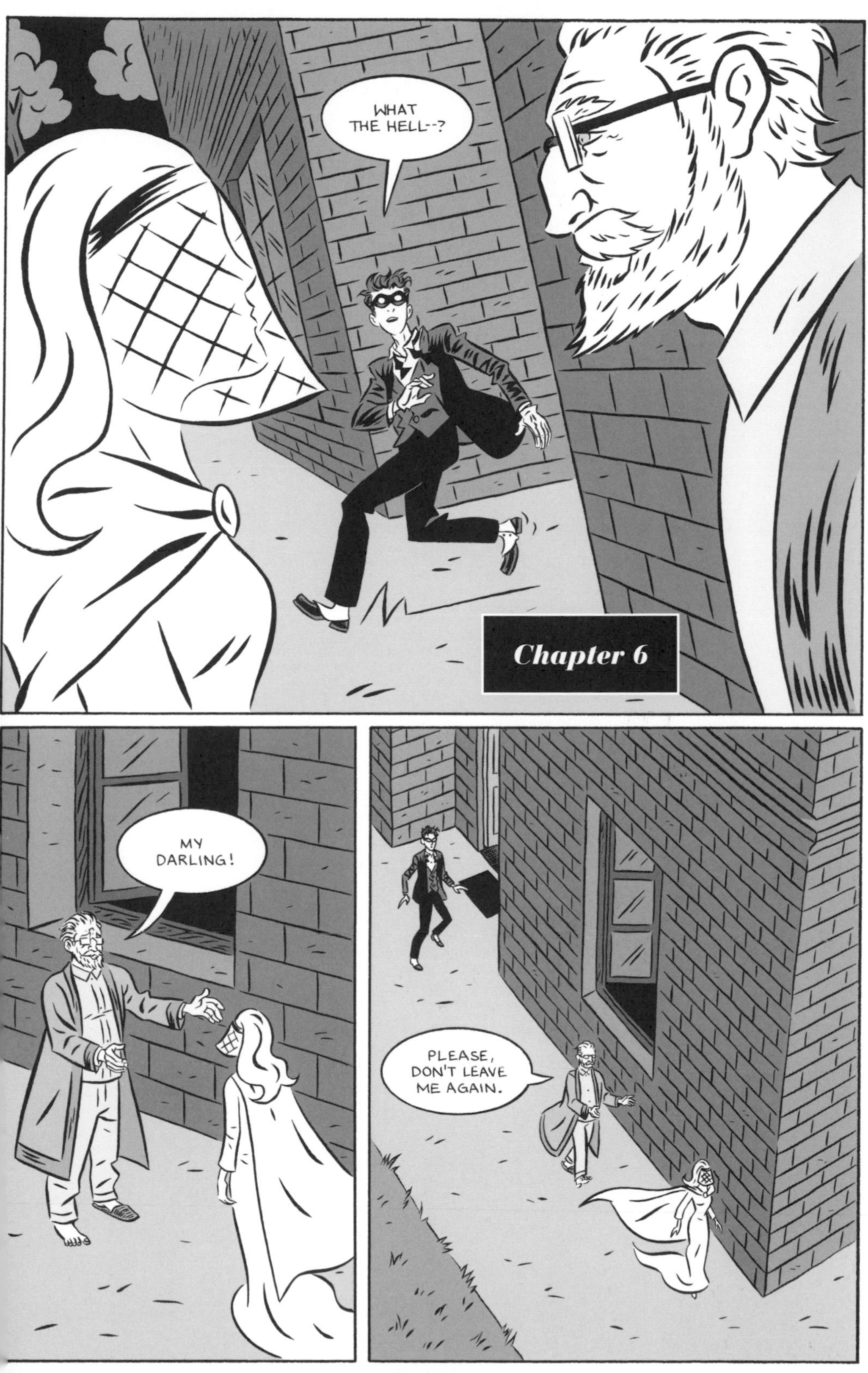
WHAT THE HELL--?
Chapter 6
MY DARLING!
PLEASE, DON'T LEAVE ME AGAIN.

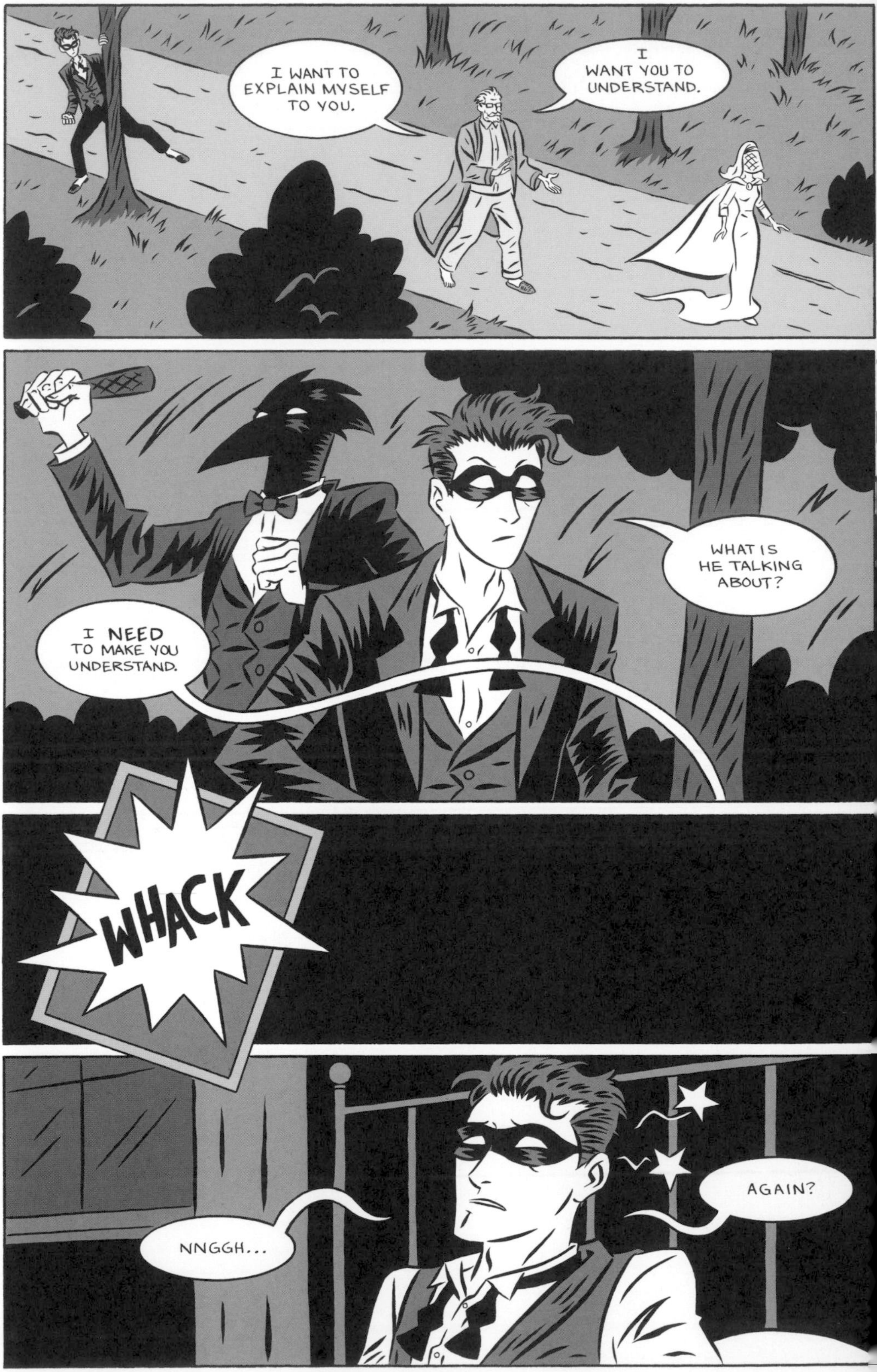
I WANT TO EXPLAIN MYSELF TO YOU.
I WANT YOU TO UNDERSTAND.
WHAT IS HE TALKING ABOUT?
I NEED TO MAKE YOU UNDERSTAND.
WHACK
NNGGH...
AGAIN?

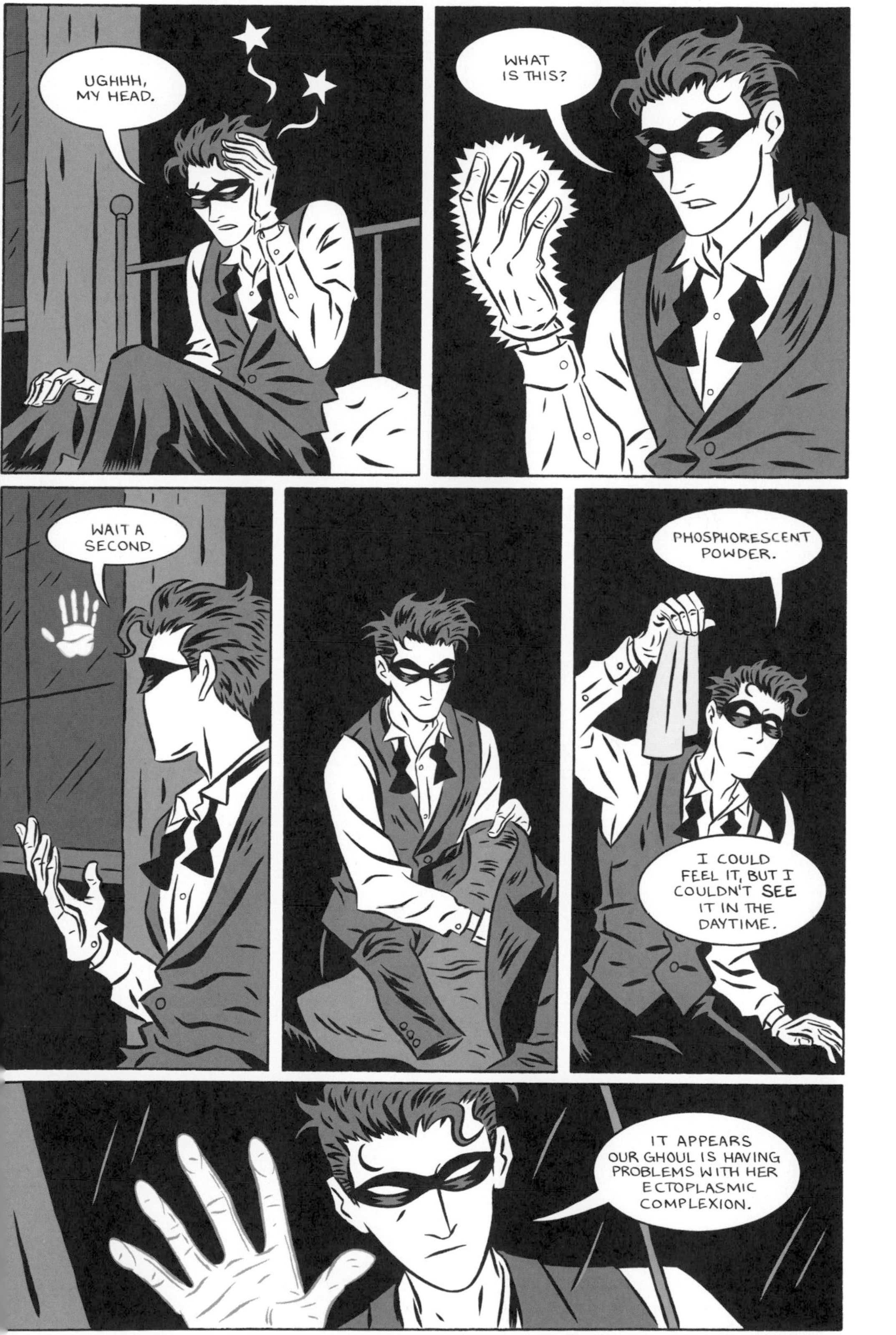
UGHHH, MY HEAD.
WHAT IS THIS?
WAIT A SECOND.
PHOSPHORESCENT POWDER.
I COULD FEEL IT, BUT I COULDN'T SEE IT IN THE DAYTIME.
IT APPEARS OUR GHOUL IS HAVING PROBLEMS WITH HER ECTOPLASMIC COMPLEXION.

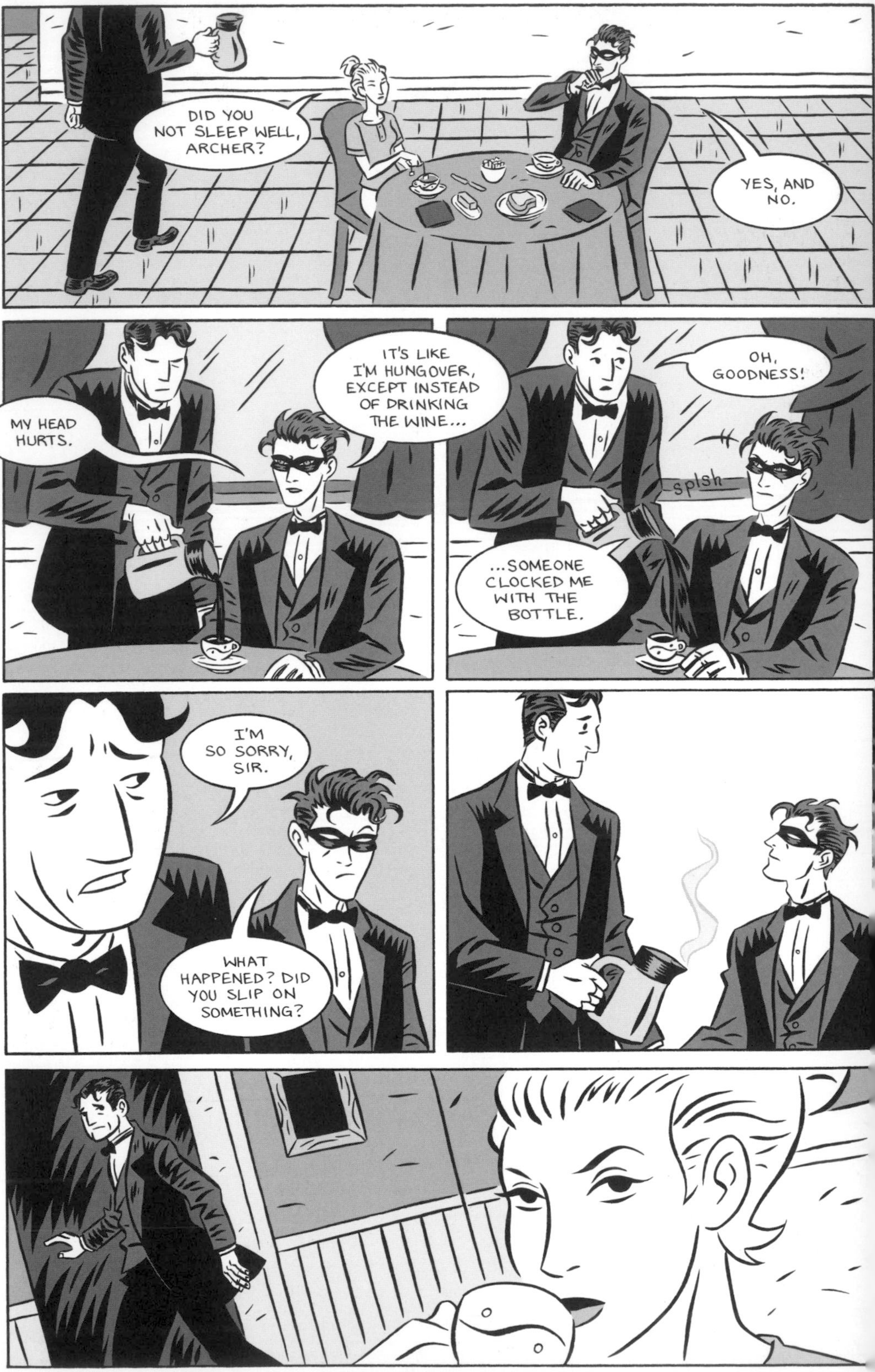
DID YOU NOT SLEEP WELL, ARCHER?
YES, AND NO.
MY HEAD HURTS.
IT'S LIKE I'M HUNGOVER, EXCEPT INSTEAD OF DRINKING THE WINE...
OH, GOODNESS!
splsh
...SOMEONE CLOCKED ME WITH THE BOTTLE.
I'M SO SORRY, SIR.
WHAT HAPPENED? DID YOU SLIP ON SOMETHING?

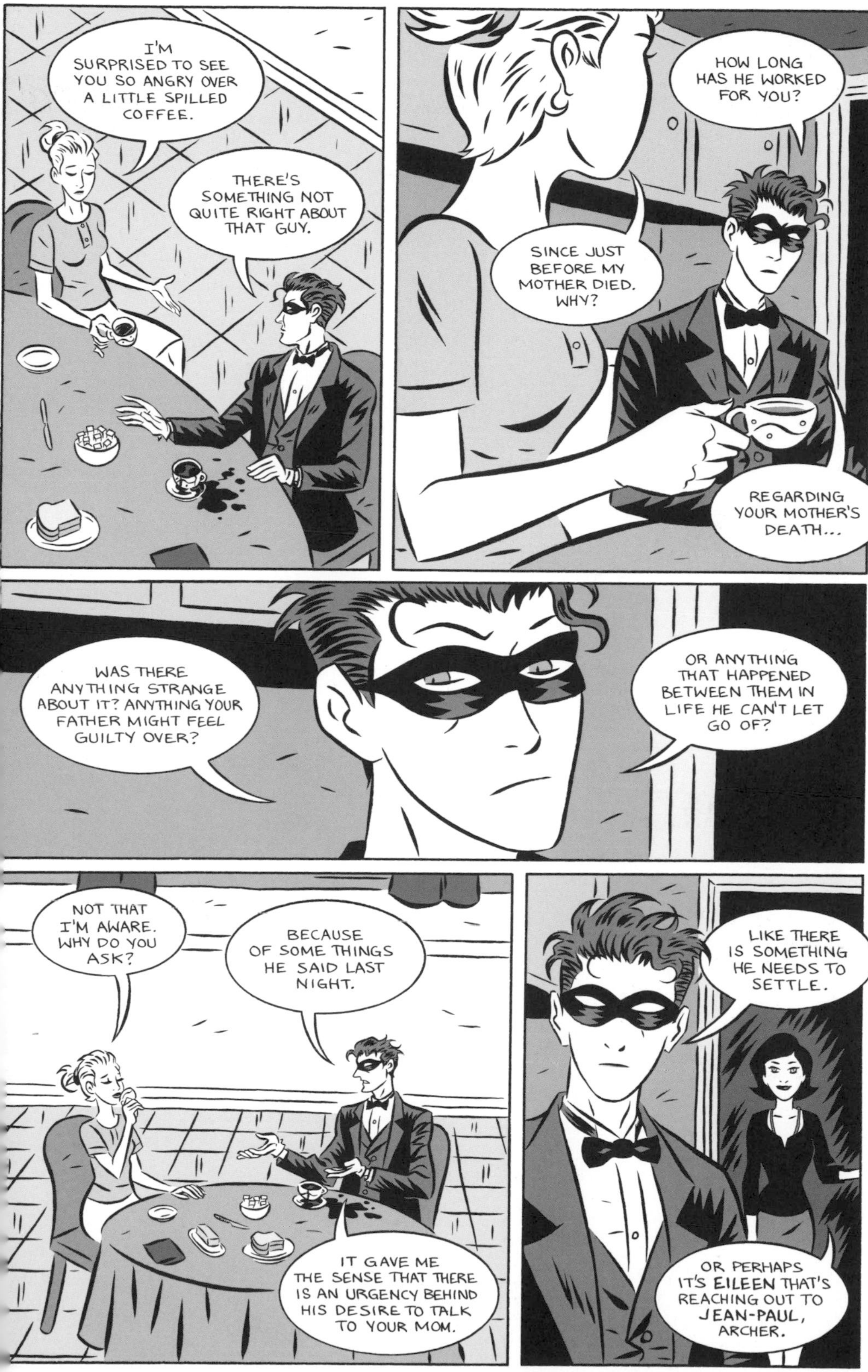
I'M SURPRISED TO SEE YOU SO ANGRY OVER A LITTLE SPILLED COFFEE.
THERE'S SOMETHING NOT QUITE RIGHT ABOUT THAT GUY.
HOW LONG HAS HE WORKED FOR YOU?
SINCE JUST BEFORE MY MOTHER DIED. WHY?
REGARDING YOUR MOTHER'S DEATH...
WAS THERE ANYTHING STRANGE ABOUT IT? ANYTHING YOUR FATHER MIGHT FEEL GUILTY OVER?
OR ANYTHING THAT HAPPENED BETWEEN THEM IN LIFE HE CAN'T LET GO OF?
NOT THAT I'M AWARE. WHY DO YOU ASK?
BECAUSE OF SOME THINGS HE SAID LAST NIGHT.
IT GAVE ME THE SENSE THAT THERE IS AN URGENCY BEHIND HIS DESIRE TO TALK TO YOUR MOM.
LIKE THERE IS SOMETHING HE NEEDS TO SETTLE.
OR PERHAPS IT'S **EILEEN** THAT'S REACHING OUT TO **JEAN-PAUL**, ARCHER.

I UNDERSTAND WHERE YOU'RE COMING FROM. YOU ONLY KNOW HOW TO WORK WITH THE LIVING.

IT IS **I** WHO HANDLE THE DEAD.

HOW'S YOUR LEG?

NOT BAD.

THERE'S A SLIGHT **PHANTOM** PAIN, BUT OTHERWISE...

HA HA HA.

YOU'RE FUNNY.

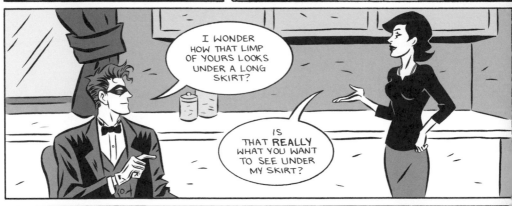

I WONDER HOW THAT LIMP OF YOURS LOOKS UNDER A LONG SKIRT?

IS THAT **REALLY** WHAT YOU WANT TO SEE UNDER MY SKIRT?

I REALLY WISH YOU TWO WOULD TAKE THIS SERIOUSLY.

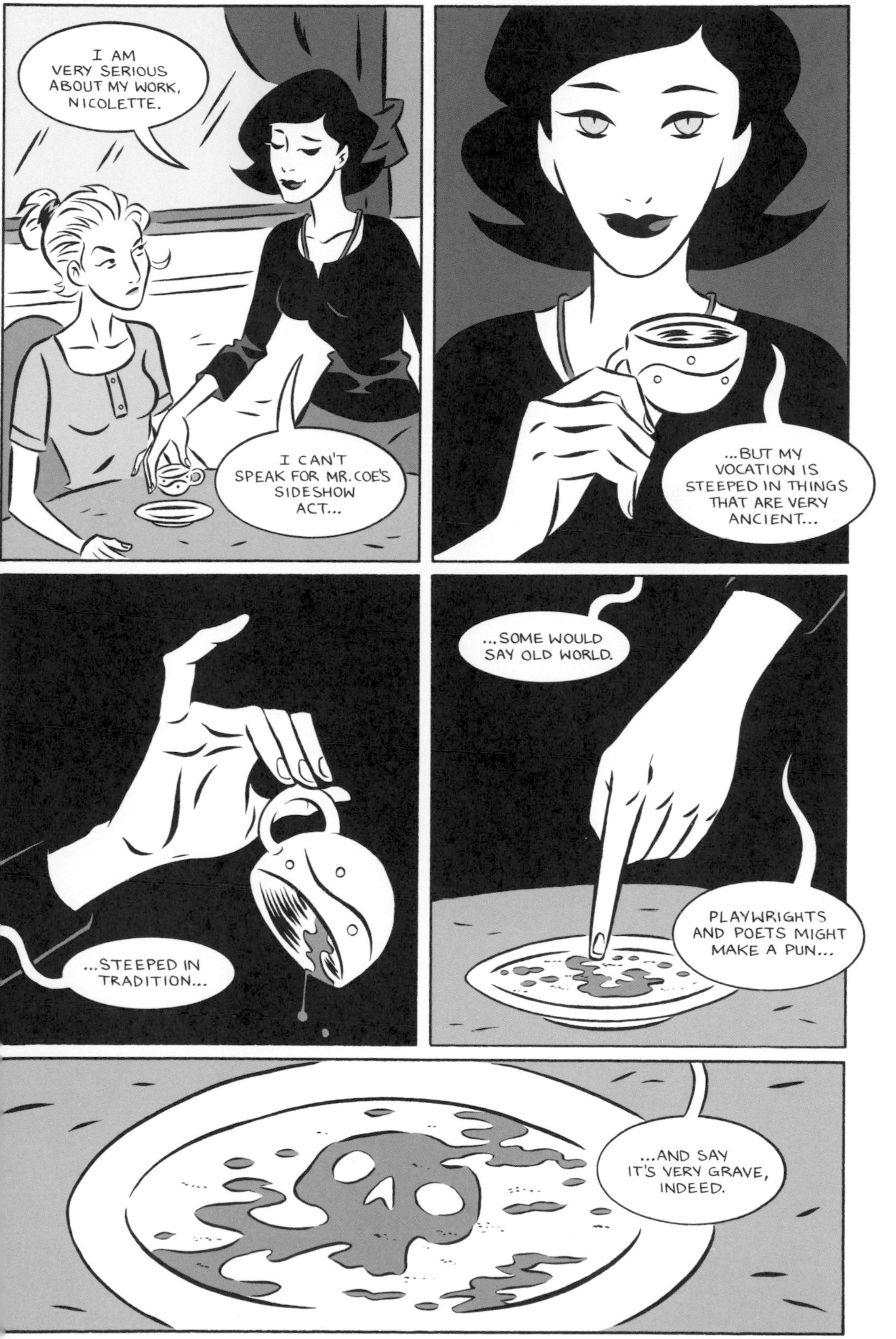
I AM VERY SERIOUS ABOUT MY WORK, NICOLETTE.
I CAN'T SPEAK FOR MR. COE'S SIDESHOW ACT...
...BUT MY VOCATION IS STEEPED IN THINGS THAT ARE VERY ANCIENT...
...STEEPED IN TRADITION...
...SOME WOULD SAY OLD WORLD.
PLAYWRIGHTS AND POETS MIGHT MAKE A PUN...
...AND SAY IT'S VERY GRAVE, INDEED.

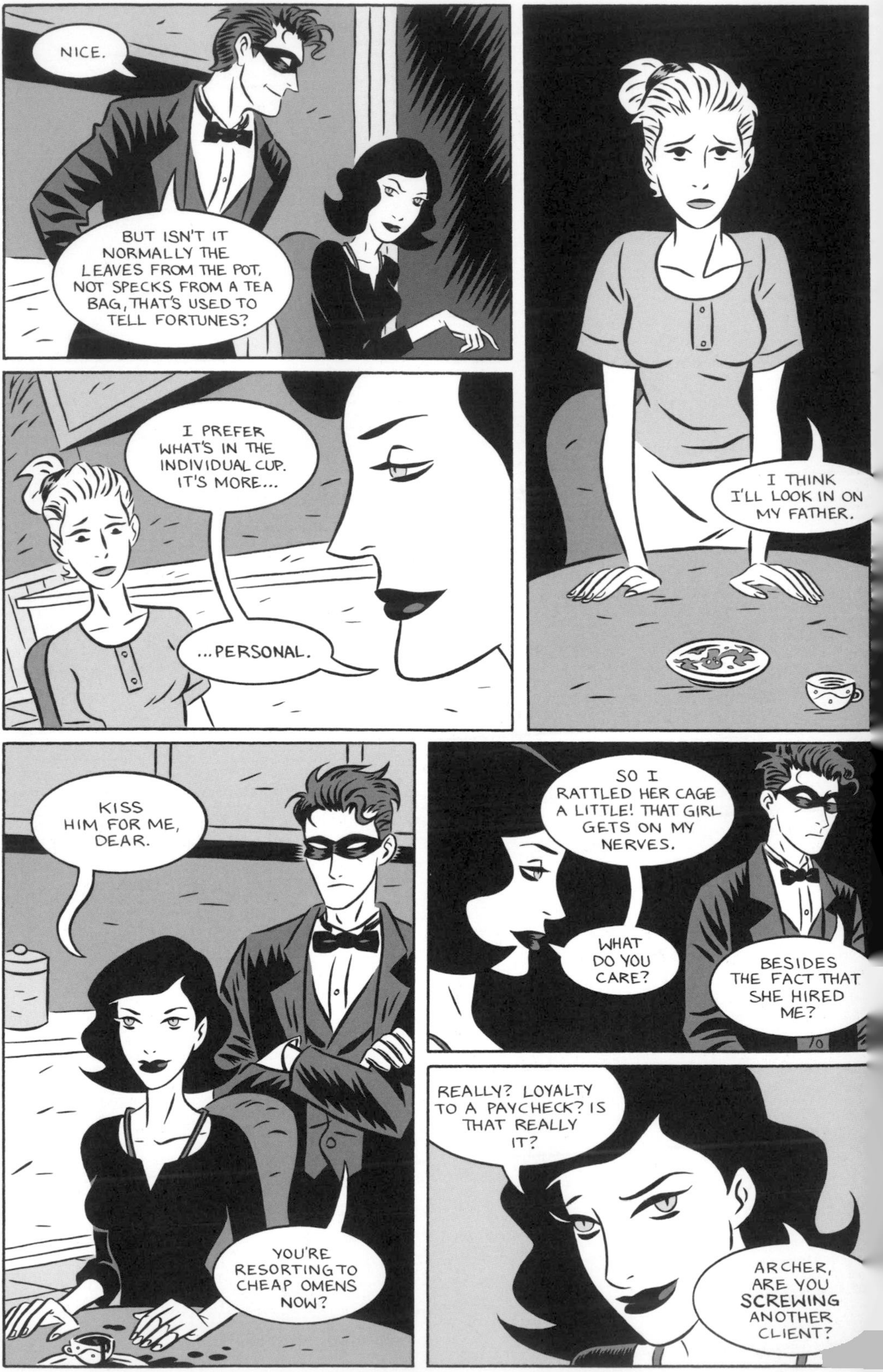
NICE.
BUT ISN'T IT NORMALLY THE LEAVES FROM THE POT, NOT SPECKS FROM A TEA BAG, THAT'S USED TO TELL FORTUNES?
I PREFER WHAT'S IN THE INDIVIDUAL CUP. IT'S MORE...
...PERSONAL.
I THINK I'LL LOOK IN ON MY FATHER.
KISS HIM FOR ME, DEAR.
YOU'RE RESORTING TO CHEAP OMENS NOW?
SO I RATTLED HER CAGE A LITTLE! THAT GIRL GETS ON MY NERVES.
WHAT DO YOU CARE?
BESIDES THE FACT THAT SHE HIRED ME?
REALLY? LOYALTY TO A PAYCHECK? IS THAT REALLY IT?
ARCHER, ARE YOU SCREWING ANOTHER CLIENT?

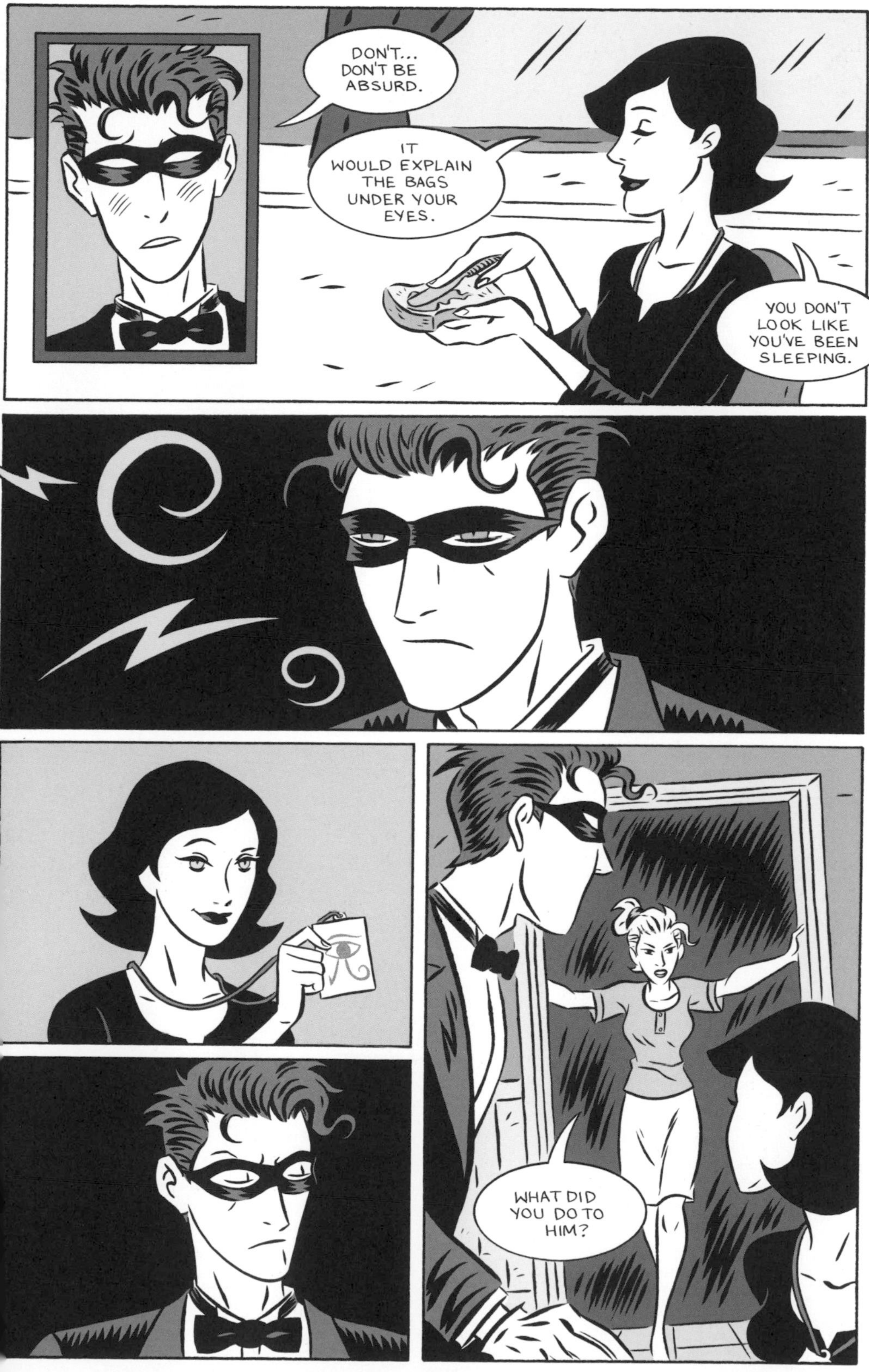
DON'T... DON'T BE ABSURD.
IT WOULD EXPLAIN THE BAGS UNDER YOUR EYES.
YOU DON'T LOOK LIKE YOU'VE BEEN SLEEPING.
WHAT DID YOU DO TO HIM?

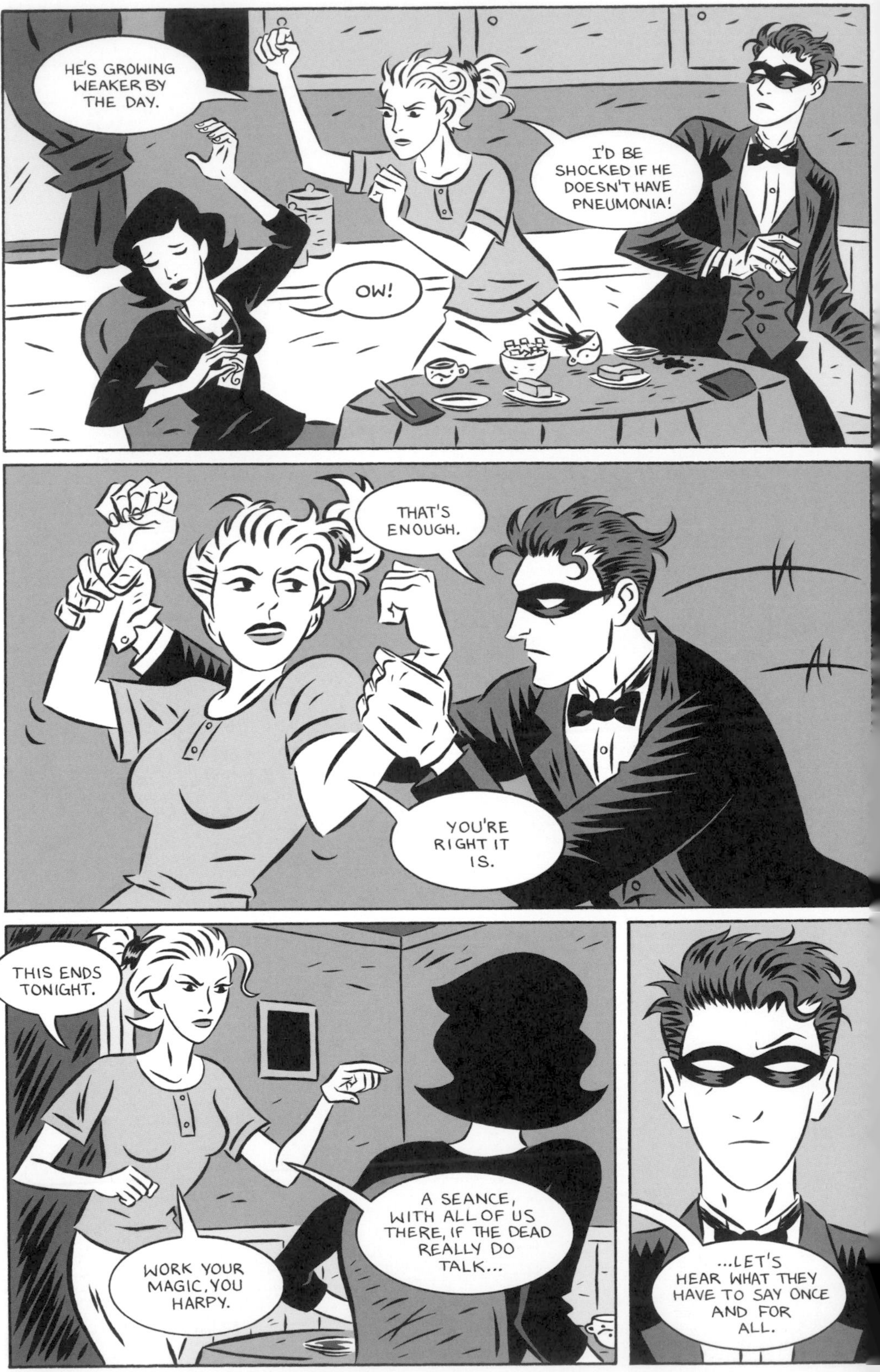
HE'S GROWING WEAKER BY THE DAY.
I'D BE SHOCKED IF HE DOESN'T HAVE PNEUMONIA!
OW!
THAT'S ENOUGH.
YOU'RE RIGHT IT IS.
THIS ENDS TONIGHT.
WORK YOUR MAGIC, YOU HARPY.
A SEANCE, WITH ALL OF US THERE, IF THE DEAD REALLY DO TALK...
...LET'S HEAR WHAT THEY HAVE TO SAY ONCE AND FOR ALL.

Chapter 7

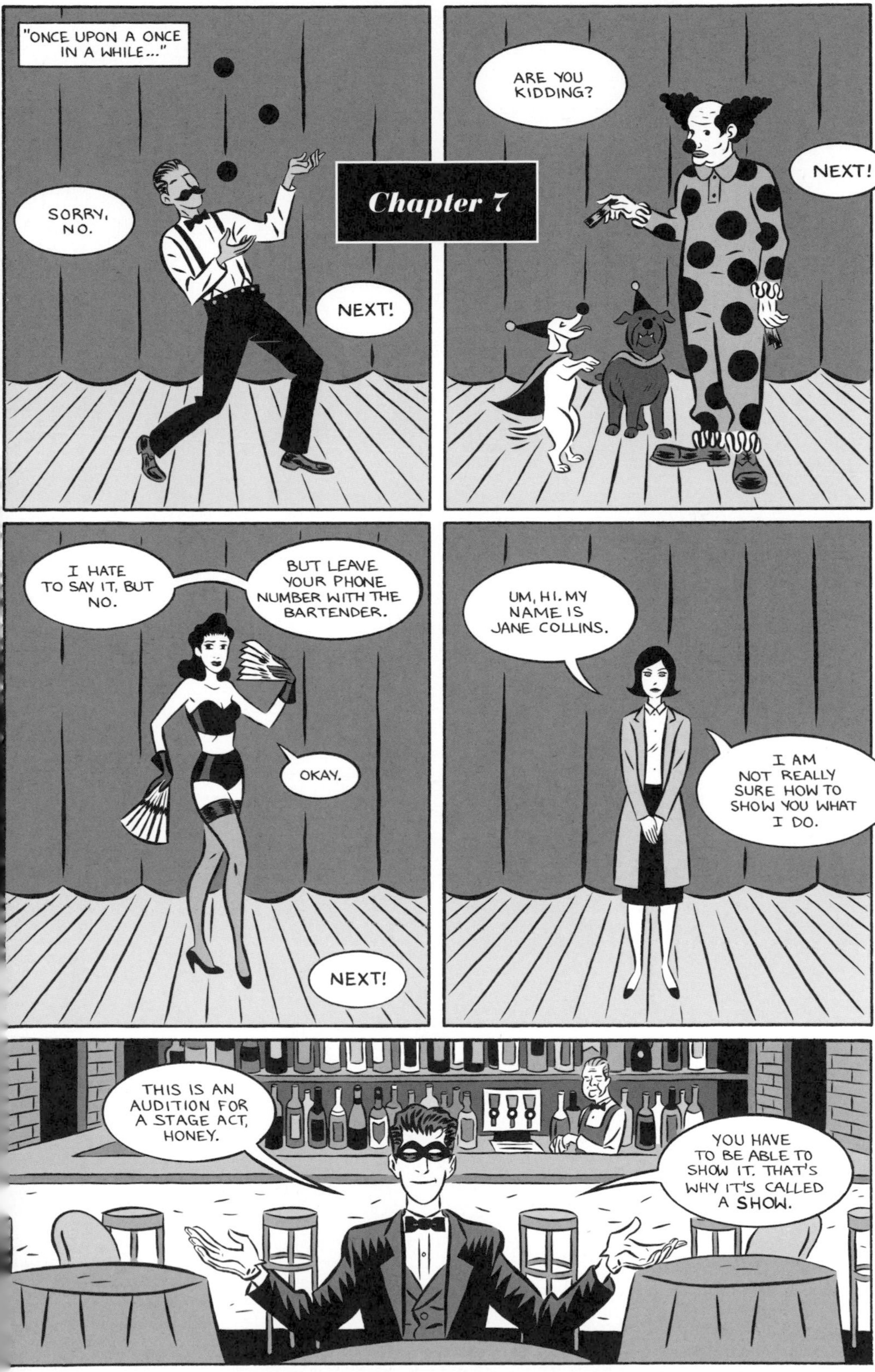
"ONCE UPON A ONCE IN A WHILE..."
SORRY, NO.
NEXT!
ARE YOU KIDDING?
NEXT!
I HATE TO SAY IT, BUT NO.
BUT LEAVE YOUR PHONE NUMBER WITH THE BARTENDER.
OKAY.
NEXT!
UM, HI. MY NAME IS JANE COLLINS.
I AM NOT REALLY SURE HOW TO SHOW YOU WHAT I DO.
THIS IS AN AUDITION FOR A STAGE ACT, HONEY.
YOU HAVE TO BE ABLE TO SHOW IT. THAT'S WHY IT'S CALLED A SHOW.

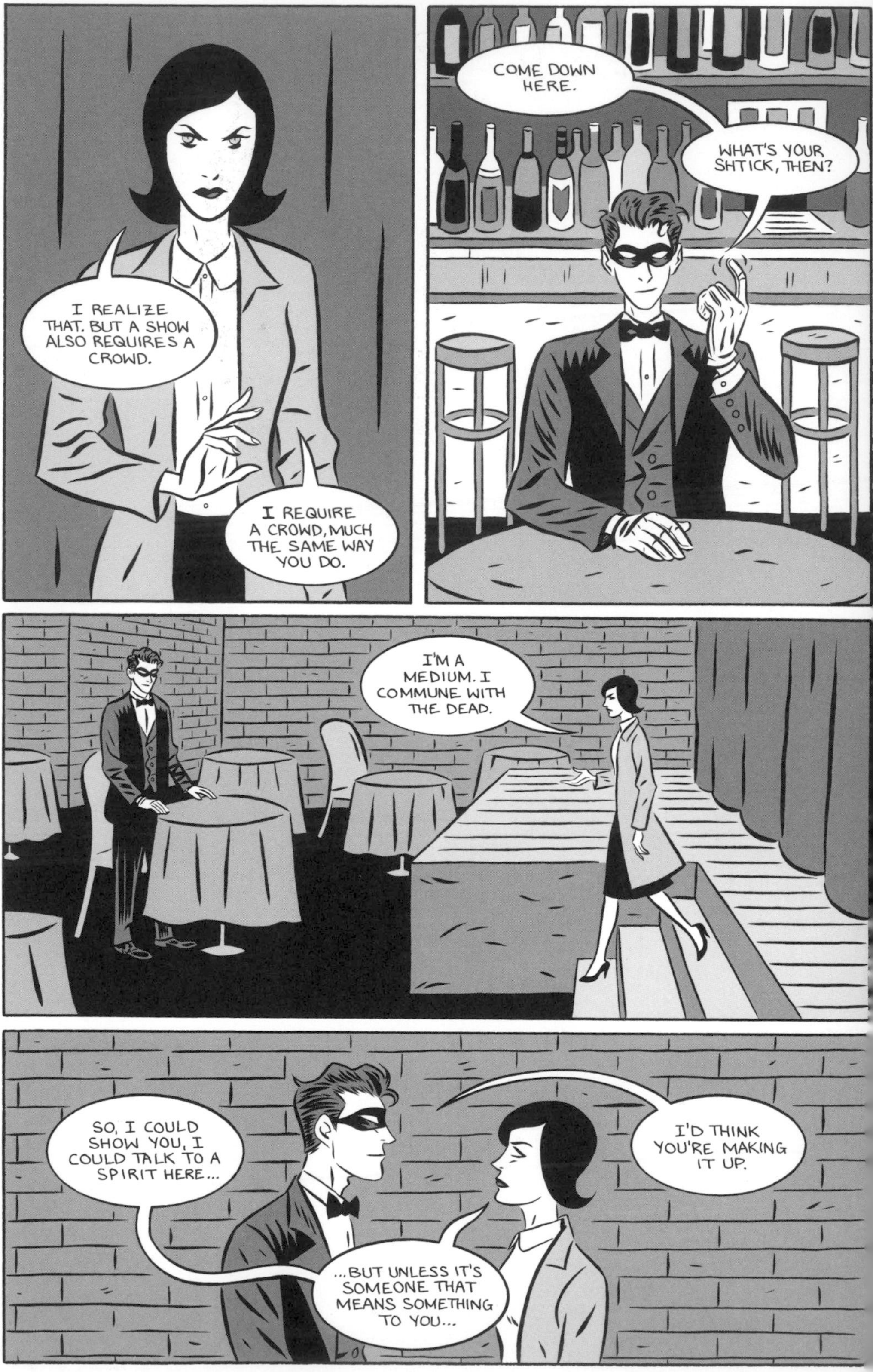
I REALIZE THAT. BUT A SHOW ALSO REQUIRES A CROWD.
I REQUIRE A CROWD, MUCH THE SAME WAY YOU DO.
COME DOWN HERE.
WHAT'S YOUR SHTICK, THEN?
I'M A MEDIUM. I COMMUNE WITH THE DEAD.
SO, I COULD SHOW YOU, I COULD TALK TO A SPIRIT HERE...
...BUT UNLESS IT'S SOMEONE THAT MEANS SOMETHING TO YOU...
I'D THINK YOU'RE MAKING IT UP.

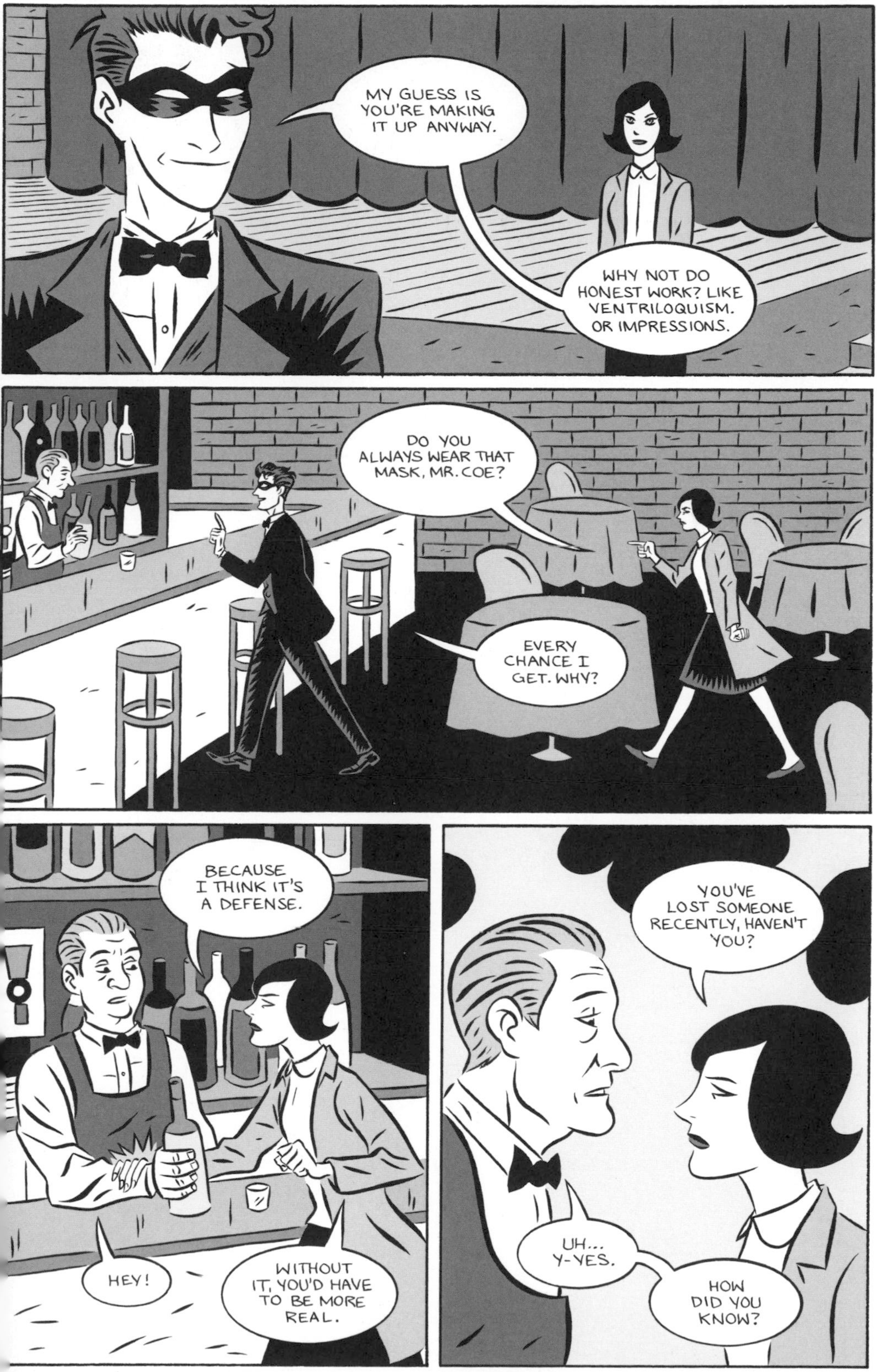
MY GUESS IS YOU'RE MAKING IT UP ANYWAY.
WHY NOT DO HONEST WORK? LIKE VENTRILOQUISM. OR IMPRESSIONS.
DO YOU ALWAYS WEAR THAT MASK, MR. COE?
EVERY CHANCE I GET. WHY?
BECAUSE I THINK IT'S A DEFENSE.
HEY!
WITHOUT IT, YOU'D HAVE TO BE MORE REAL.
YOU'VE LOST SOMEONE RECENTLY, HAVEN'T YOU?
UH... Y-YES.
HOW DID YOU KNOW?

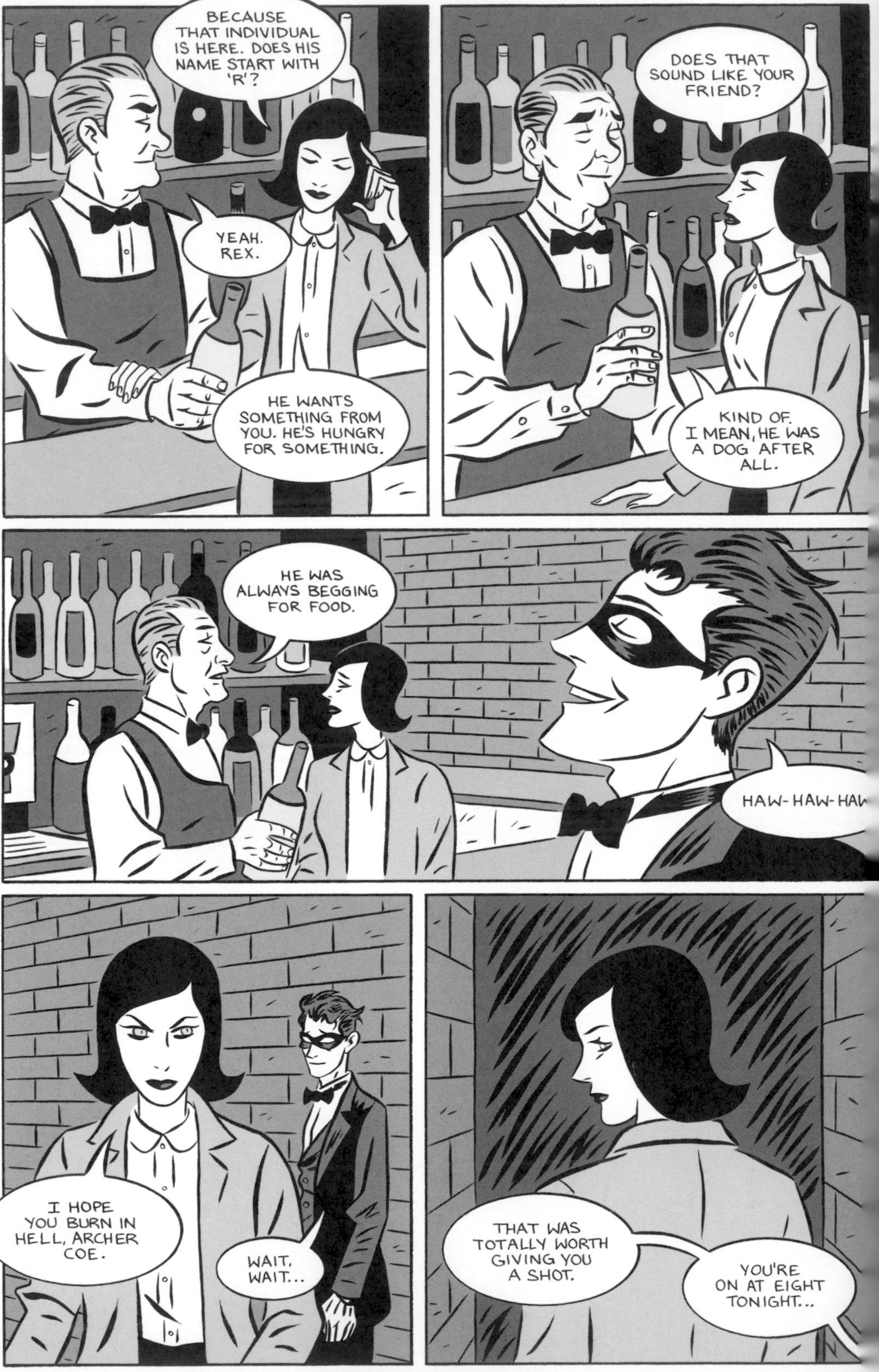
BECAUSE THAT INDIVIDUAL IS HERE. DOES HIS NAME START WITH 'R'?
YEAH. REX.
HE WANTS SOMETHING FROM YOU. HE'S HUNGRY FOR SOMETHING.
DOES THAT SOUND LIKE YOUR FRIEND?
KIND OF. I MEAN, HE WAS A DOG AFTER ALL.
HE WAS ALWAYS BEGGING FOR FOOD.
HAW-HAW-HAW
I HOPE YOU BURN IN HELL, ARCHER COE.
WAIT, WAIT...
THAT WAS TOTALLY WORTH GIVING YOU A SHOT.
YOU'RE ON AT EIGHT TONIGHT...

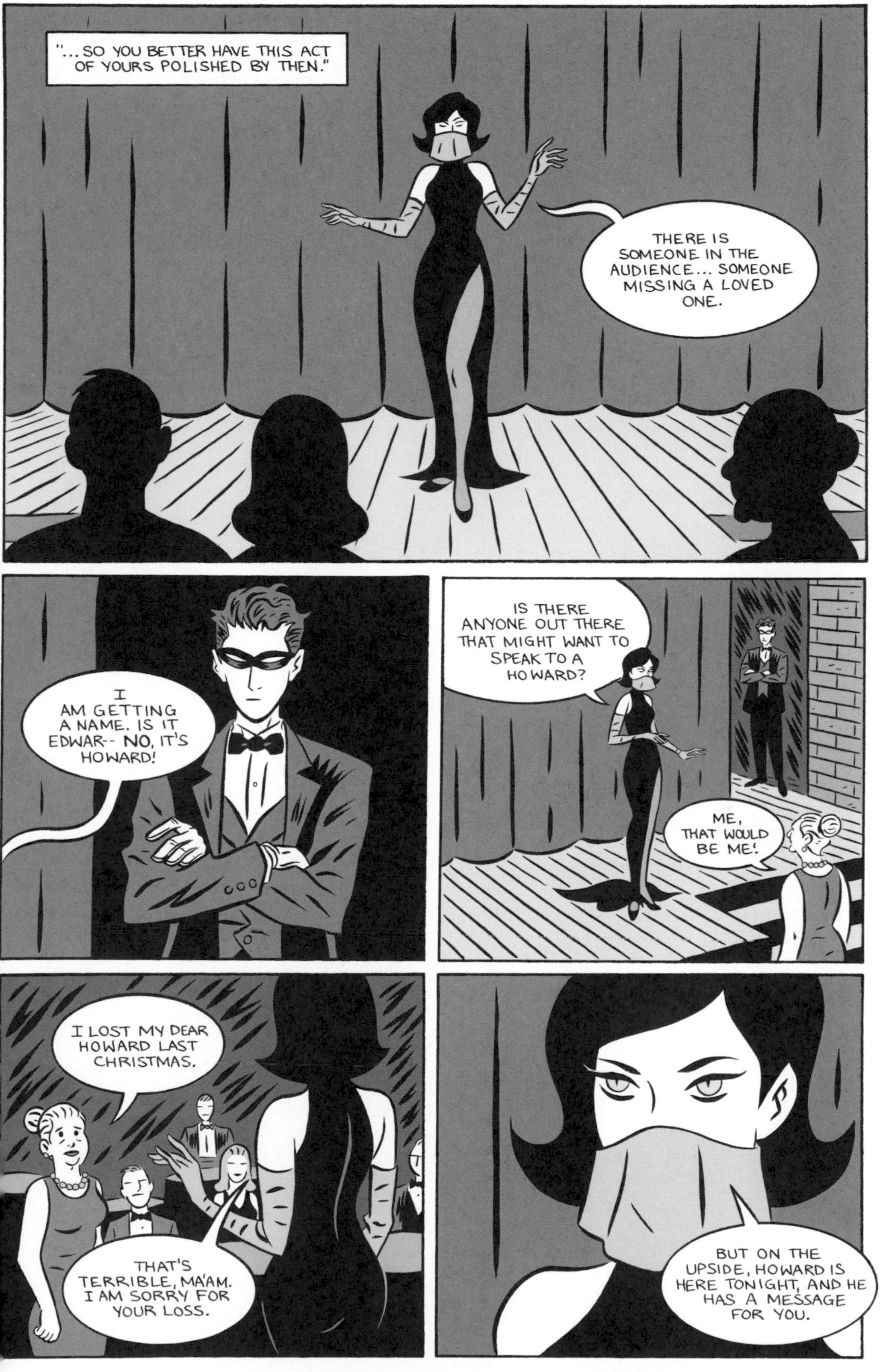
"...SO YOU BETTER HAVE THIS ACT OF YOURS POLISHED BY THEN."
THERE IS SOMEONE IN THE AUDIENCE... SOMEONE MISSING A LOVED ONE.
I AM GETTING A NAME. IS IT EDWAR-- NO, IT'S HOWARD!
IS THERE ANYONE OUT THERE THAT MIGHT WANT TO SPEAK TO A HOWARD?
ME, THAT WOULD BE ME!
I LOST MY DEAR HOWARD LAST CHRISTMAS.
THAT'S TERRIBLE, MA'AM. I AM SORRY FOR YOUR LOSS.
BUT ON THE UPSIDE, HOWARD IS HERE TONIGHT, AND HE HAS A MESSAGE FOR YOU.

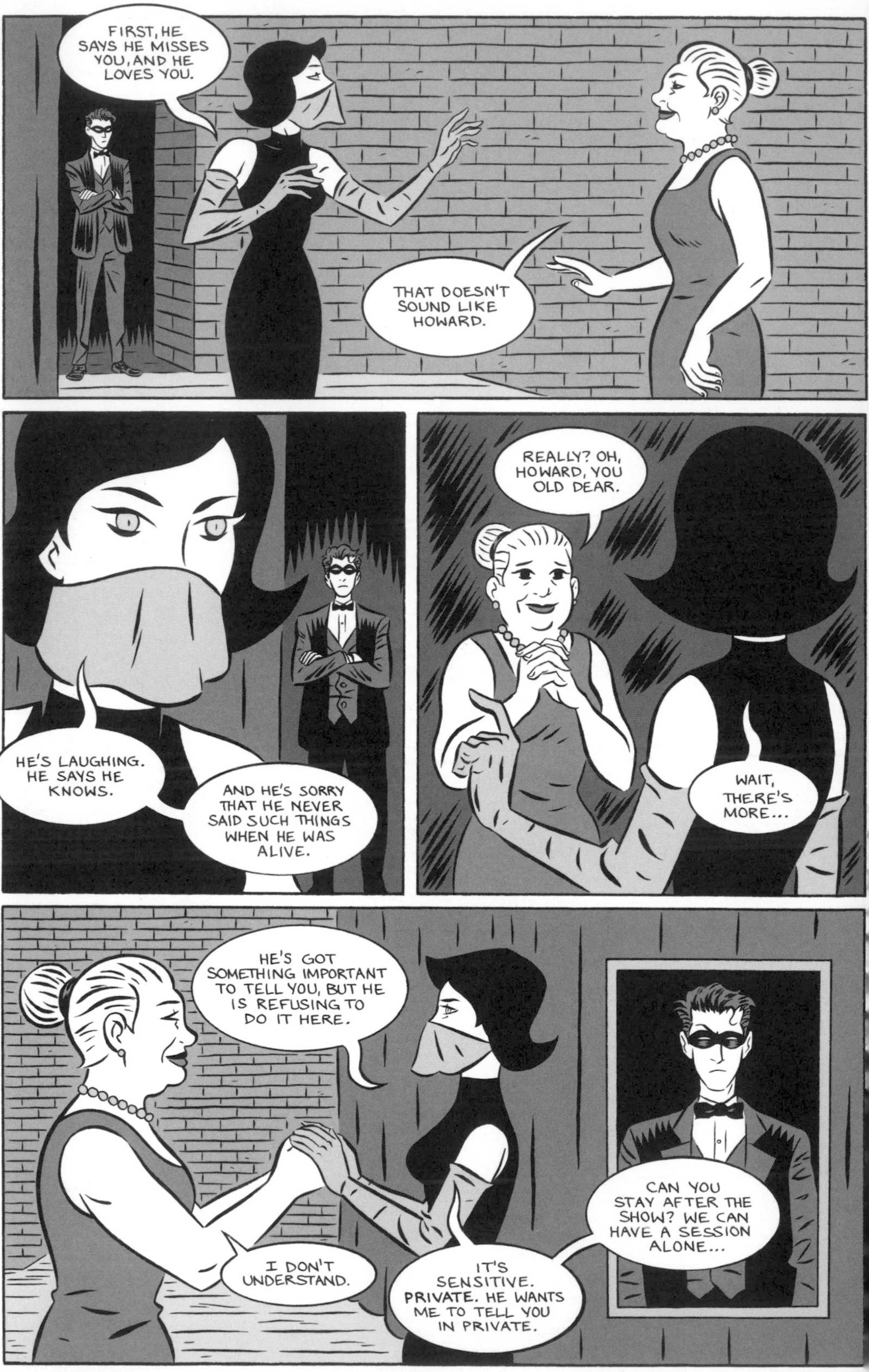
FIRST, HE SAYS HE MISSES YOU, AND HE LOVES YOU.
THAT DOESN'T SOUND LIKE HOWARD.
HE'S LAUGHING. HE SAYS HE KNOWS.
AND HE'S SORRY THAT HE NEVER SAID SUCH THINGS WHEN HE WAS ALIVE.
REALLY? OH, HOWARD, YOU OLD DEAR.
WAIT, THERE'S MORE...
HE'S GOT SOMETHING IMPORTANT TO TELL YOU, BUT HE IS REFUSING TO DO IT HERE.
I DON'T UNDERSTAND.
IT'S SENSITIVE. PRIVATE. HE WANTS ME TO TELL YOU IN PRIVATE.
CAN YOU STAY AFTER THE SHOW? WE CAN HAVE A SESSION ALONE...

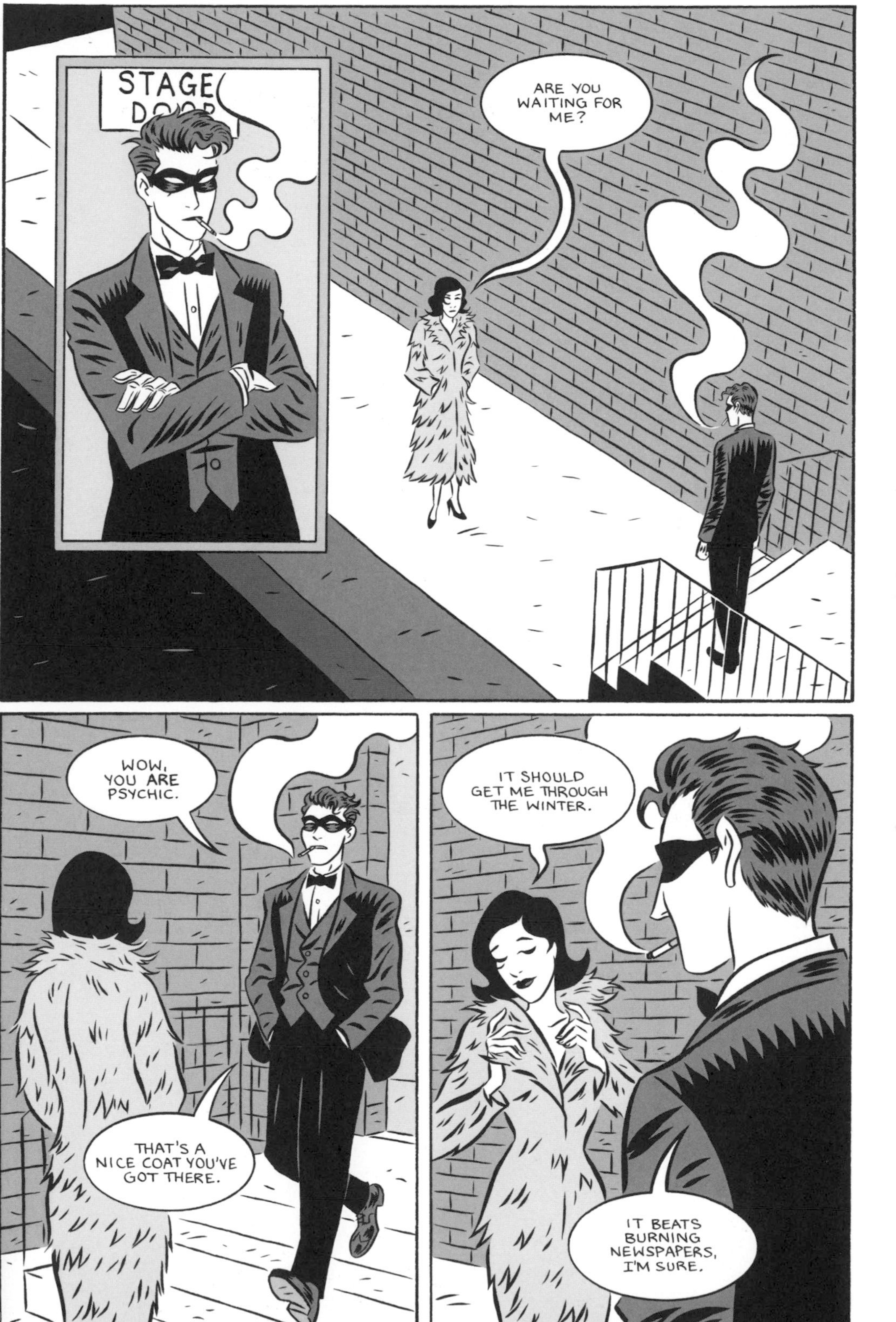
STAGE DOOR
ARE YOU WAITING FOR ME?
WOW, YOU ARE PSYCHIC.
THAT'S A NICE COAT YOU'VE GOT THERE.
IT SHOULD GET ME THROUGH THE WINTER.
IT BEATS BURNING NEWSPAPERS, I'M SURE.

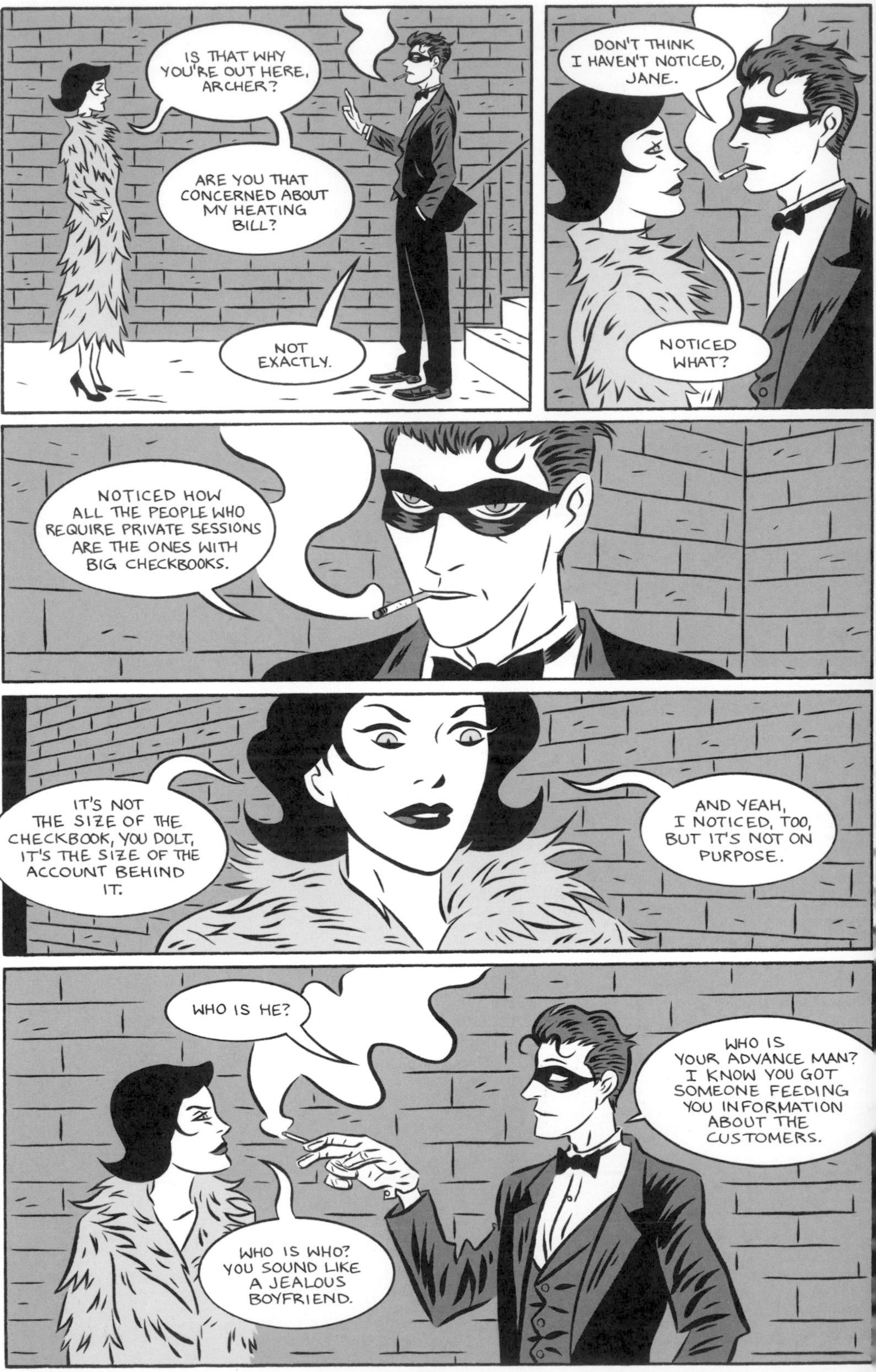
IS THAT WHY YOU'RE OUT HERE, ARCHER?
ARE YOU THAT CONCERNED ABOUT MY HEATING BILL?
NOT EXACTLY.
DON'T THINK I HAVEN'T NOTICED, JANE.
NOTICED WHAT?
NOTICED HOW ALL THE PEOPLE WHO REQUIRE PRIVATE SESSIONS ARE THE ONES WITH BIG CHECKBOOKS.
IT'S NOT THE SIZE OF THE CHECKBOOK, YOU DOLT, IT'S THE SIZE OF THE ACCOUNT BEHIND IT.
AND YEAH, I NOTICED, TOO, BUT IT'S NOT ON PURPOSE.
WHO IS HE?
WHO IS YOUR ADVANCE MAN? I KNOW YOU GOT SOMEONE FEEDING YOU INFORMATION ABOUT THE CUSTOMERS.
WHO IS WHO? YOU SOUND LIKE A JEALOUS BOYFRIEND.

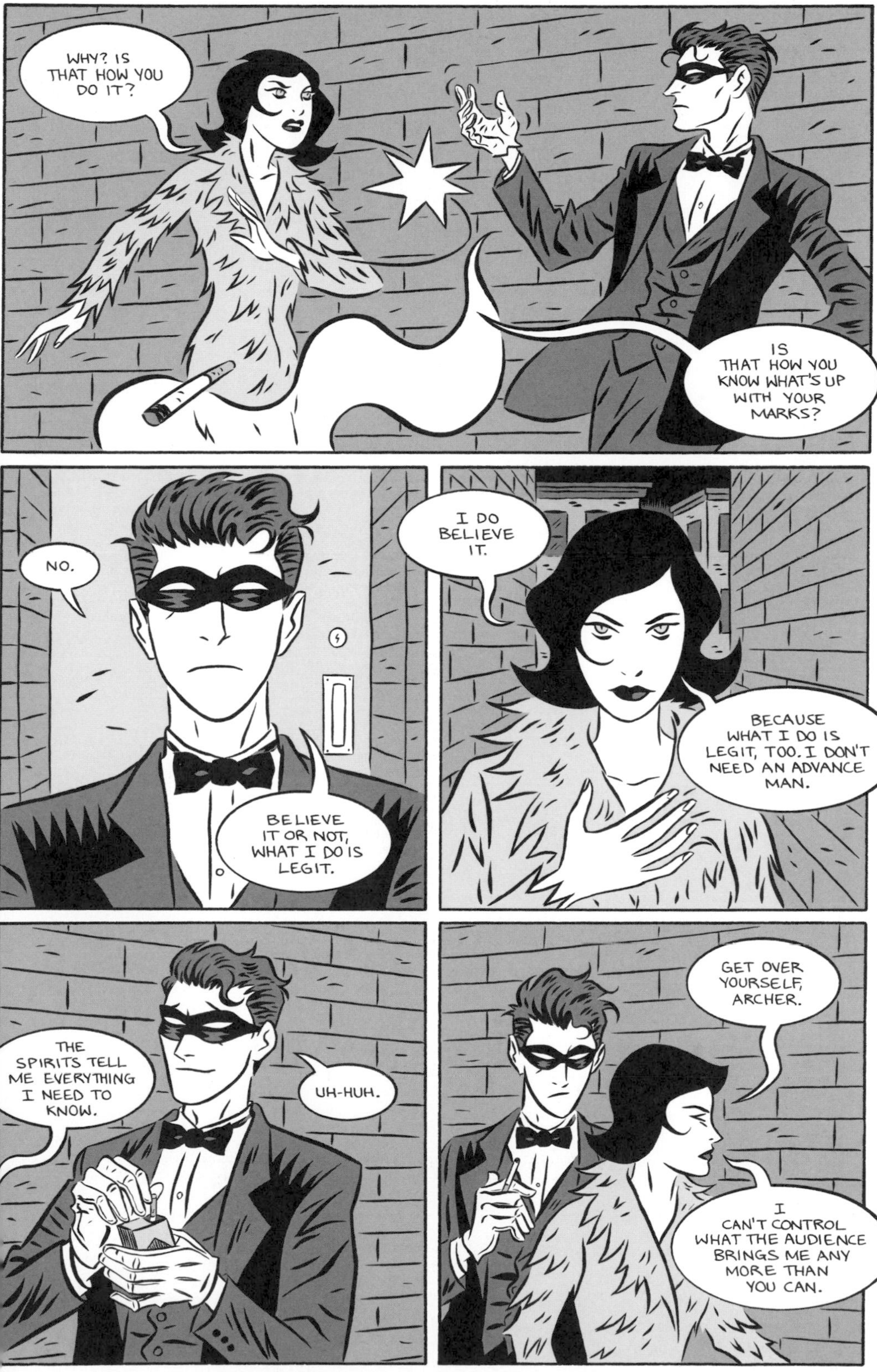
WHY? IS THAT HOW YOU DO IT?
IS THAT HOW YOU KNOW WHAT'S UP WITH YOUR MARKS?
NO.
BELIEVE IT OR NOT, WHAT I DO IS LEGIT.
I DO BELIEVE IT.
BECAUSE WHAT I DO IS LEGIT, TOO. I DON'T NEED AN ADVANCE MAN.
THE SPIRITS TELL ME EVERYTHING I NEED TO KNOW.
UH-HUH.
GET OVER YOURSELF, ARCHER.
I CAN'T CONTROL WHAT THE AUDIENCE BRINGS ME ANY MORE THAN YOU CAN.

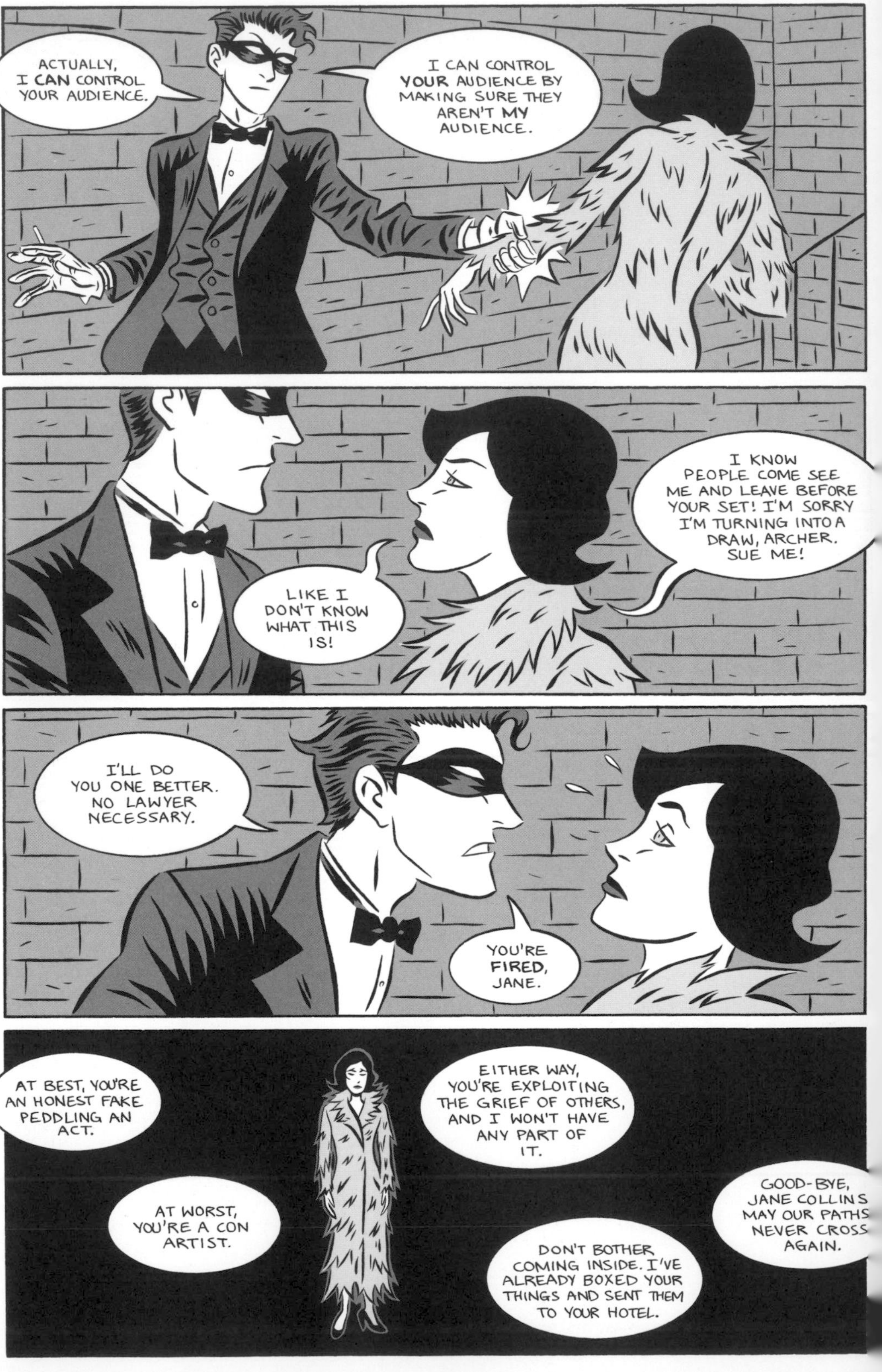
ACTUALLY, I CAN CONTROL YOUR AUDIENCE.
I CAN CONTROL YOUR AUDIENCE BY MAKING SURE THEY AREN'T MY AUDIENCE.
I KNOW PEOPLE COME SEE ME AND LEAVE BEFORE YOUR SET! I'M SORRY I'M TURNING INTO A DRAW, ARCHER. SUE ME!
LIKE I DON'T KNOW WHAT THIS IS!
I'LL DO YOU ONE BETTER. NO LAWYER NECESSARY.
YOU'RE FIRED, JANE.
AT BEST, YOU'RE AN HONEST FAKE PEDDLING AN ACT.
AT WORST, YOU'RE A CON ARTIST.
EITHER WAY, YOU'RE EXPLOITING THE GRIEF OF OTHERS, AND I WON'T HAVE ANY PART OF IT.
DON'T BOTHER COMING INSIDE. I'VE ALREADY BOXED YOUR THINGS AND SENT THEM TO YOUR HOTEL.
GOOD-BYE, JANE COLLINS MAY OUR PATHS NEVER CROSS AGAIN.

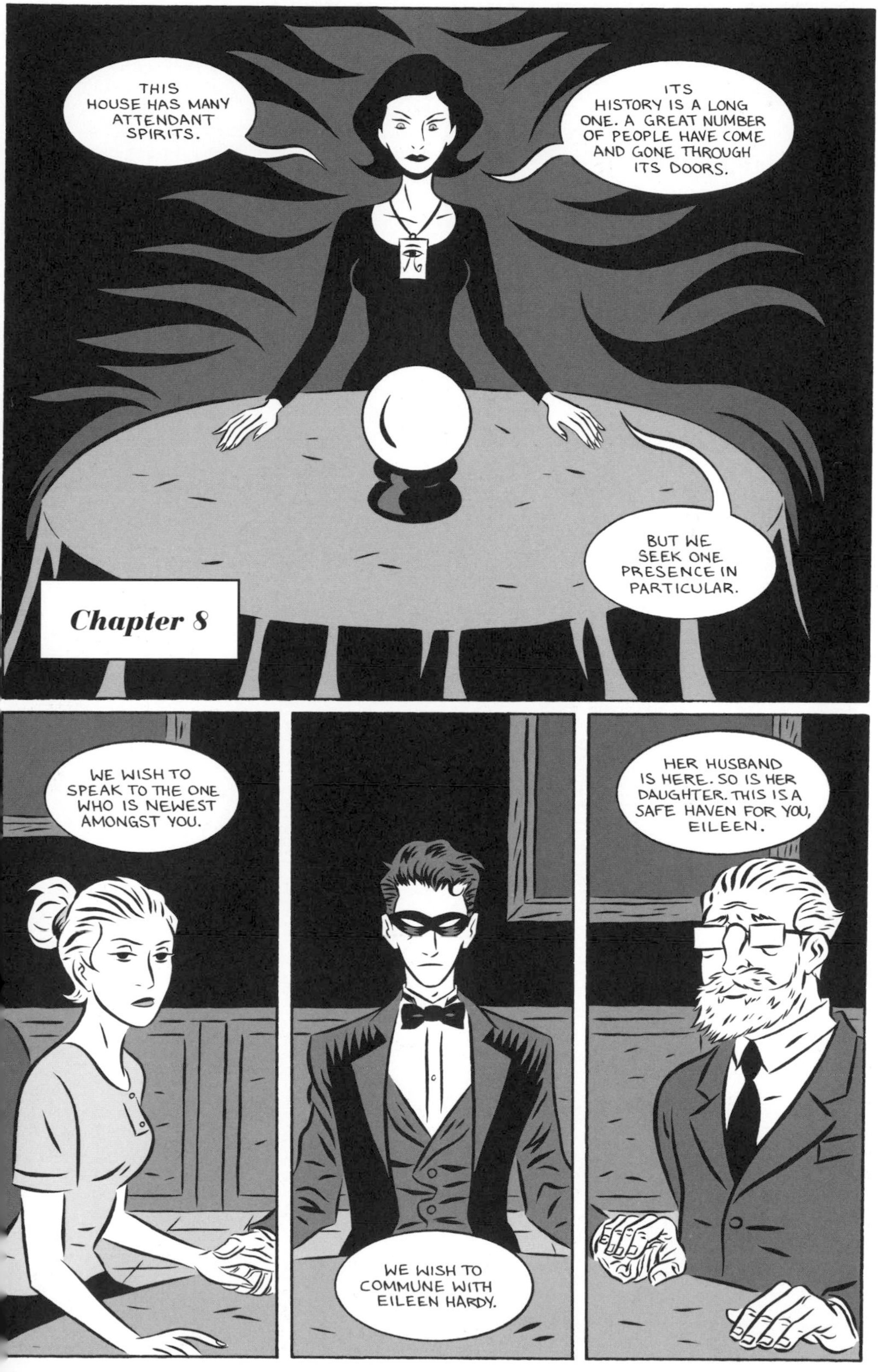
THIS HOUSE HAS MANY ATTENDANT SPIRITS.
ITS HISTORY IS A LONG ONE. A GREAT NUMBER OF PEOPLE HAVE COME AND GONE THROUGH ITS DOORS.
BUT WE SEEK ONE PRESENCE IN PARTICULAR.
Chapter 8
WE WISH TO SPEAK TO THE ONE WHO IS NEWEST AMONGST YOU.
WE WISH TO COMMUNE WITH EILEEN HARDY.
HER HUSBAND IS HERE. SO IS HER DAUGHTER. THIS IS A SAFE HAVEN FOR YOU, EILEEN.

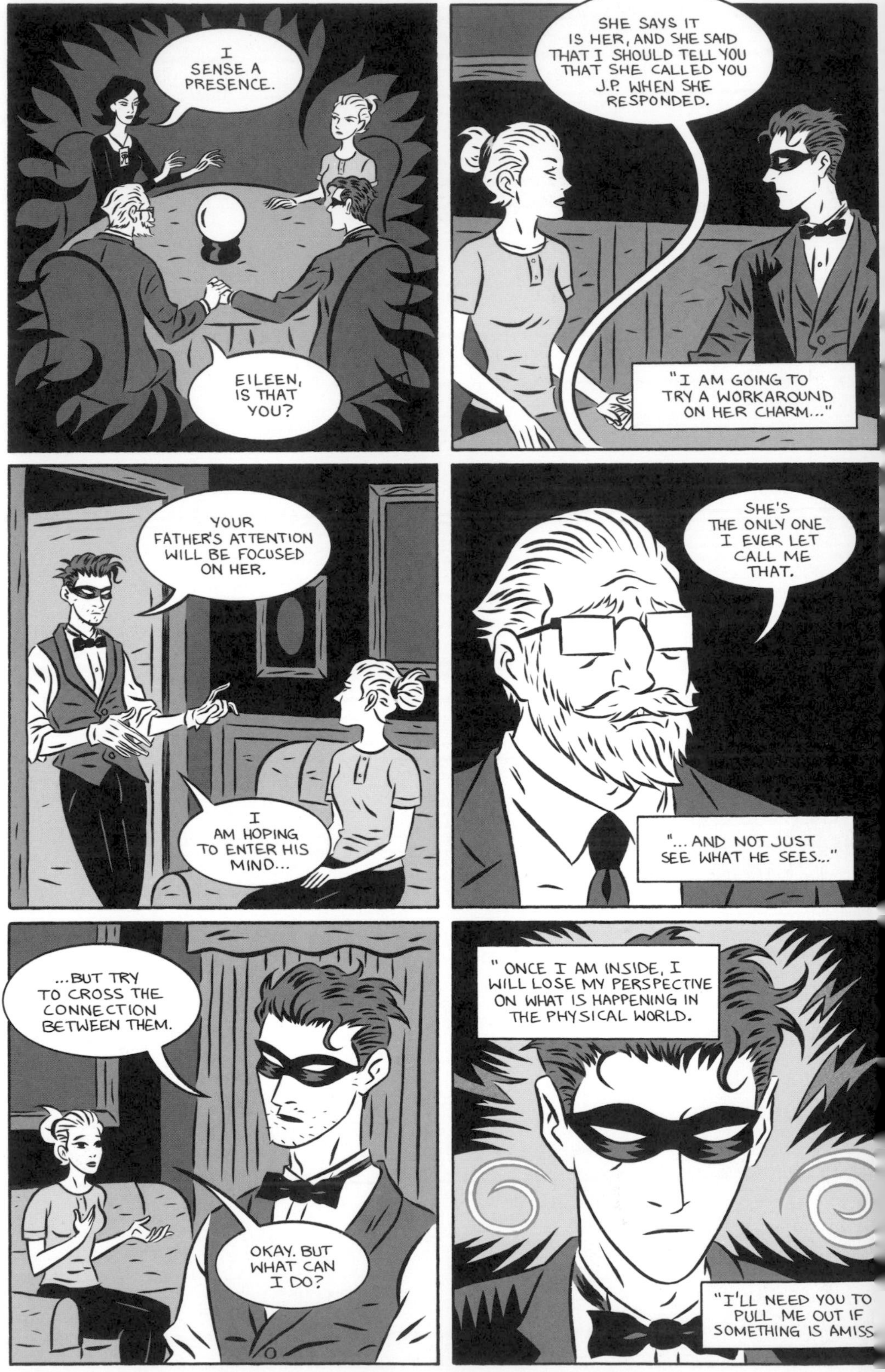
I SENSE A PRESENCE.
EILEEN, IS THAT YOU?
SHE SAYS IT IS HER, AND SHE SAID THAT I SHOULD TELL YOU THAT SHE CALLED YOU J.P. WHEN SHE RESPONDED.
"I AM GOING TO TRY A WORKAROUND ON HER CHARM..."
YOUR FATHER'S ATTENTION WILL BE FOCUSED ON HER.
I AM HOPING TO ENTER HIS MIND...
SHE'S THE ONLY ONE I EVER LET CALL ME THAT.
"... AND NOT JUST SEE WHAT HE SEES..."
...BUT TRY TO CROSS THE CONNECTION BETWEEN THEM.
OKAY. BUT WHAT CAN I DO?
" ONCE I AM INSIDE, I WILL LOSE MY PERSPECTIVE ON WHAT IS HAPPENING IN THE PHYSICAL WORLD.
"I'LL NEED YOU TO PULL ME OUT IF SOMETHING IS AMISS

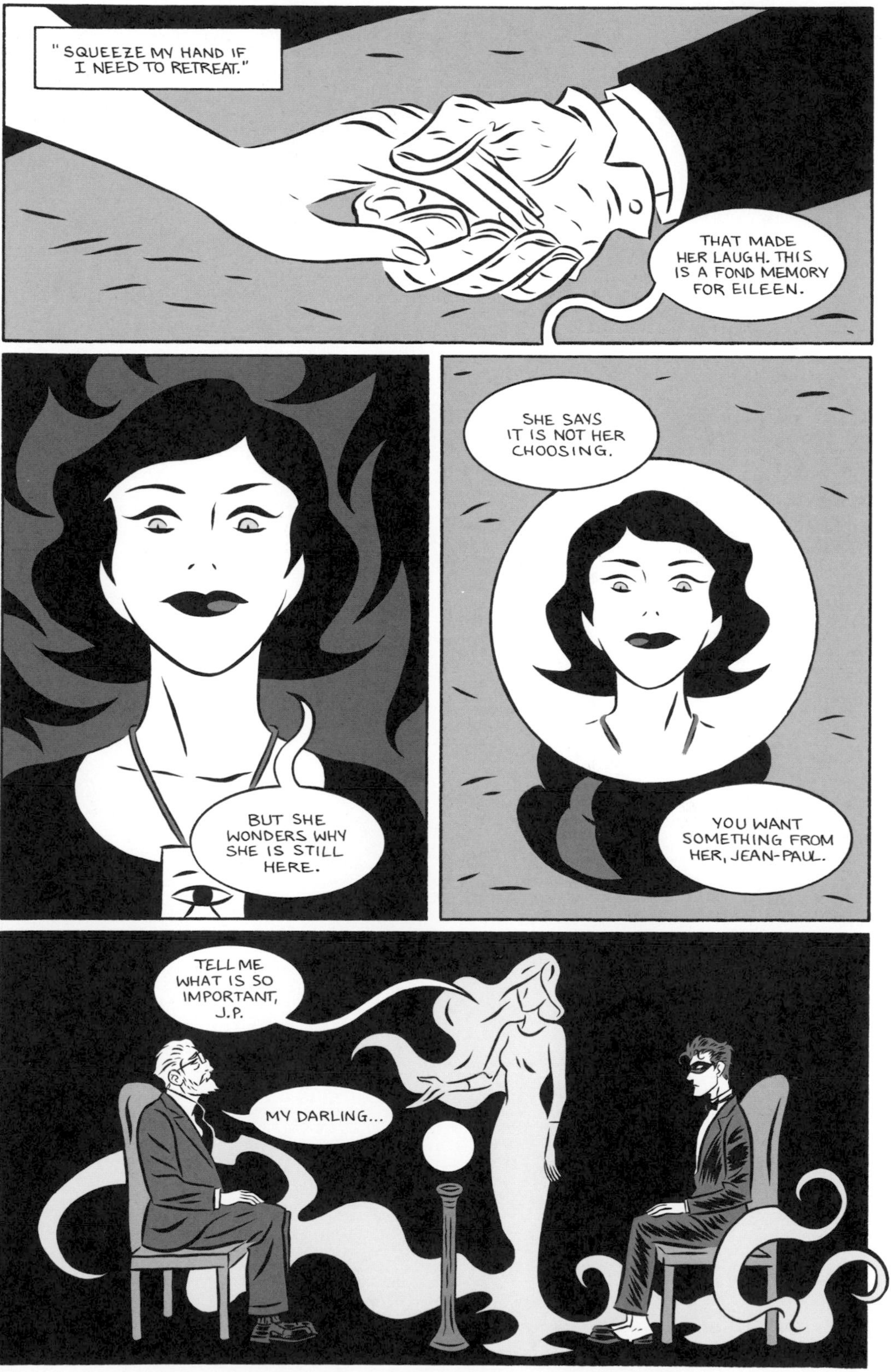
"SQUEEZE MY HAND IF I NEED TO RETREAT."
THAT MADE HER LAUGH. THIS IS A FOND MEMORY FOR EILEEN.
BUT SHE WONDERS WHY SHE IS STILL HERE.
SHE SAYS IT IS NOT HER CHOOSING.
YOU WANT SOMETHING FROM HER, JEAN-PAUL.
TELL ME WHAT IS SO IMPORTANT, J.P.
MY DARLING...

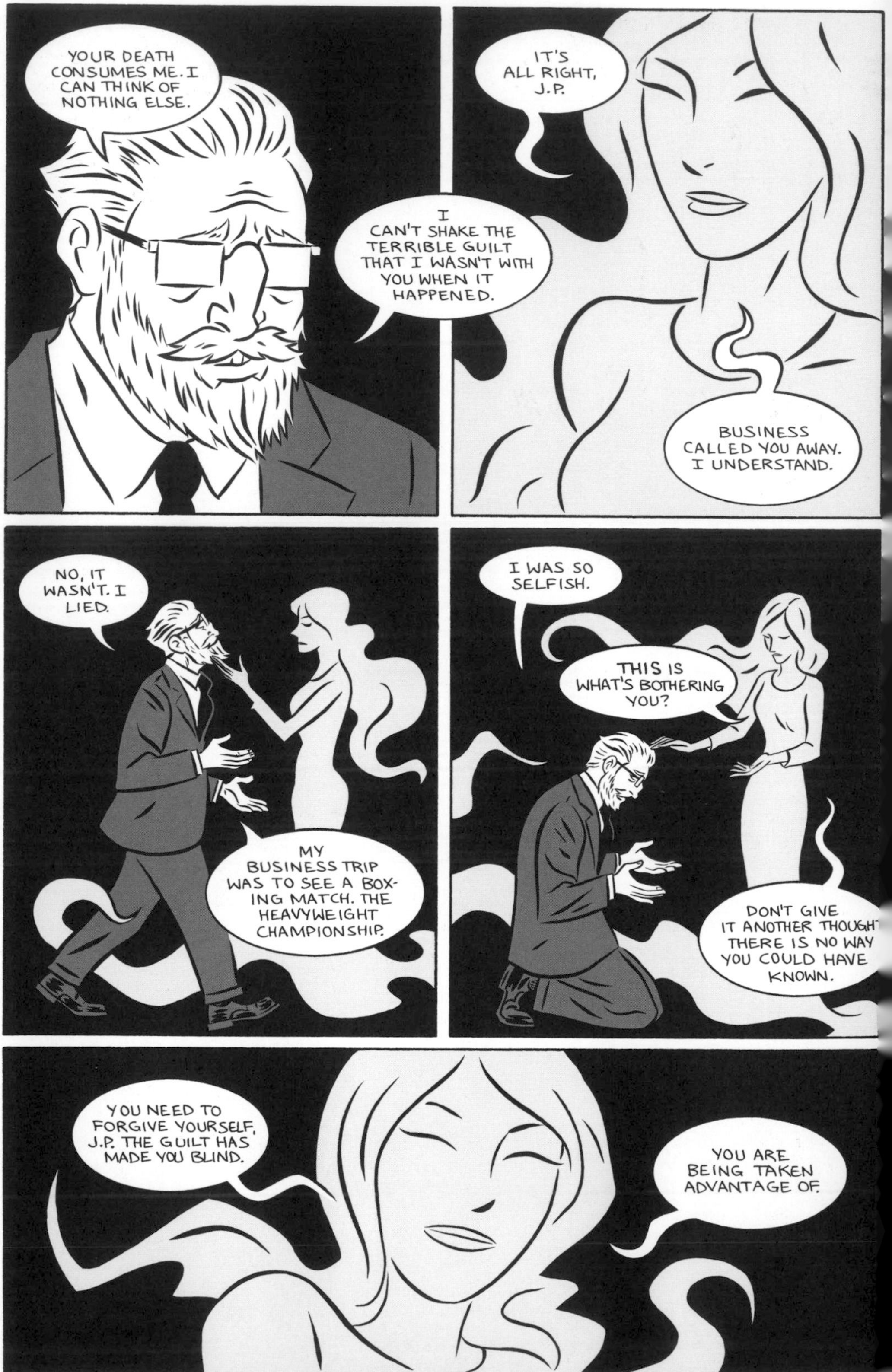
YOUR DEATH CONSUMES ME. I CAN THINK OF NOTHING ELSE.
I CAN'T SHAKE THE TERRIBLE GUILT THAT I WASN'T WITH YOU WHEN IT HAPPENED.
IT'S ALL RIGHT, J.P.
BUSINESS CALLED YOU AWAY. I UNDERSTAND.
NO, IT WASN'T. I LIED.
MY BUSINESS TRIP WAS TO SEE A BOX-ING MATCH. THE HEAVYWEIGHT CHAMPIONSHIP.
I WAS SO SELFISH.
THIS IS WHAT'S BOTHERING YOU?
DON'T GIVE IT ANOTHER THOUGHT. THERE IS NO WAY YOU COULD HAVE KNOWN.
YOU NEED TO FORGIVE YOURSELF, J.P. THE GUILT HAS MADE YOU BLIND.
YOU ARE BEING TAKEN ADVANTAGE OF.

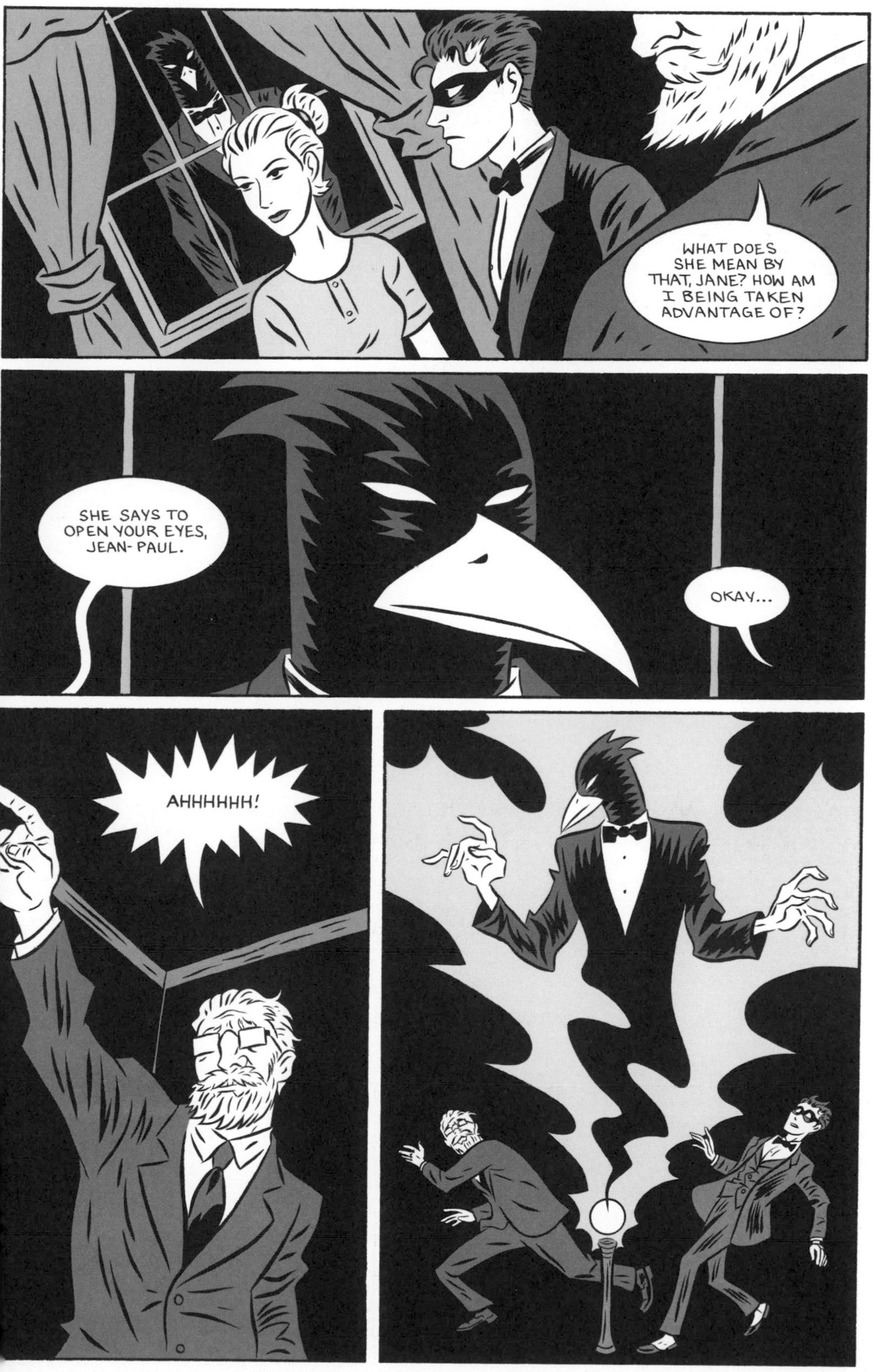
WHAT DOES SHE MEAN BY THAT, JANE? HOW AM I BEING TAKEN ADVANTAGE OF?
SHE SAYS TO OPEN YOUR EYES, JEAN-PAUL.
OKAY...
AHHHHHH!

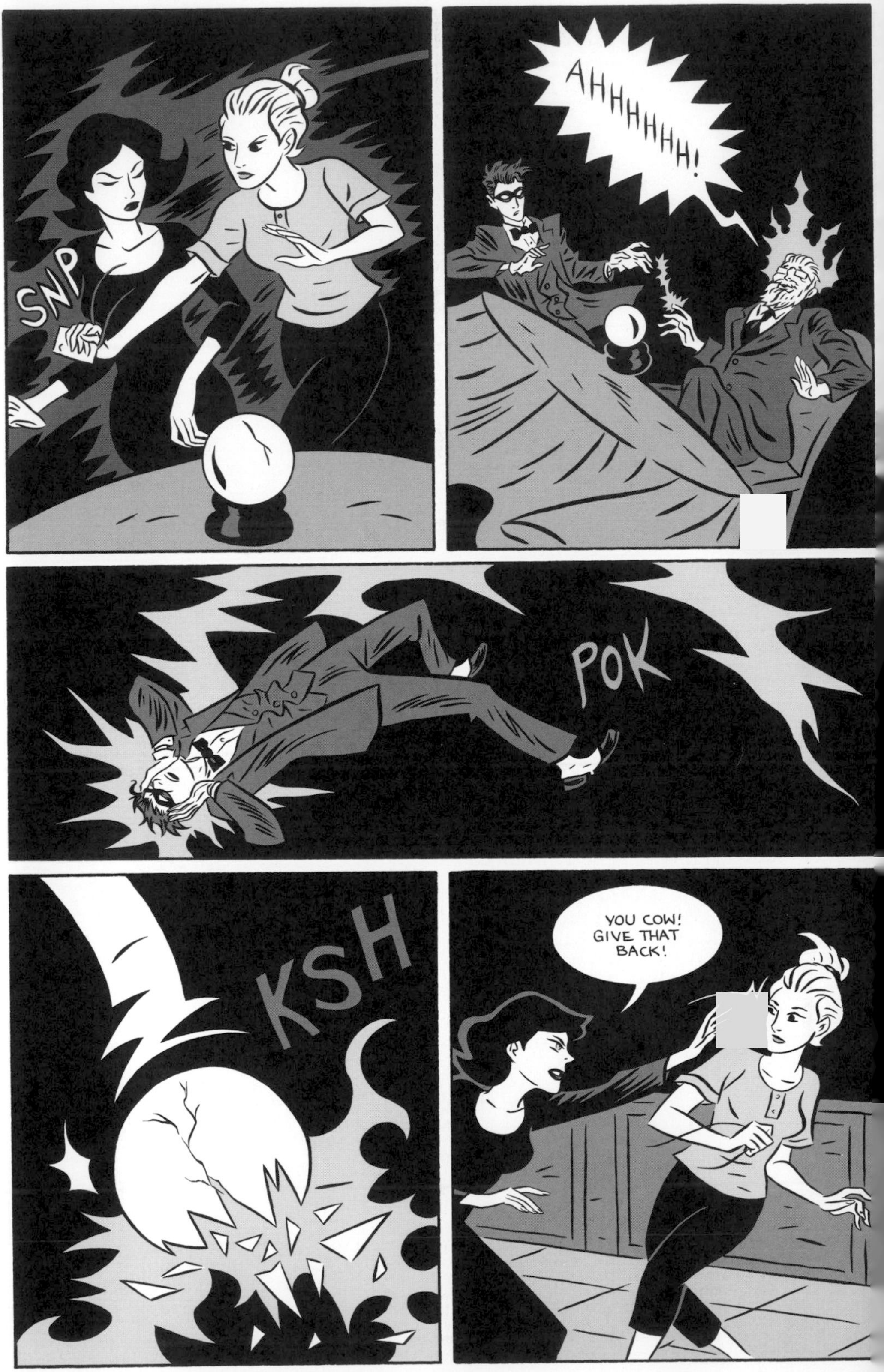
SNP
AHHHHHHH!
POK
KSH
YOU COW! GIVE THAT BACK!

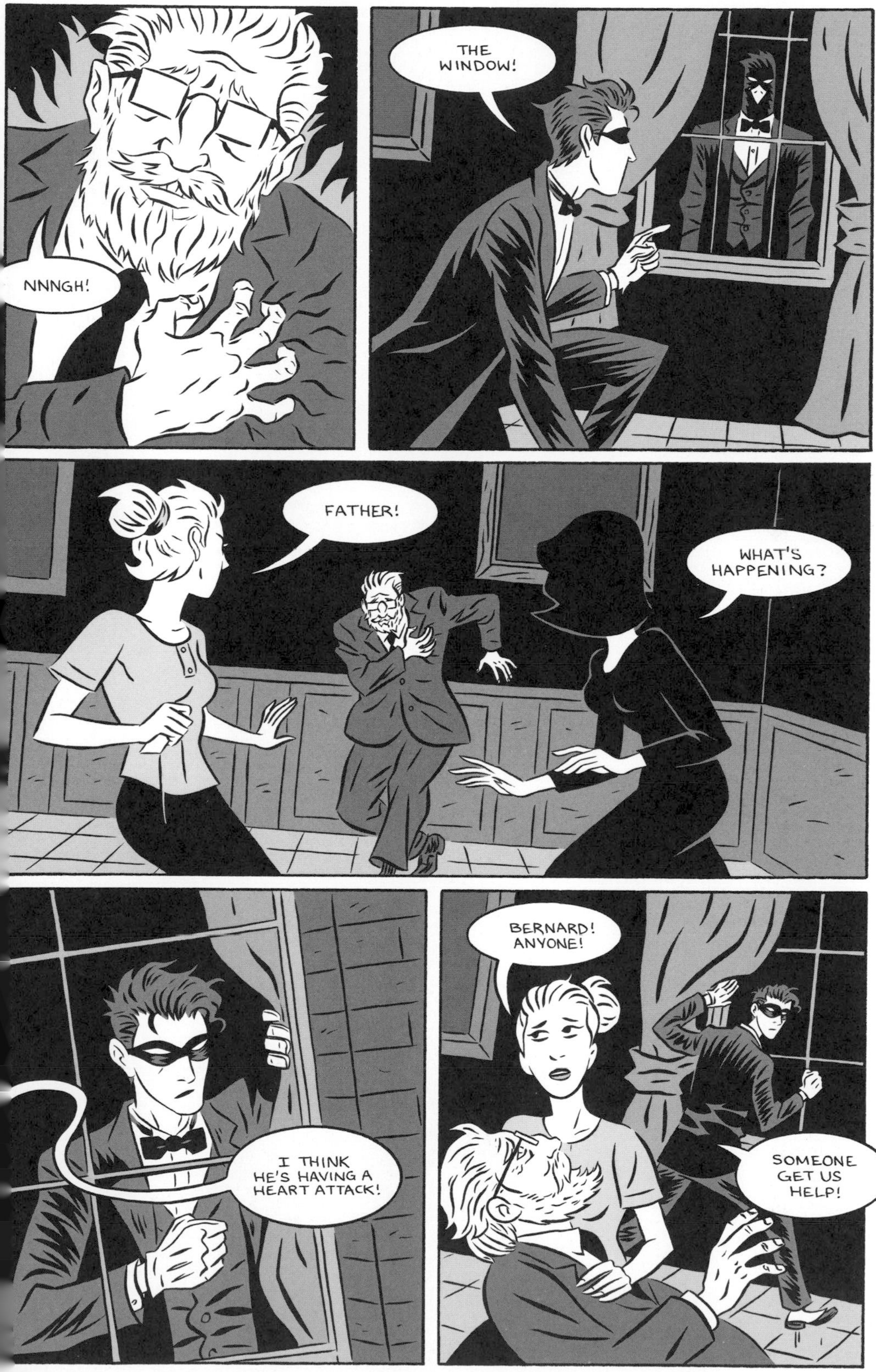
NNNGH!
THE WINDOW!
FATHER!
WHAT'S HAPPENING?
I THINK HE'S HAVING A HEART ATTACK!
BERNARD! ANYONE!
SOMEONE GET US HELP!

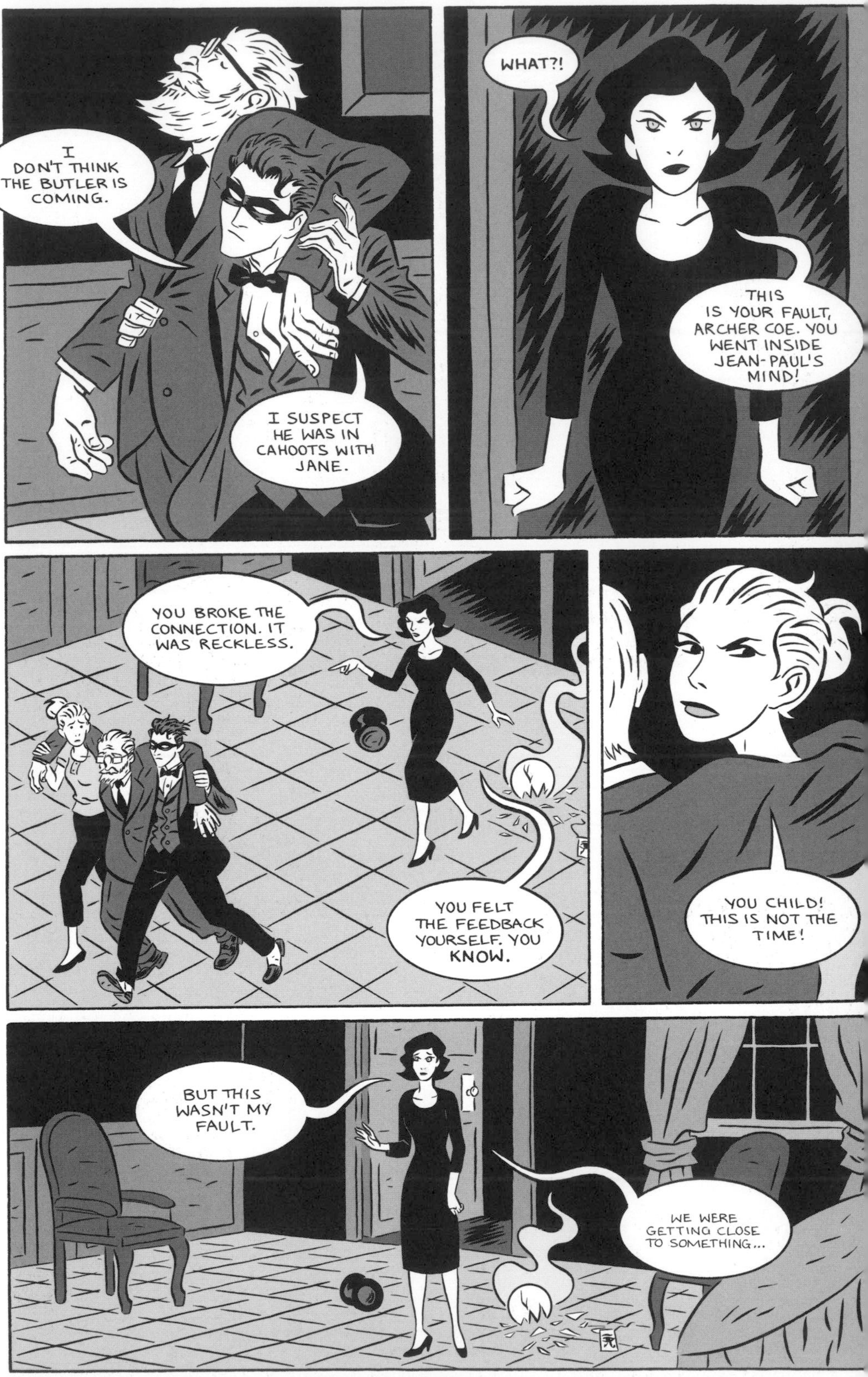
I DON'T THINK THE BUTLER IS COMING.
I SUSPECT HE WAS IN CAHOOTS WITH JANE.
WHAT?!
THIS IS YOUR FAULT, ARCHER COE. YOU WENT INSIDE JEAN-PAUL'S MIND!
YOU BROKE THE CONNECTION. IT WAS RECKLESS.
YOU FELT THE FEEDBACK YOURSELF. YOU KNOW.
YOU CHILD! THIS IS NOT THE TIME!
BUT THIS WASN'T MY FAULT.
WE WERE GETTING CLOSE TO SOMETHING...

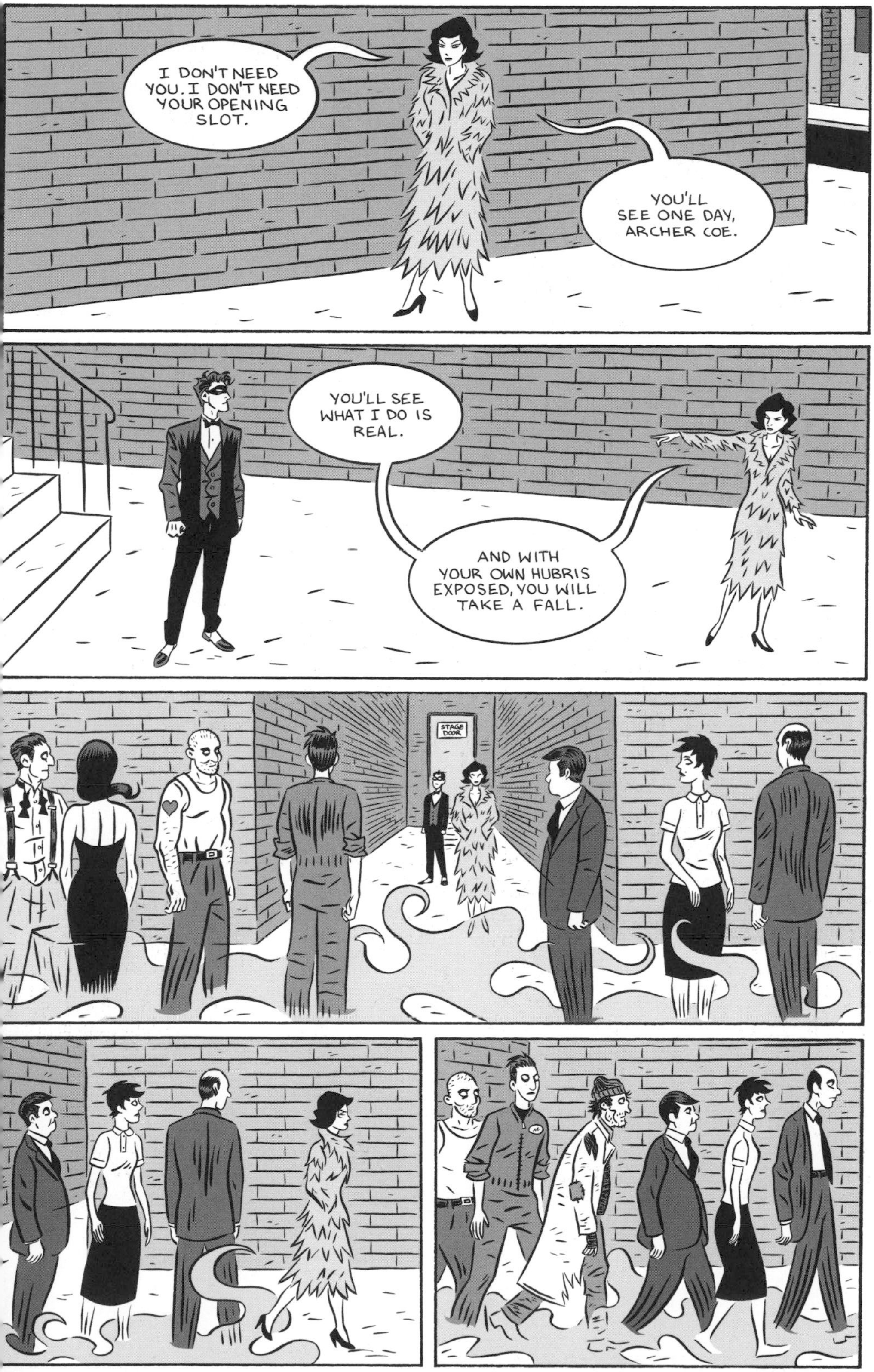
I DON'T NEED YOU. I DON'T NEED YOUR OPENING SLOT.
YOU'LL SEE ONE DAY, ARCHER COE.
YOU'LL SEE WHAT I DO IS REAL.
AND WITH YOUR OWN HUBRIS EXPOSED, YOU WILL TAKE A FALL.
STAGE DOOR

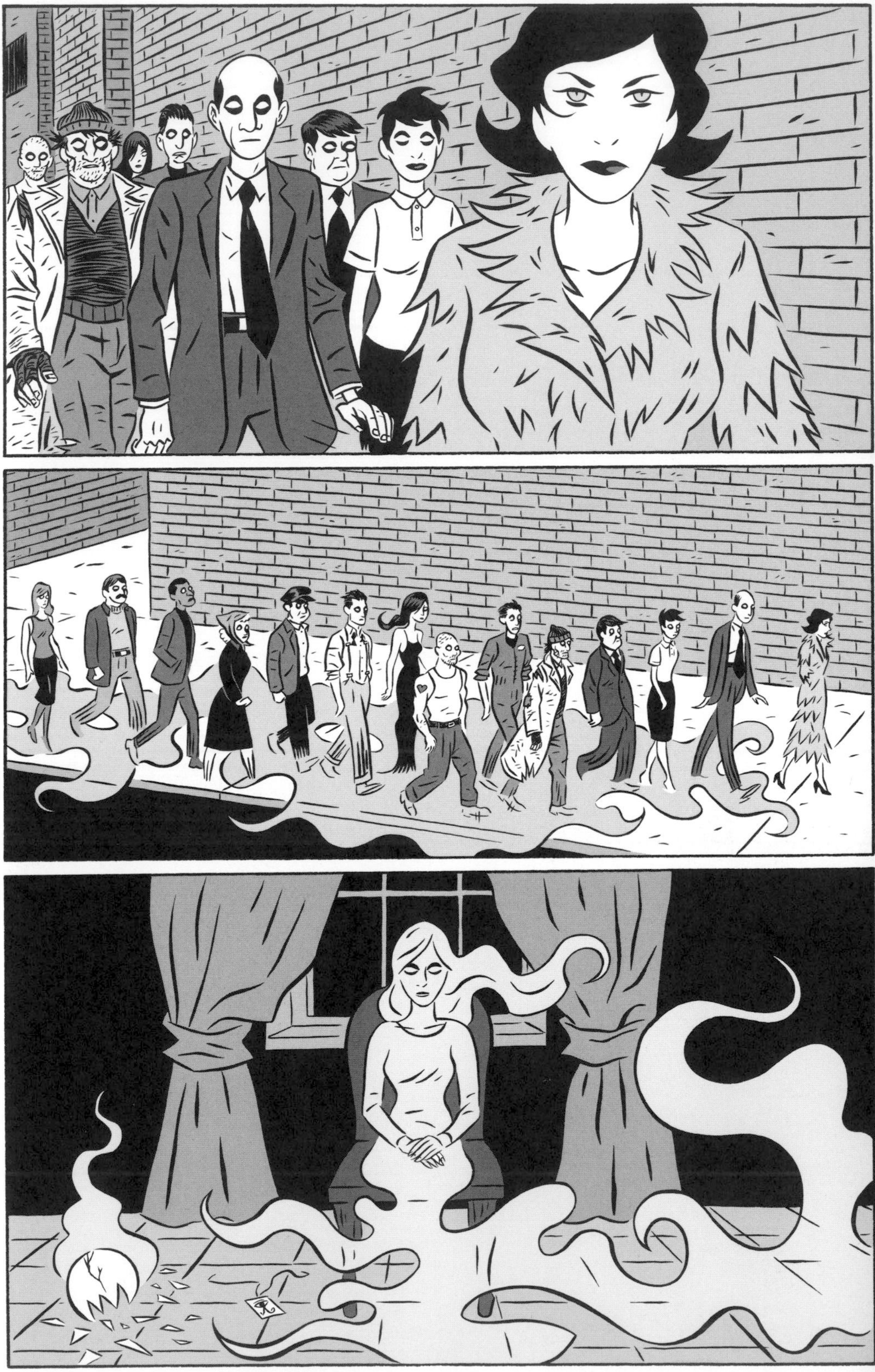

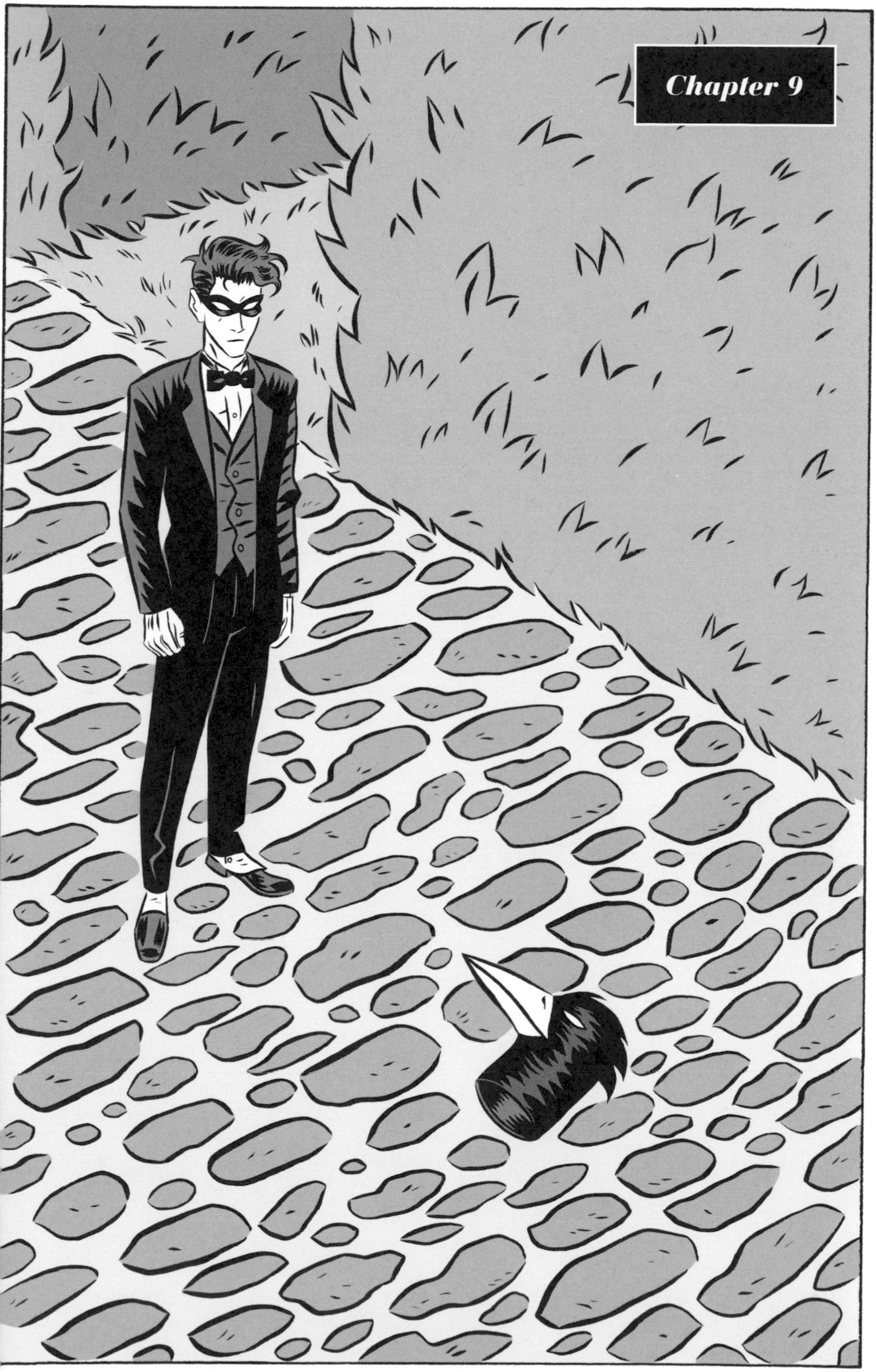
Chapter 9

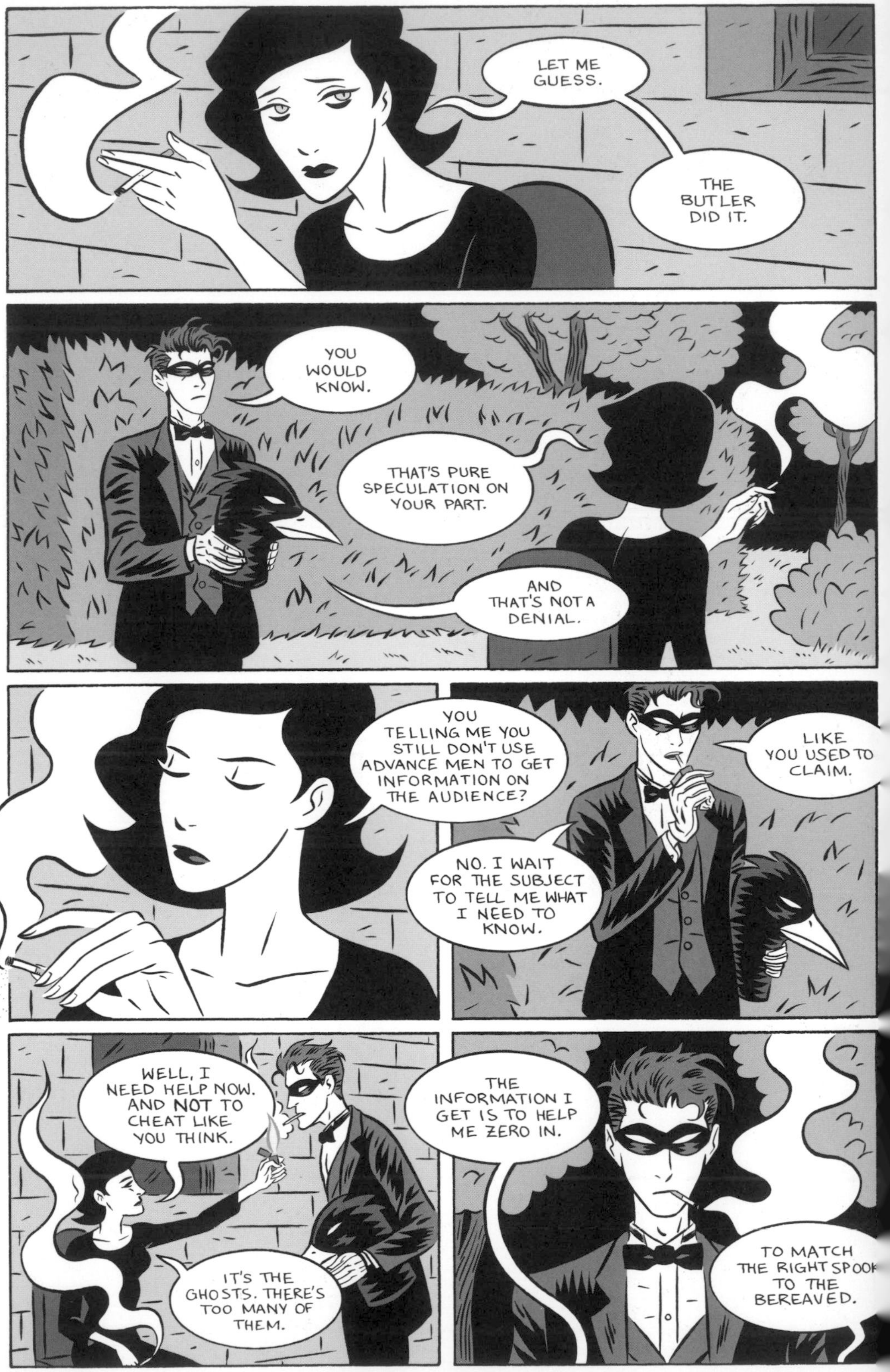
LET ME GUESS.
THE BUTLER DID IT.
YOU WOULD KNOW.
THAT'S PURE SPECULATION ON YOUR PART.
AND THAT'S NOT A DENIAL.
YOU TELLING ME YOU STILL DON'T USE ADVANCE MEN TO GET INFORMATION ON THE AUDIENCE?
LIKE YOU USED TO CLAIM.
NO. I WAIT FOR THE SUBJECT TO TELL ME WHAT I NEED TO KNOW.
WELL, I NEED HELP NOW. AND **NOT** TO CHEAT LIKE YOU THINK.
IT'S THE GHOSTS. THERE'S TOO MANY OF THEM.
THE INFORMATION I GET IS TO HELP ME ZERO IN.
TO MATCH THE RIGHT SPOOK TO THE BEREAVED.

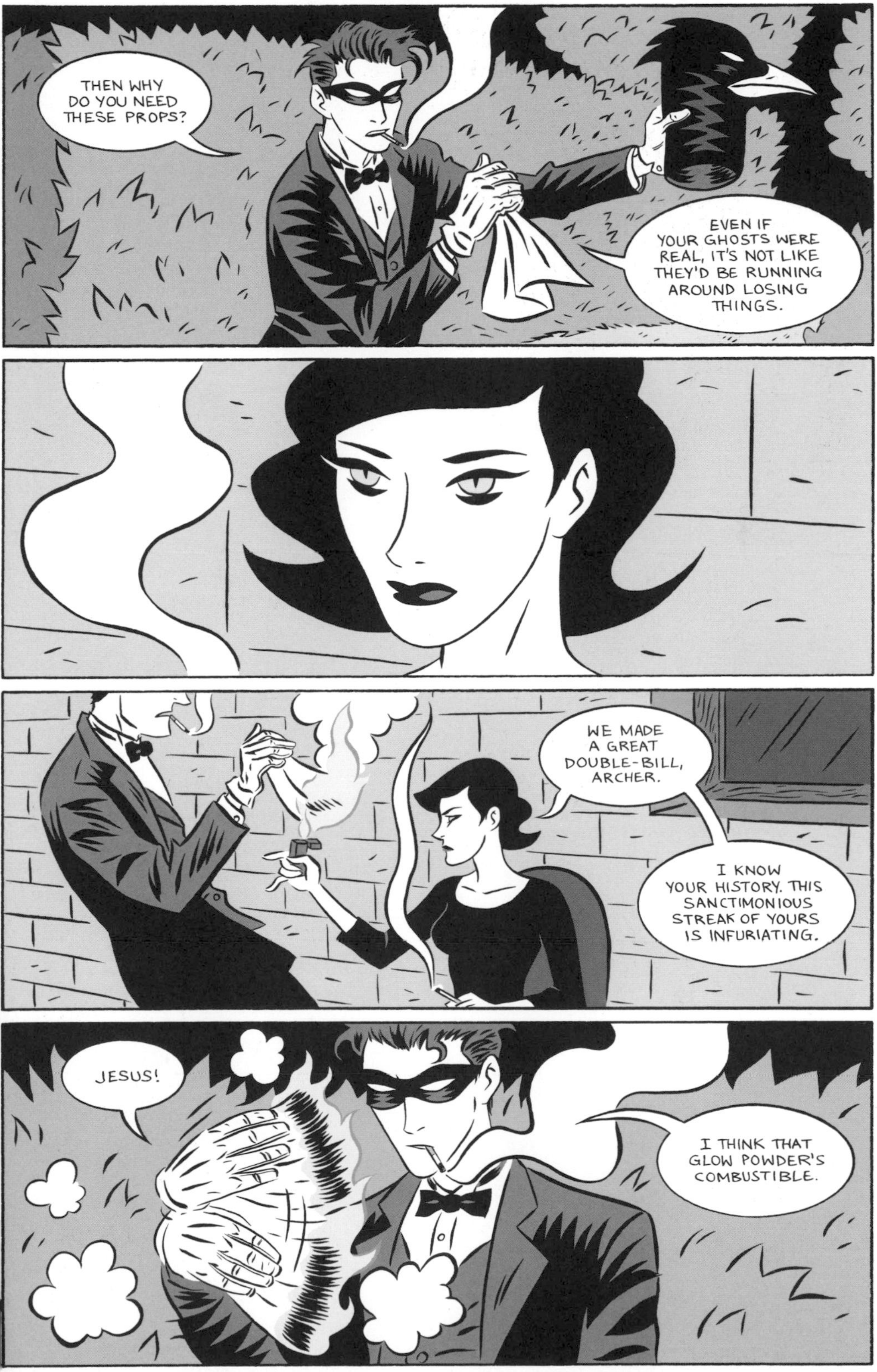
THEN WHY DO YOU NEED THESE PROPS?
EVEN IF YOUR GHOSTS WERE REAL, IT'S NOT LIKE THEY'D BE RUNNING AROUND LOSING THINGS.
WE MADE A GREAT DOUBLE-BILL, ARCHER.
I KNOW YOUR HISTORY. THIS SANCTIMONIOUS STREAK OF YOURS IS INFURIATING.
JESUS!
I THINK THAT GLOW POWDER'S COMBUSTIBLE.

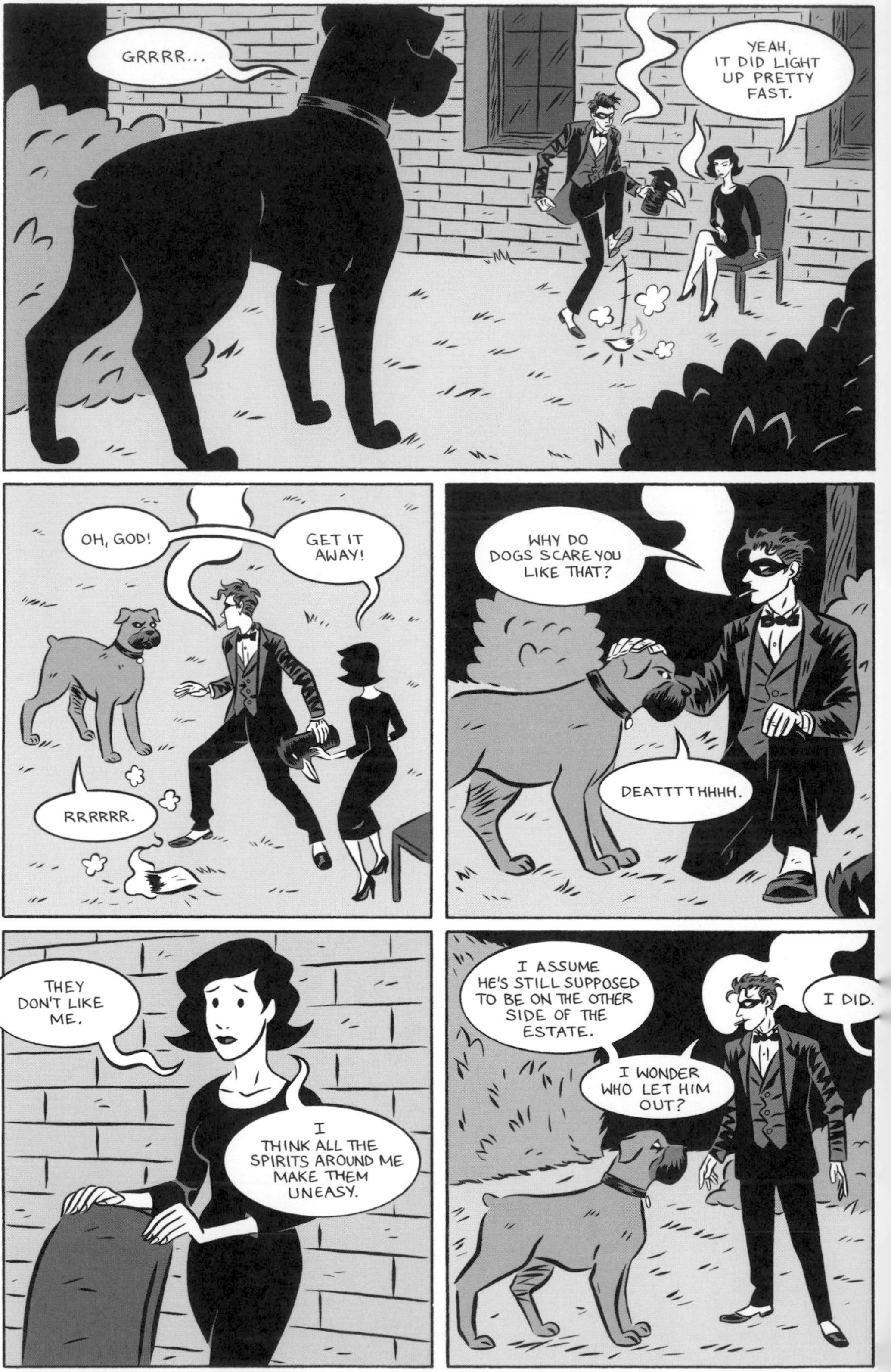
GRRRR...
YEAH, IT DID LIGHT UP PRETTY FAST.
OH, GOD!
GET IT AWAY!
RRRRRR.
WHY DO DOGS SCARE YOU LIKE THAT?
DEATTTTHHHH.
THEY DON'T LIKE ME.
I THINK ALL THE SPIRITS AROUND ME MAKE THEM UNEASY.
I ASSUME HE'S STILL SUPPOSED TO BE ON THE OTHER SIDE OF THE ESTATE.
I WONDER WHO LET HIM OUT?
I DID.

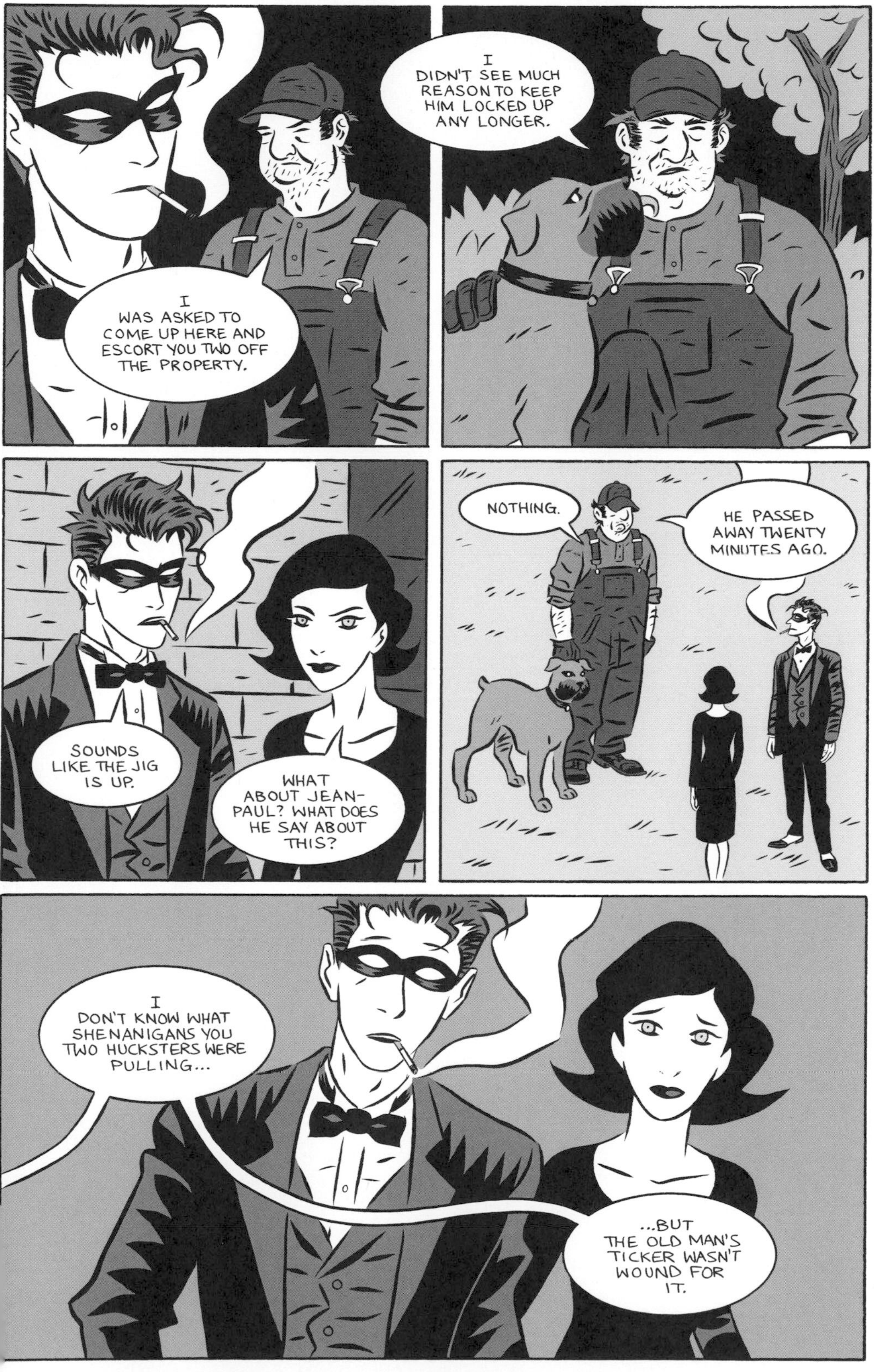
I WAS ASKED TO COME UP HERE AND ESCORT YOU TWO OFF THE PROPERTY.
I DIDN'T SEE MUCH REASON TO KEEP HIM LOCKED UP ANY LONGER.
SOUNDS LIKE THE JIG IS UP.
WHAT ABOUT JEAN-PAUL? WHAT DOES HE SAY ABOUT THIS?
NOTHING.
HE PASSED AWAY TWENTY MINUTES AGO.
I DON'T KNOW WHAT SHENANIGANS YOU TWO HUCKSTERS WERE PULLING...
...BUT THE OLD MAN'S TICKER WASN'T WOUND FOR IT.

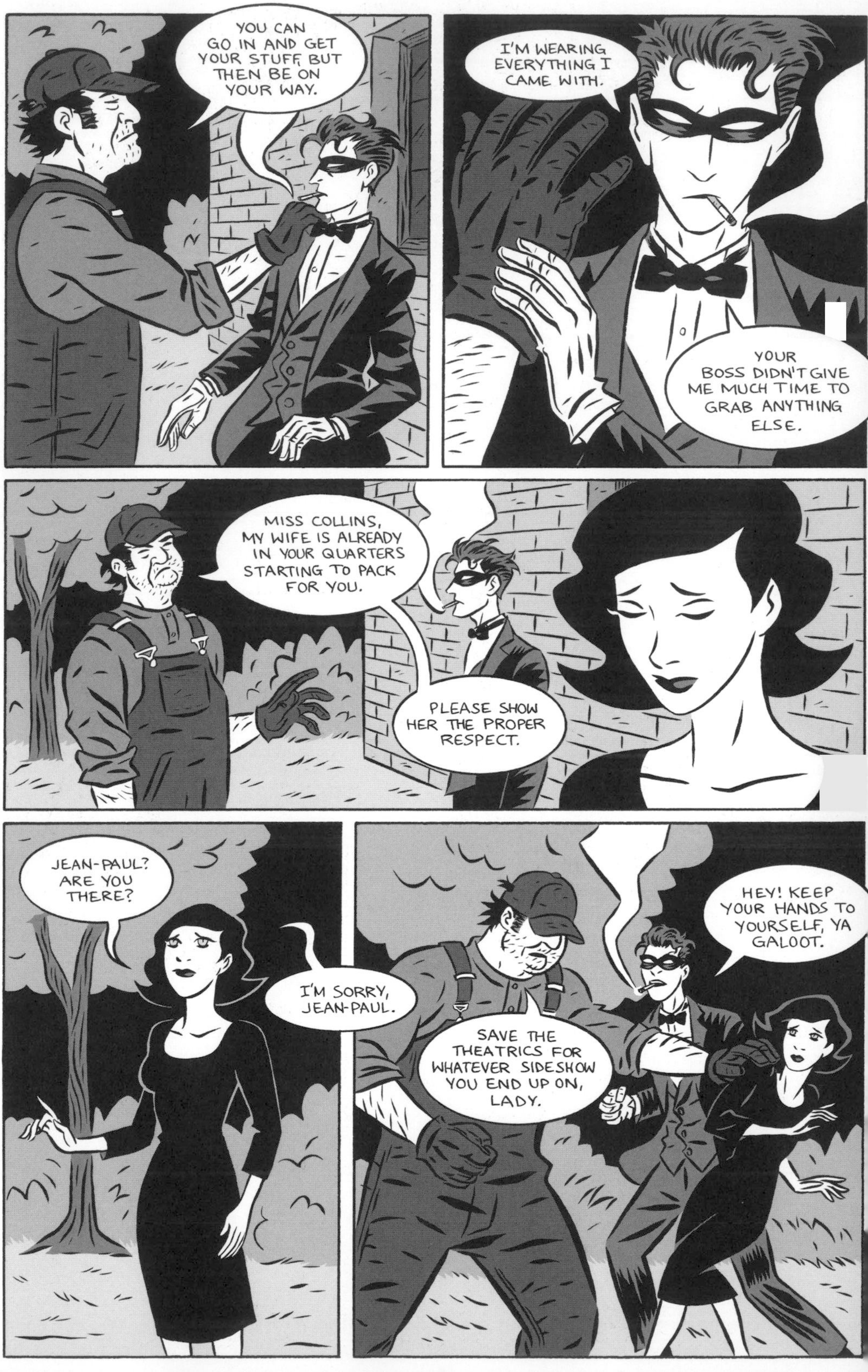
YOU CAN GO IN AND GET YOUR STUFF, BUT THEN BE ON YOUR WAY.
I'M WEARING EVERYTHING I CAME WITH.
YOUR BOSS DIDN'T GIVE ME MUCH TIME TO GRAB ANYTHING ELSE.
MISS COLLINS, MY WIFE IS ALREADY IN YOUR QUARTERS STARTING TO PACK FOR YOU.
PLEASE SHOW HER THE PROPER RESPECT.
JEAN-PAUL? ARE YOU THERE?
I'M SORRY, JEAN-PAUL.
HEY! KEEP YOUR HANDS TO YOURSELF, YA GALOOT.
SAVE THE THEATRICS FOR WHATEVER SIDESHOW YOU END UP ON, LADY.

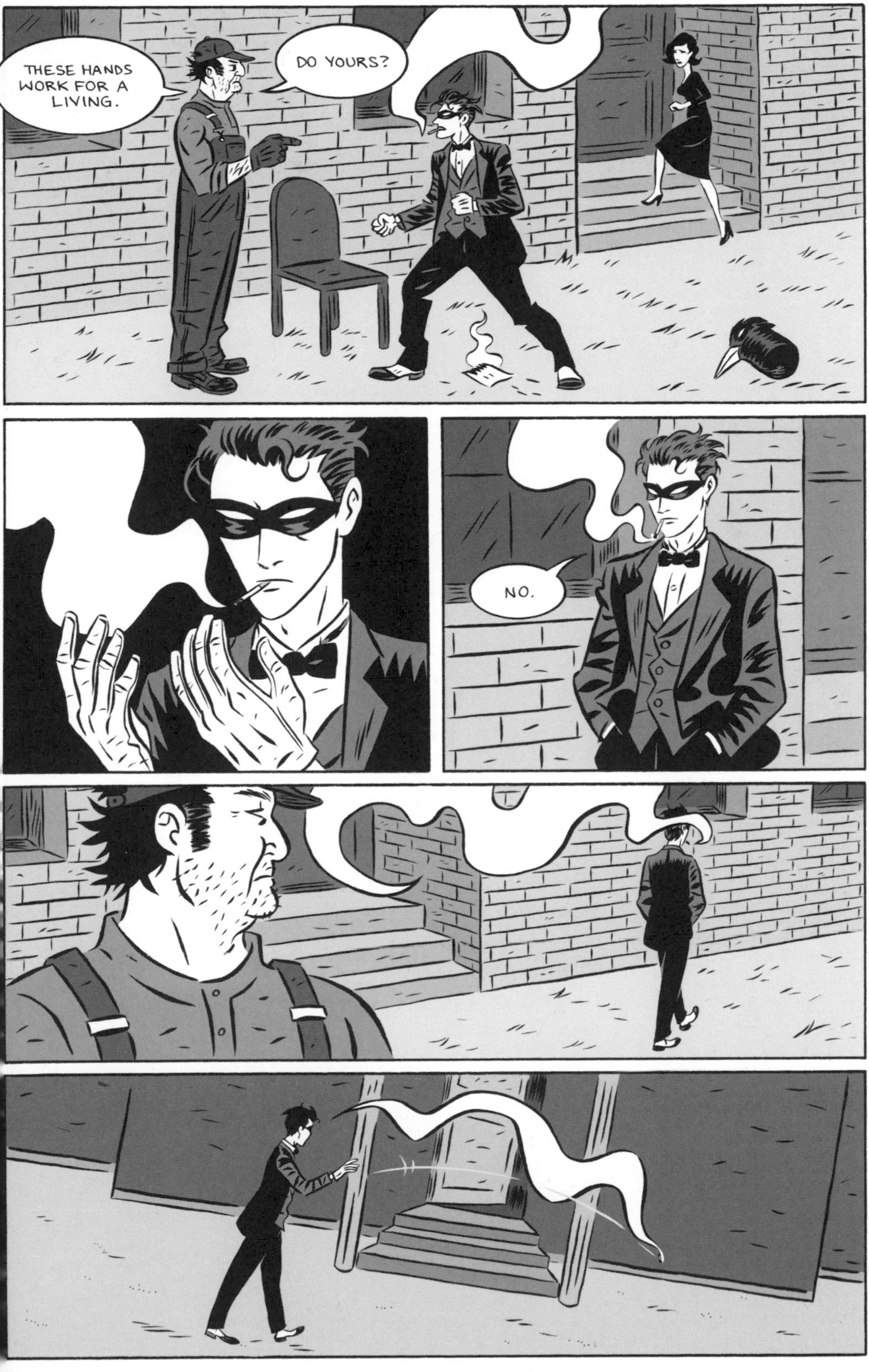
THESE HANDS WORK FOR A LIVING.
DO YOURS?
NO.

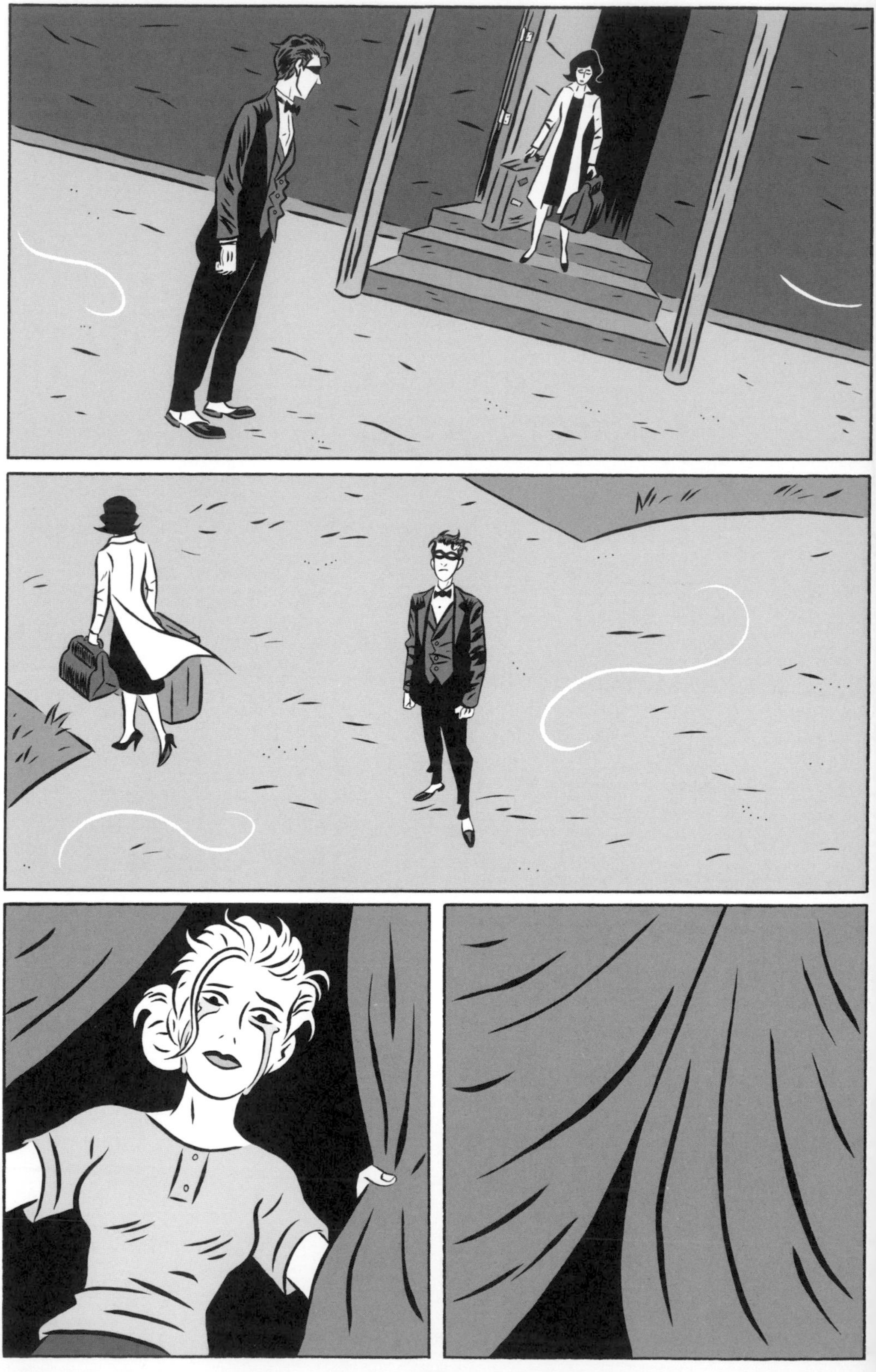

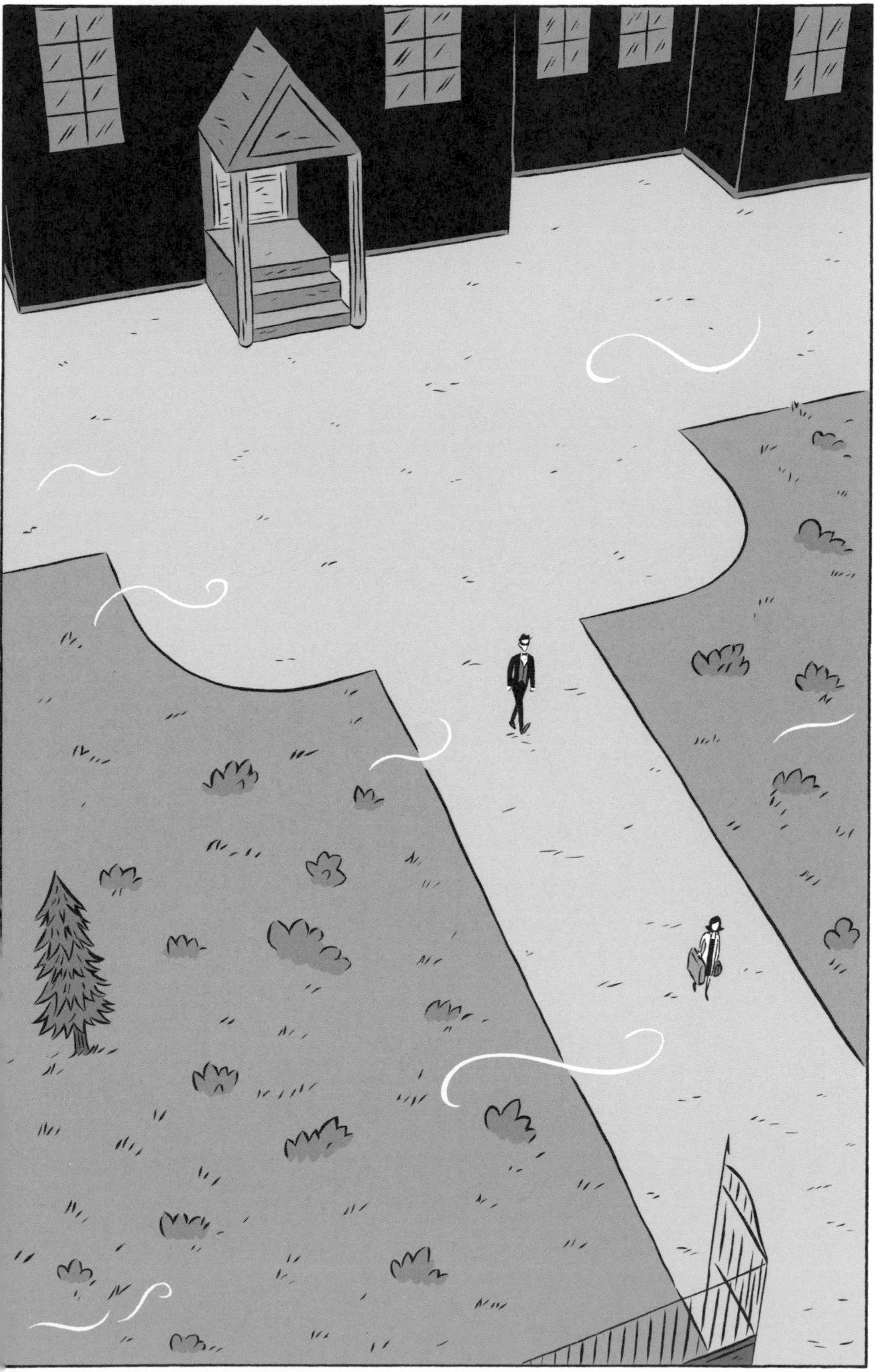

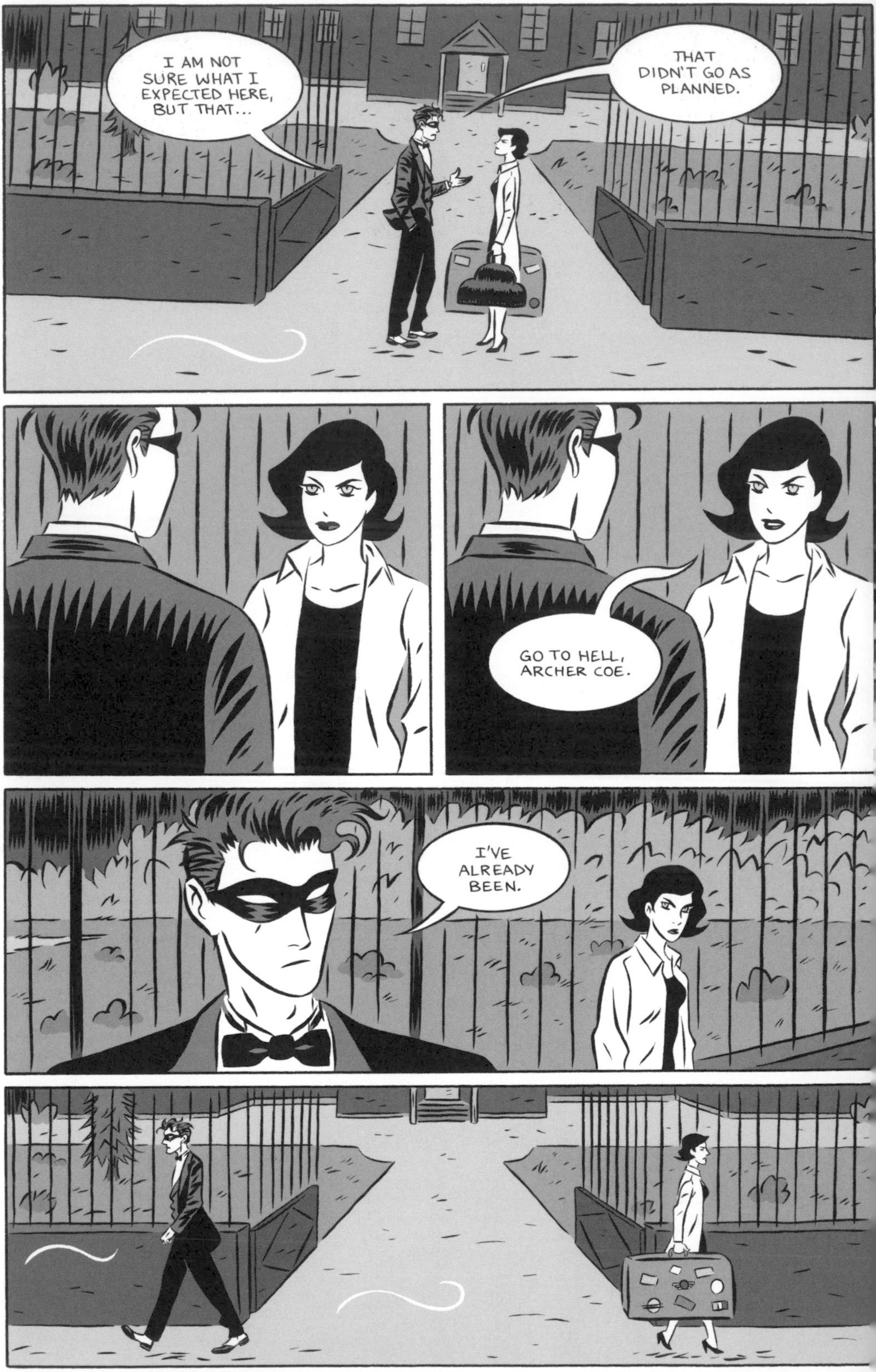
I AM NOT SURE WHAT I EXPECTED HERE, BUT THAT...
THAT DIDN'T GO AS PLANNED.
GO TO HELL, ARCHER COE.
I'VE ALREADY BEEN.

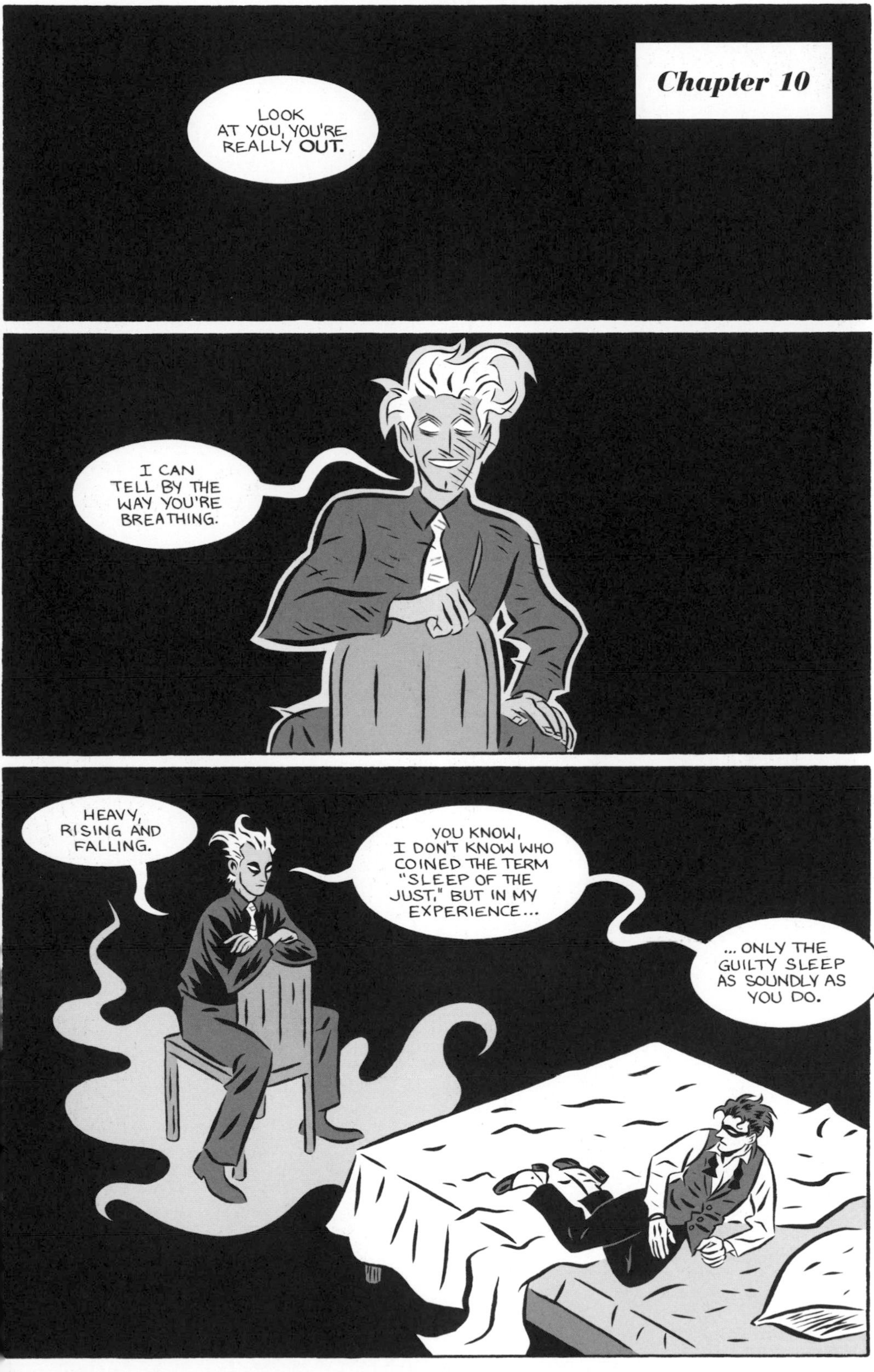
Chapter 10
LOOK AT YOU, YOU'RE REALLY OUT.
I CAN TELL BY THE WAY YOU'RE BREATHING.
HEAVY, RISING AND FALLING.
YOU KNOW, I DON'T KNOW WHO COINED THE TERM "SLEEP OF THE JUST," BUT IN MY EXPERIENCE...
...ONLY THE GUILTY SLEEP AS SOUNDLY AS YOU DO.

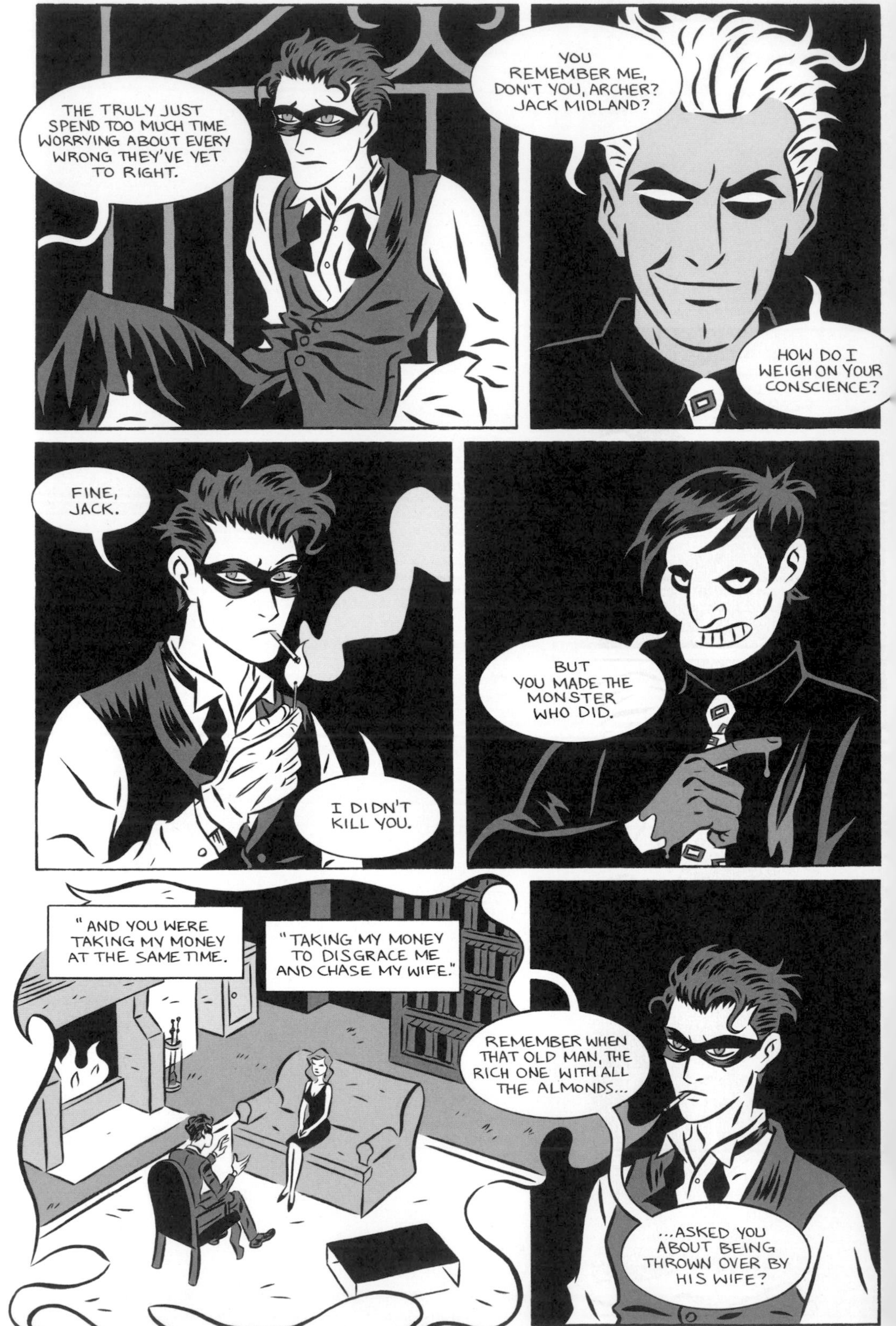
THE TRULY JUST SPEND TOO MUCH TIME WORRYING ABOUT EVERY WRONG THEY'VE YET TO RIGHT.
YOU REMEMBER ME, DON'T YOU, ARCHER? JACK MIDLAND?
HOW DO I WEIGH ON YOUR CONSCIENCE?
FINE, JACK.
I DIDN'T KILL YOU.
BUT YOU MADE THE MONSTER WHO DID.
"AND YOU WERE TAKING MY MONEY AT THE SAME TIME.
"TAKING MY MONEY TO DISGRACE ME AND CHASE MY WIFE."
REMEMBER WHEN THAT OLD MAN, THE RICH ONE WITH ALL THE ALMONDS...
...ASKED YOU ABOUT BEING THROWN OVER BY HIS WIFE?

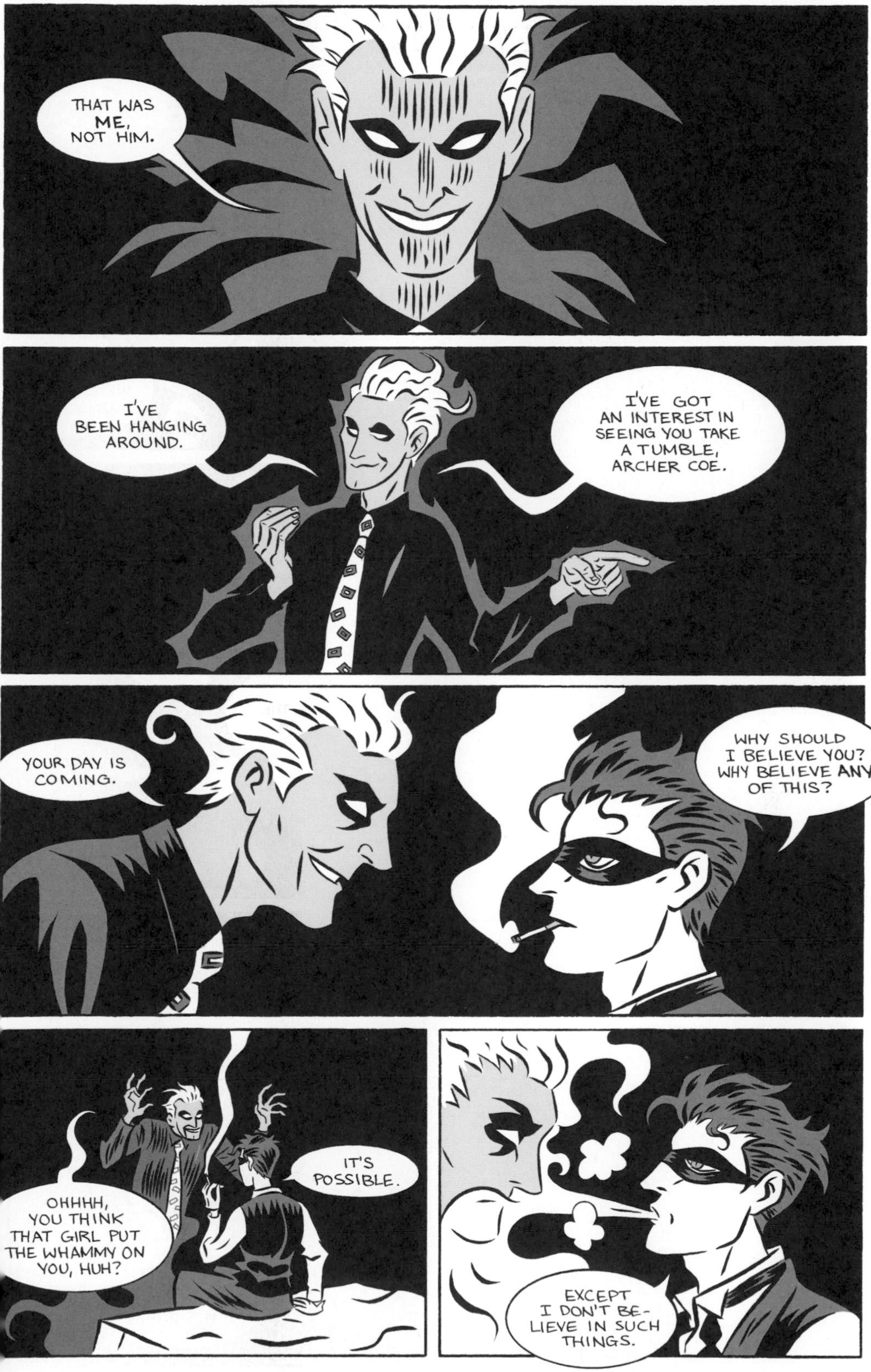
THAT WAS ME, NOT HIM.
I'VE BEEN HANGING AROUND.
I'VE GOT AN INTEREST IN SEEING YOU TAKE A TUMBLE, ARCHER COE.
YOUR DAY IS COMING.
WHY SHOULD I BELIEVE YOU? WHY BELIEVE ANY OF THIS?
OHHHH, YOU THINK THAT GIRL PUT THE WHAMMY ON YOU, HUH?
IT'S POSSIBLE.
EXCEPT I DON'T BE- LIEVE IN SUCH THINGS.

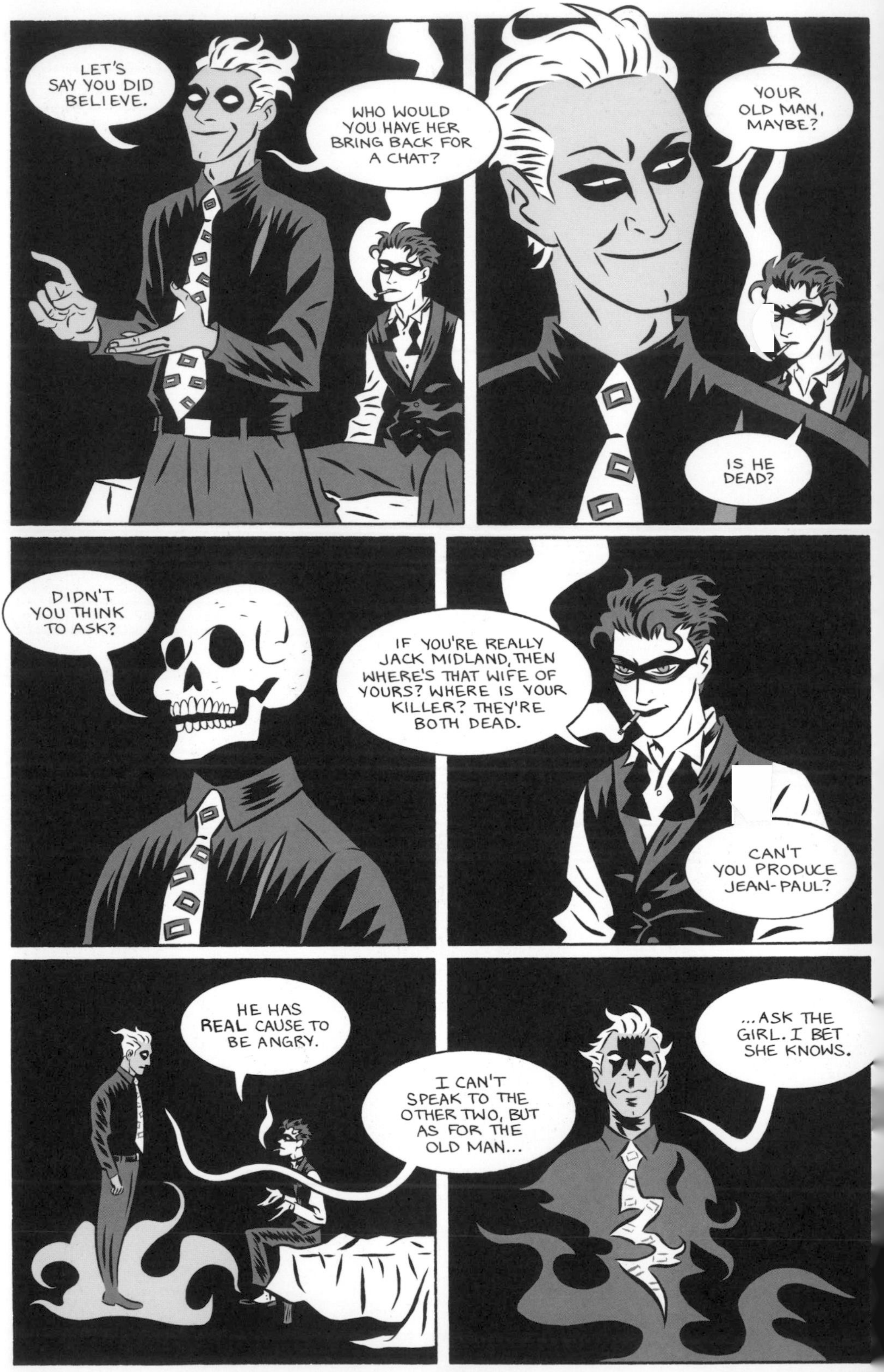
LET'S SAY YOU DID BELIEVE.
WHO WOULD YOU HAVE HER BRING BACK FOR A CHAT?
YOUR OLD MAN, MAYBE?
IS HE DEAD?
DIDN'T YOU THINK TO ASK?
IF YOU'RE REALLY JACK MIDLAND, THEN WHERE'S THAT WIFE OF YOURS? WHERE IS YOUR KILLER? THEY'RE BOTH DEAD.
CAN'T YOU PRODUCE JEAN-PAUL?
HE HAS REAL CAUSE TO BE ANGRY.
I CAN'T SPEAK TO THE OTHER TWO, BUT AS FOR THE OLD MAN...
...ASK THE GIRL. I BET SHE KNOWS.

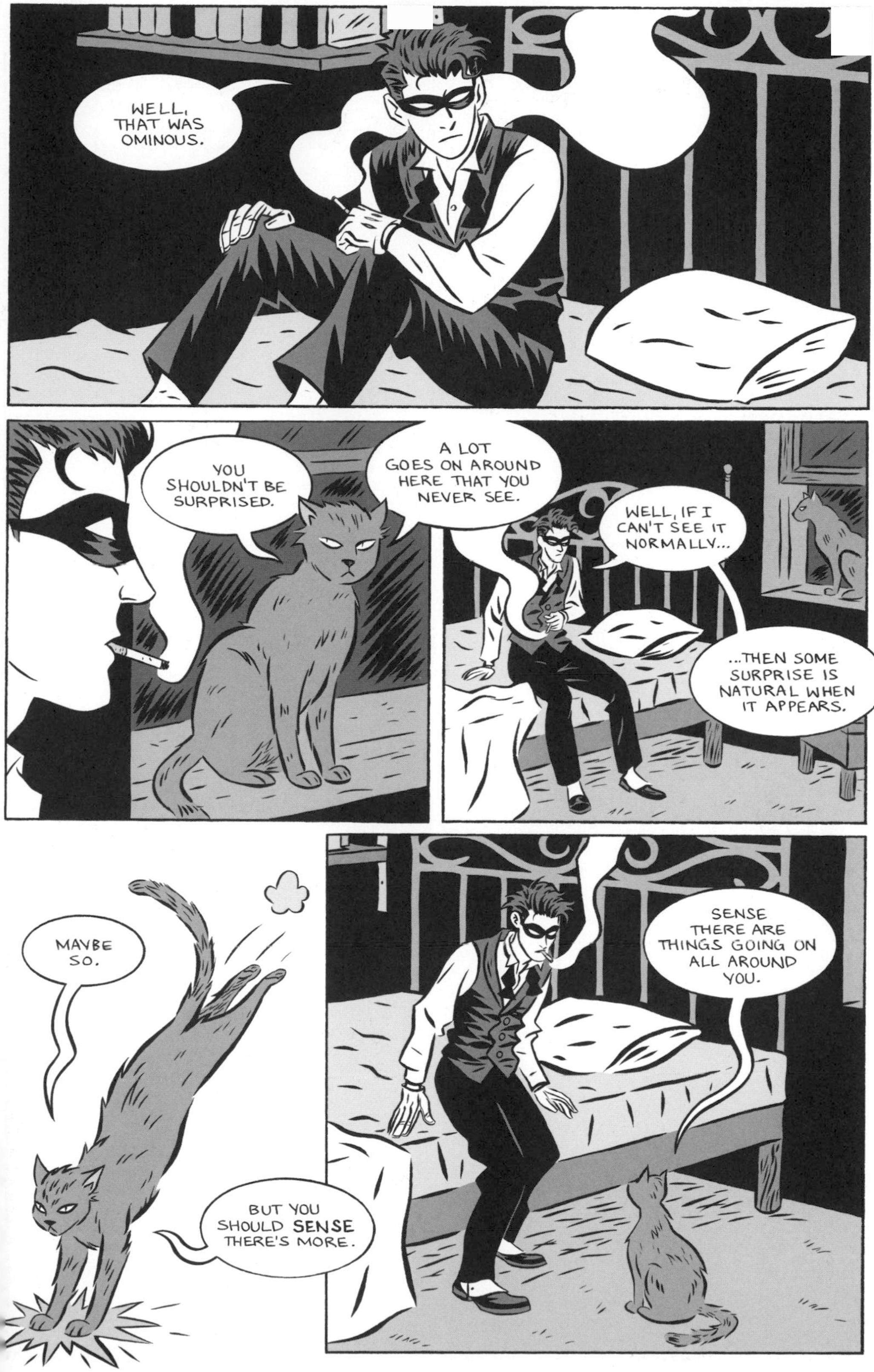
WELL, THAT WAS OMINOUS.
YOU SHOULDN'T BE SURPRISED.
A LOT GOES ON AROUND HERE THAT YOU NEVER SEE.
WELL, IF I CAN'T SEE IT NORMALLY...
...THEN SOME SURPRISE IS NATURAL WHEN IT APPEARS.
MAYBE SO.
BUT YOU SHOULD SENSE THERE'S MORE.
SENSE THERE ARE THINGS GOING ON ALL AROUND YOU.

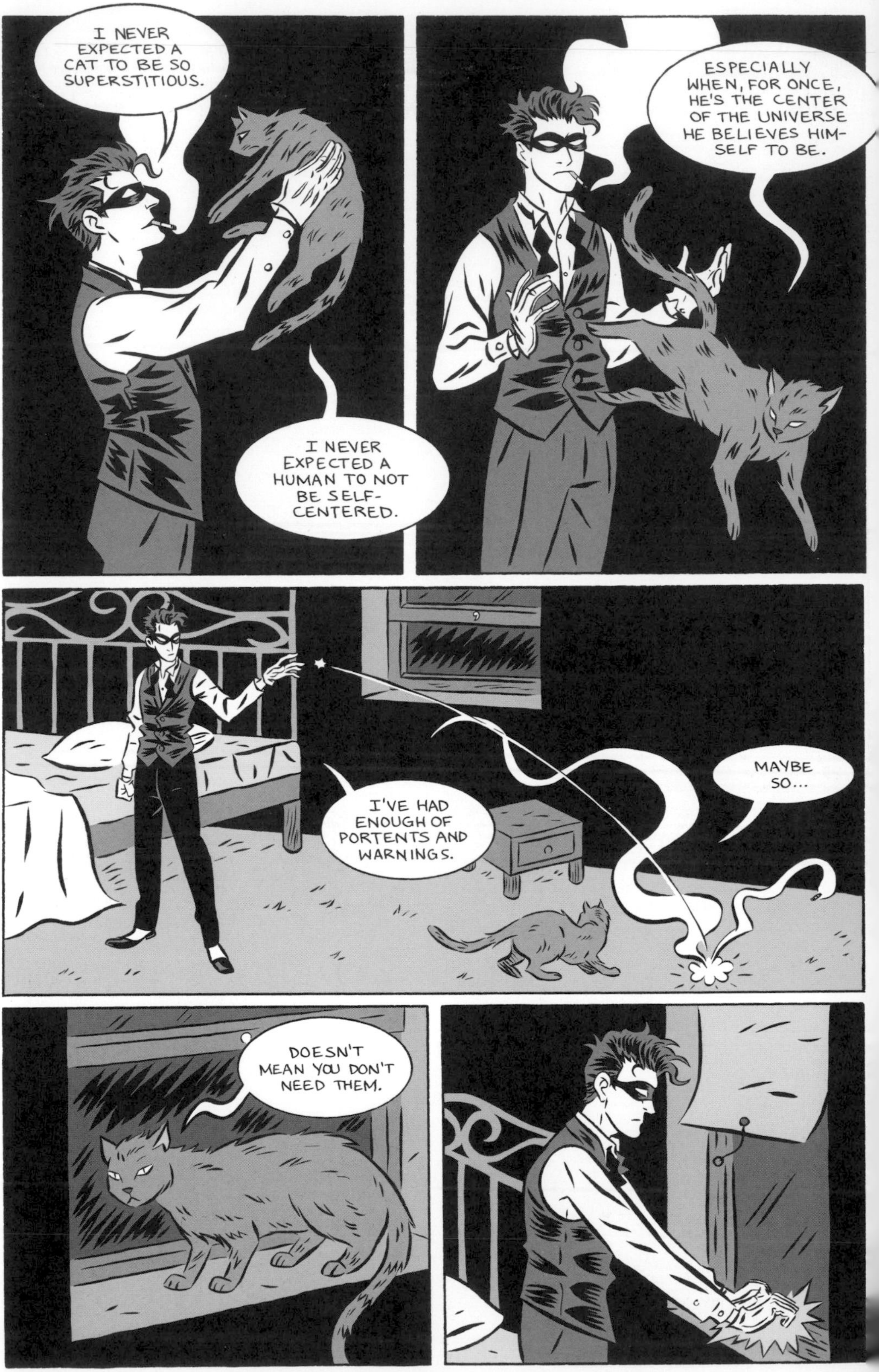
I NEVER EXPECTED A CAT TO BE SO SUPERSTITIOUS.
I NEVER EXPECTED A HUMAN TO NOT BE SELF-CENTERED.
ESPECIALLY WHEN, FOR ONCE, HE'S THE CENTER OF THE UNIVERSE HE BELIEVES HIMSELF TO BE.
I'VE HAD ENOUGH OF PORTENTS AND WARNINGS.
MAYBE SO...
DOESN'T MEAN YOU DON'T NEED THEM.

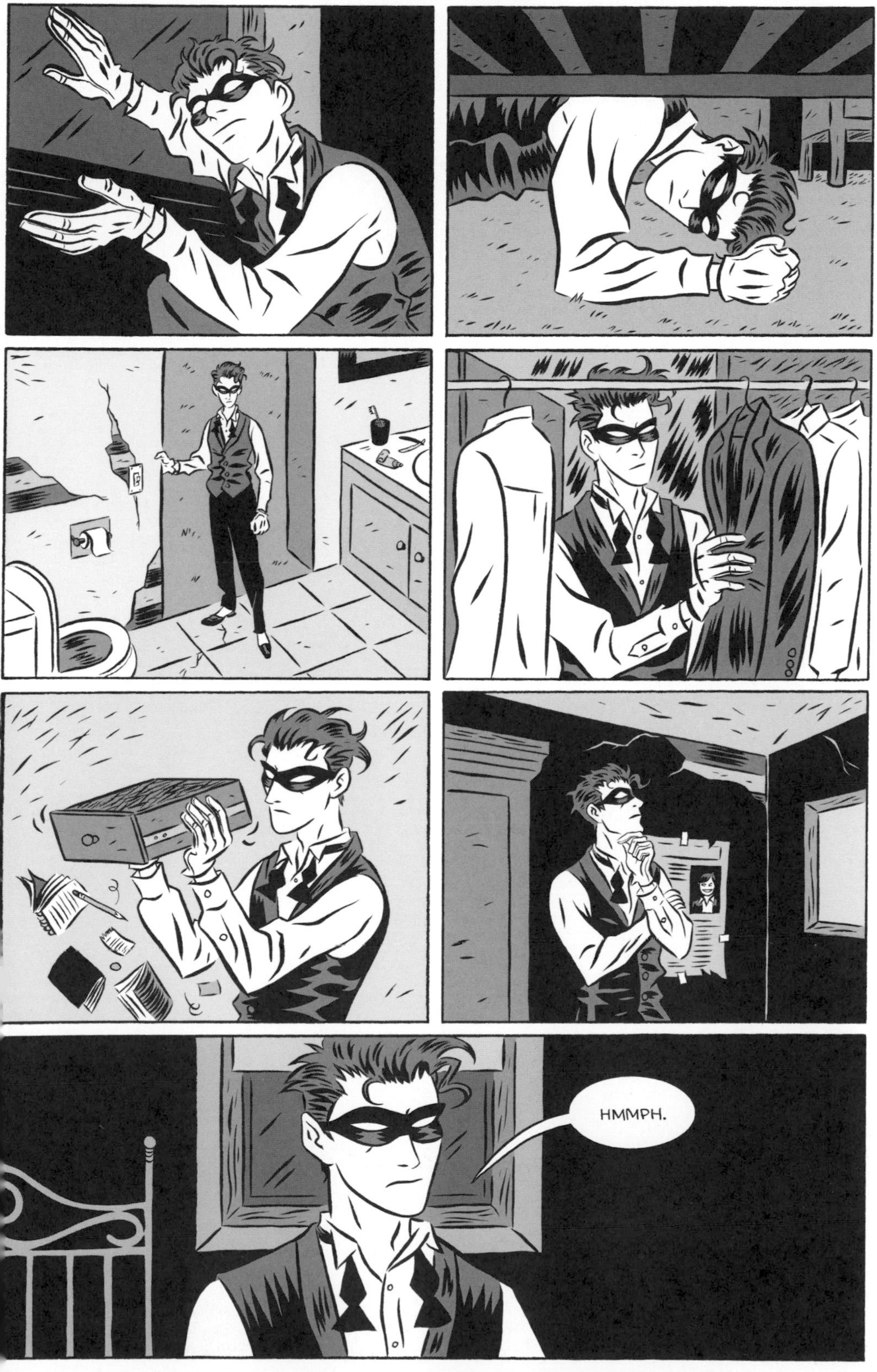
HMMPH.

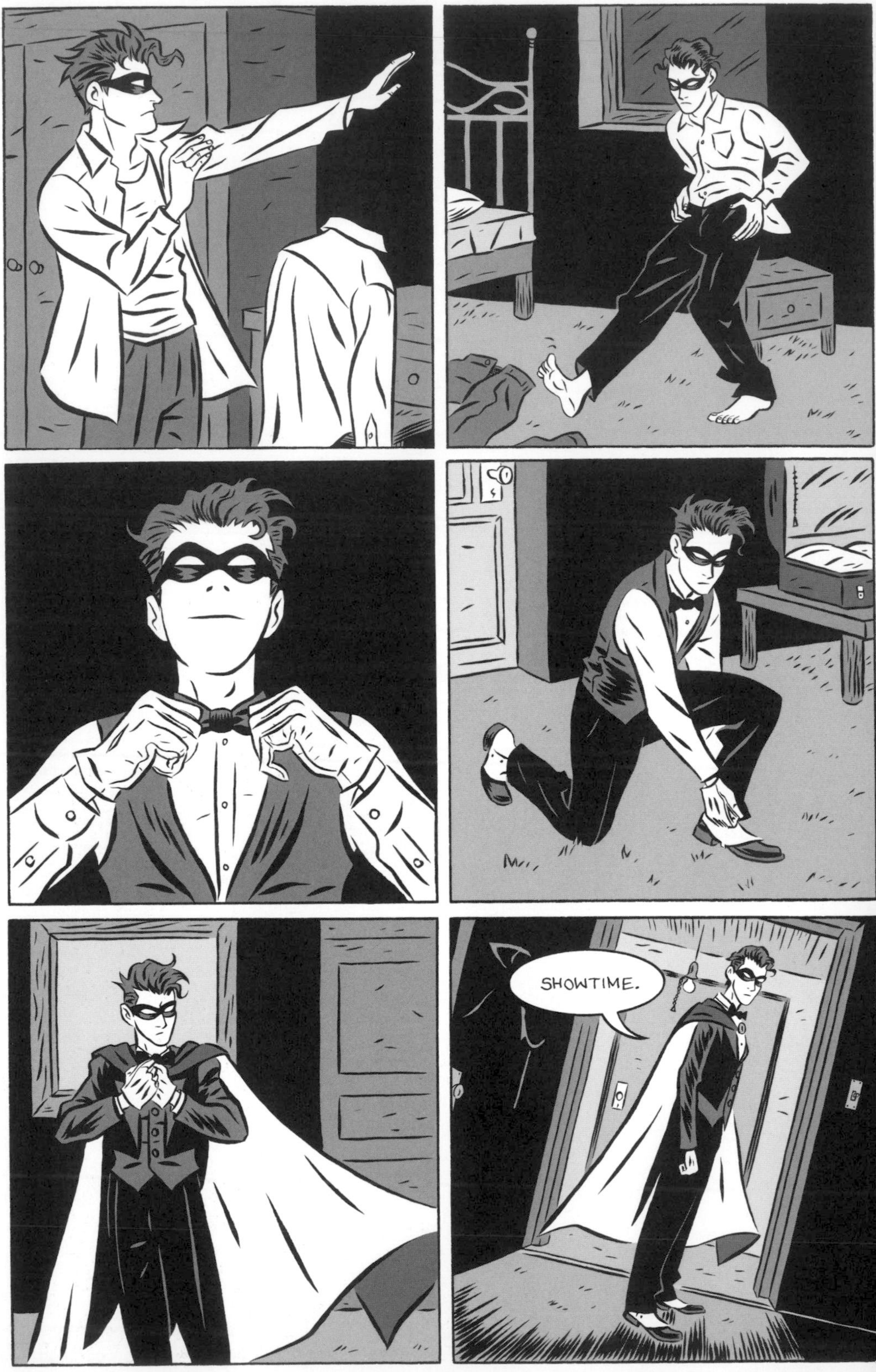
SHOWTIME.

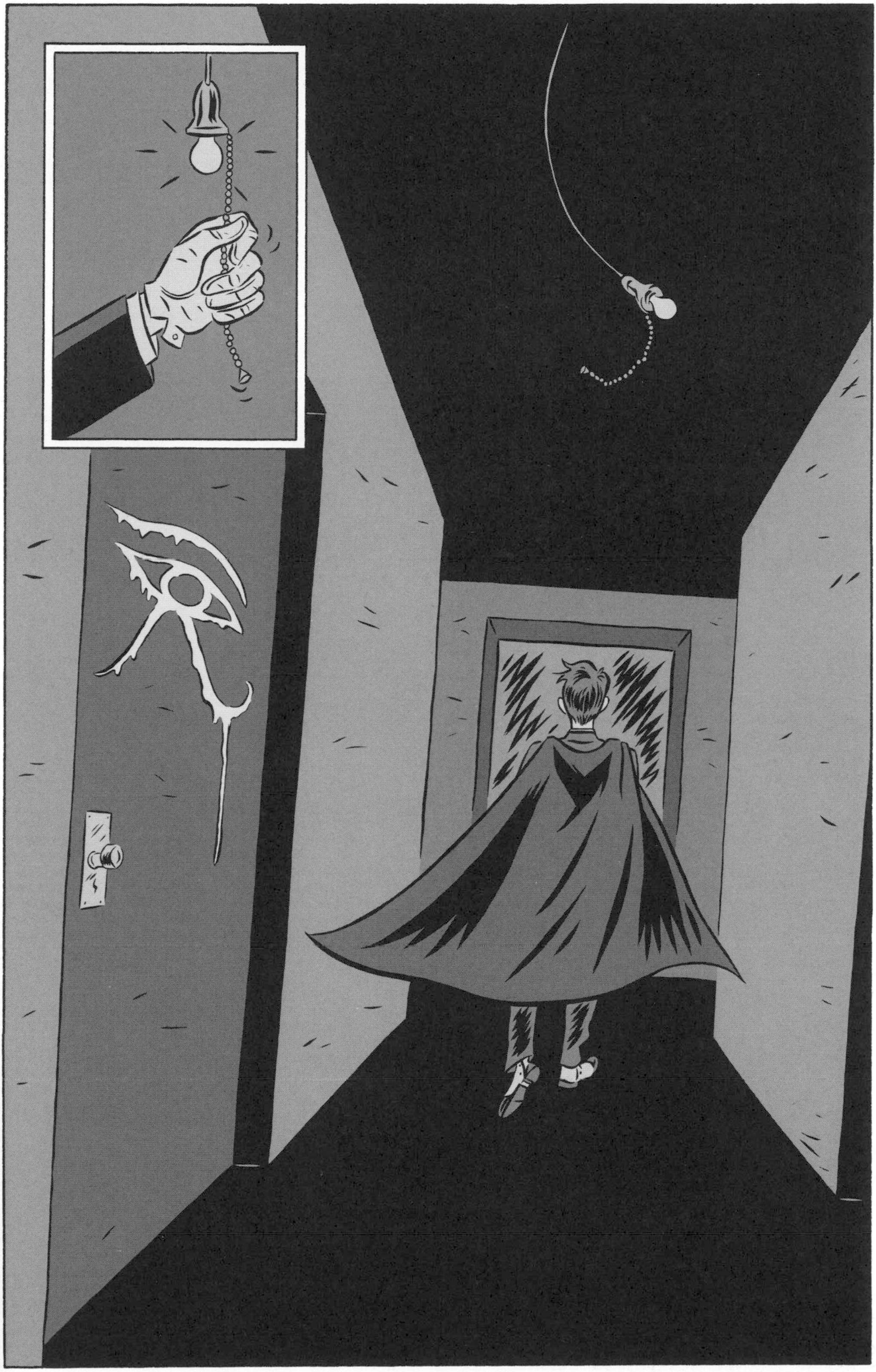

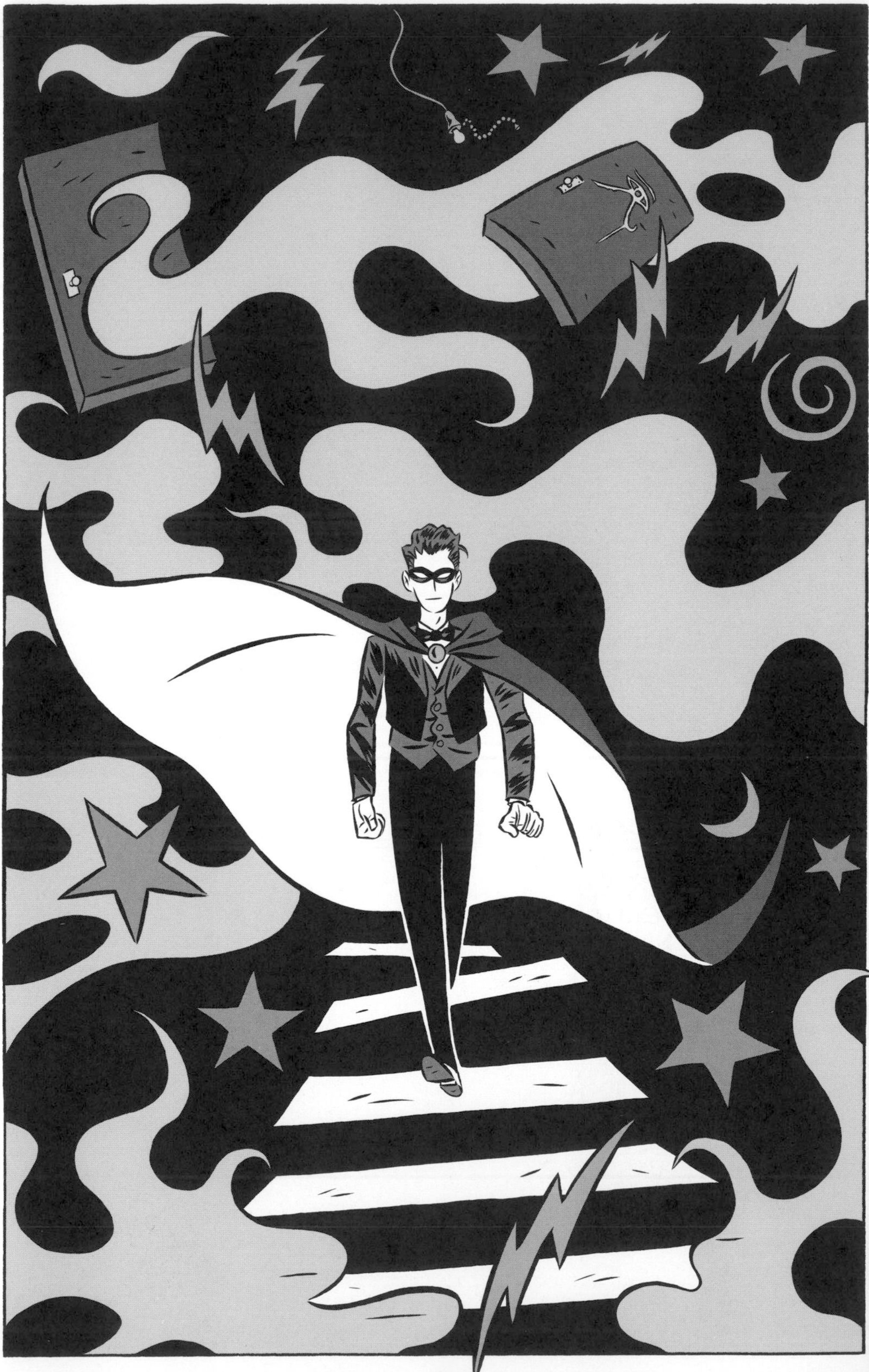

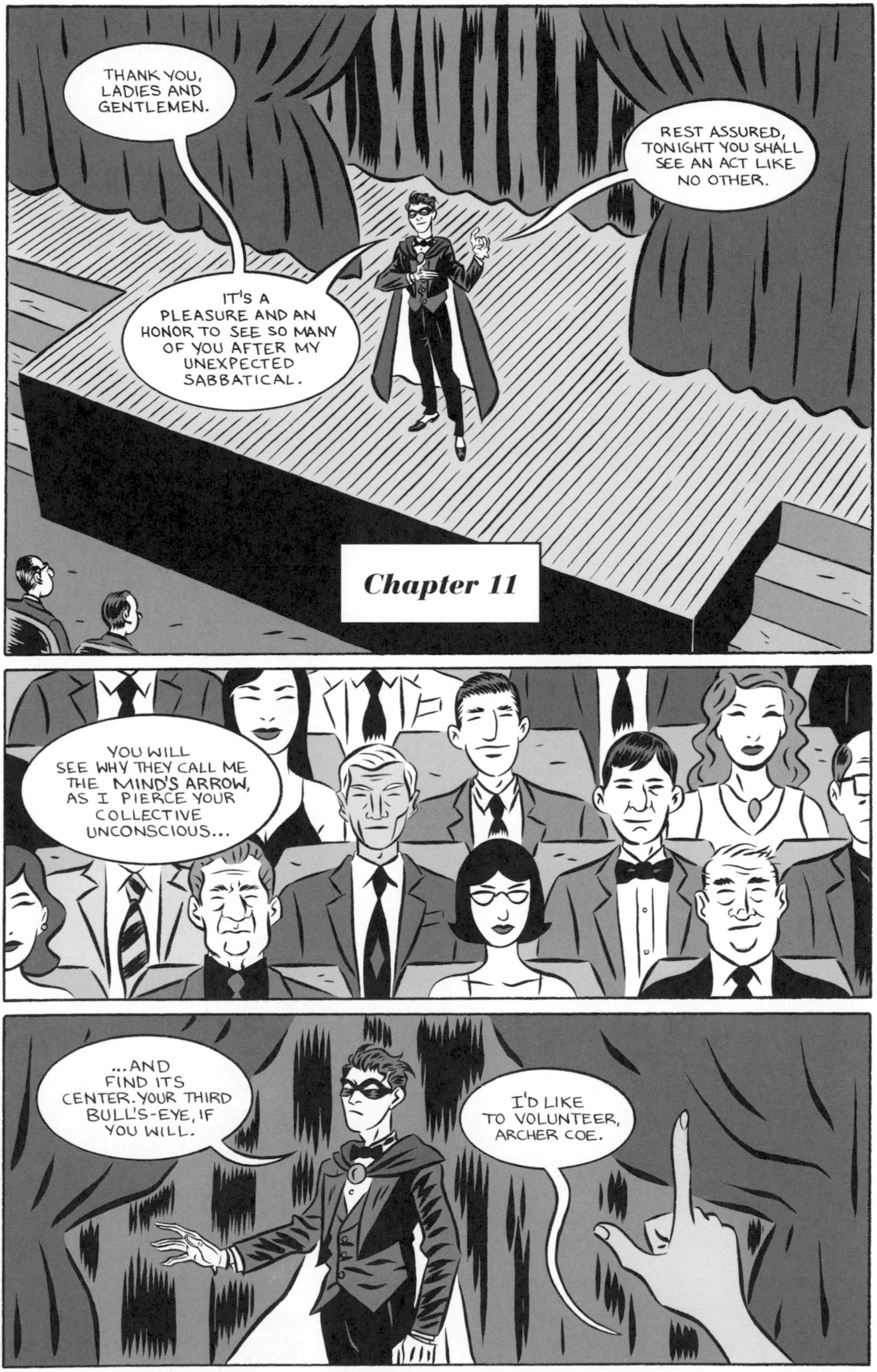
THANK YOU, LADIES AND GENTLEMEN.
IT'S A PLEASURE AND AN HONOR TO SEE SO MANY OF YOU AFTER MY UNEXPECTED SABBATICAL.
REST ASSURED, TONIGHT YOU SHALL SEE AN ACT LIKE NO OTHER.
Chapter 11
YOU WILL SEE WHY THEY CALL ME THE MIND'S ARROW, AS I PIERCE YOUR COLLECTIVE UNCONSCIOUS...
...AND FIND ITS CENTER. YOUR THIRD BULL'S-EYE, IF YOU WILL.
I'D LIKE TO VOLUNTEER, ARCHER COE.

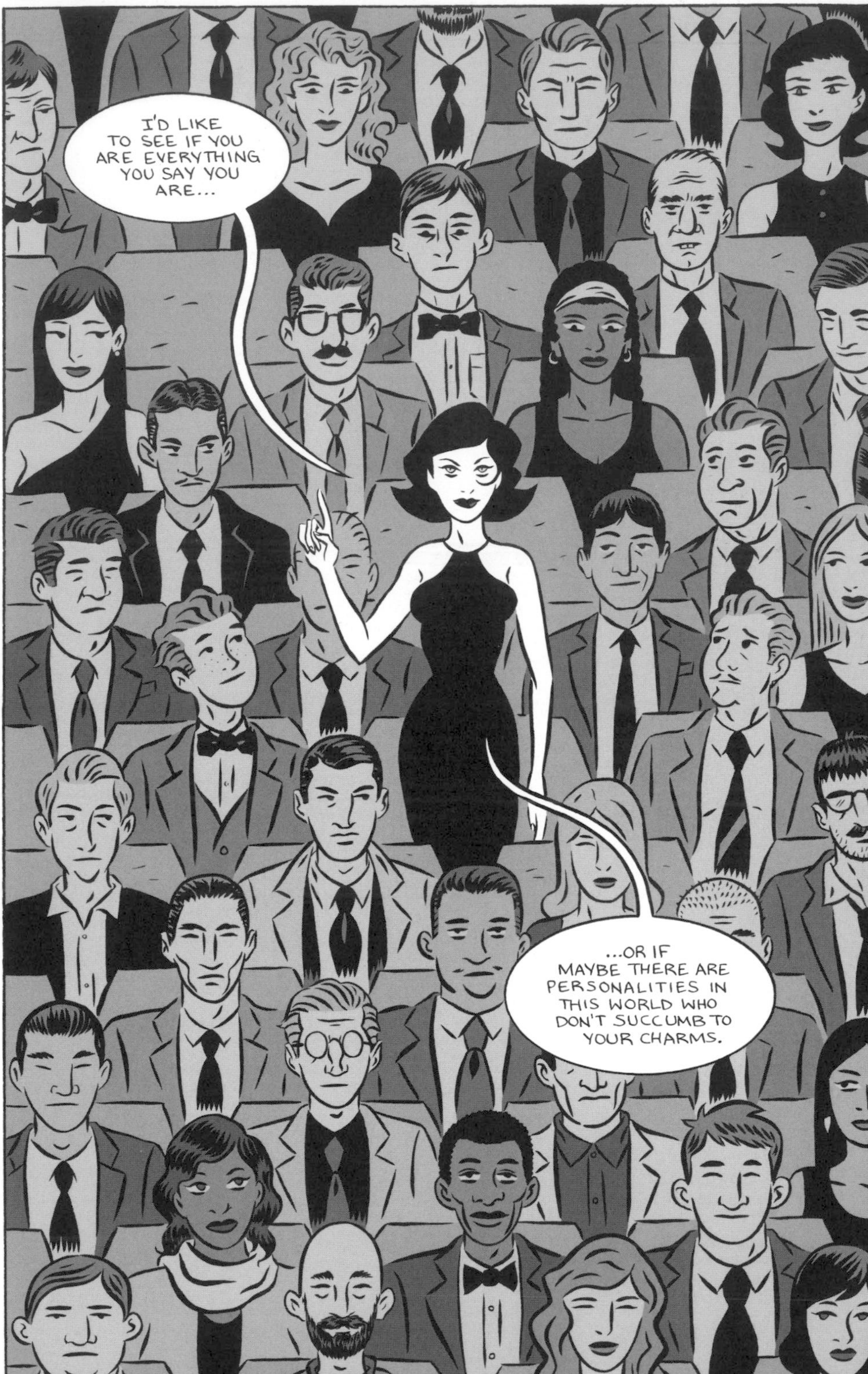
I'D LIKE TO SEE IF YOU ARE EVERYTHING YOU SAY YOU ARE...
...OR IF MAYBE THERE ARE PERSONALITIES IN THIS WORLD WHO DON'T SUCCUMB TO YOUR CHARMS.

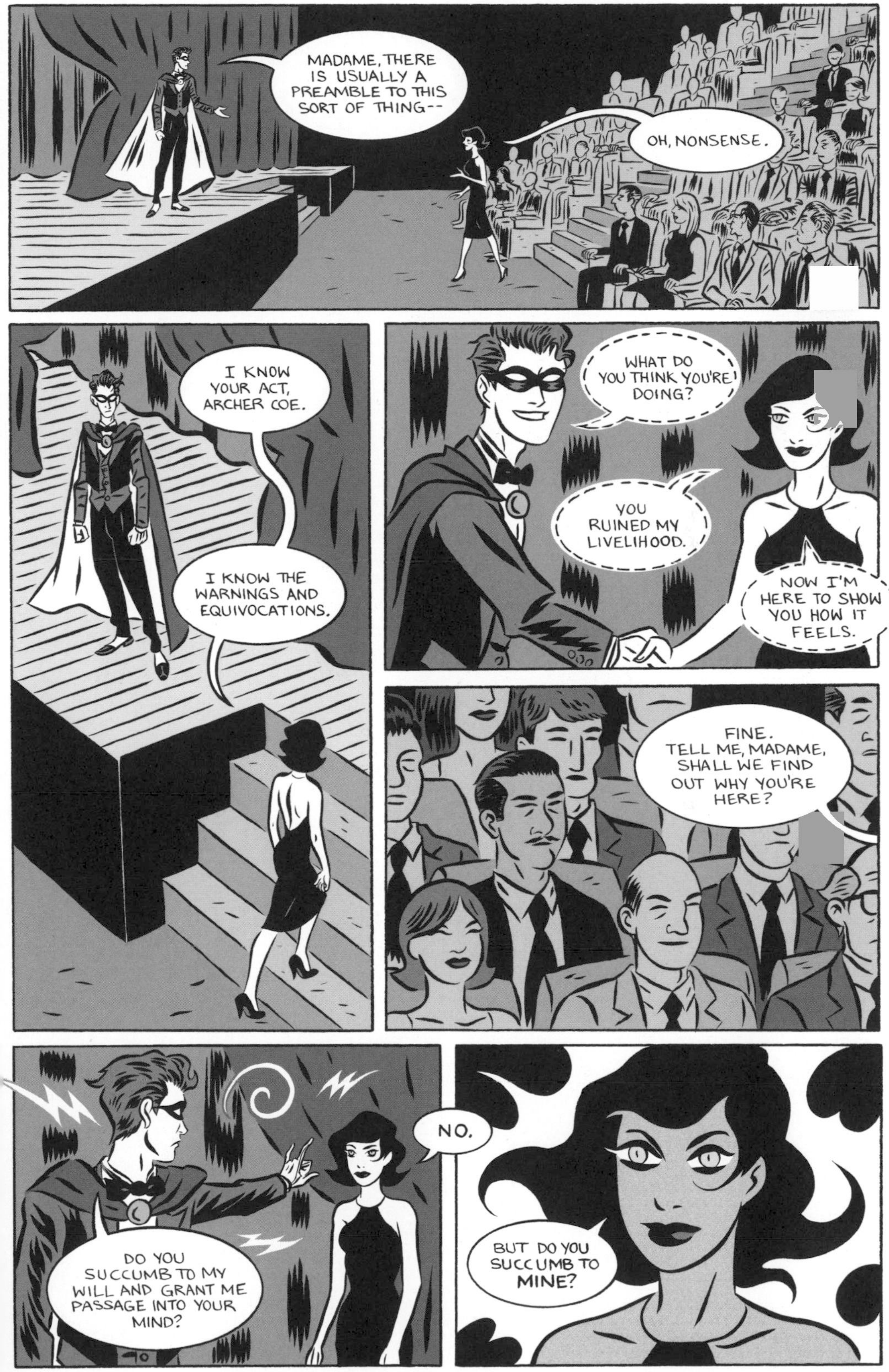
MADAME, THERE IS USUALLY A PREAMBLE TO THIS SORT OF THING--
OH, NONSENSE.
I KNOW YOUR ACT, ARCHER COE.
I KNOW THE WARNINGS AND EQUIVOCATIONS.
WHAT DO YOU THINK YOU'RE DOING?
YOU RUINED MY LIVELIHOOD.
NOW I'M HERE TO SHOW YOU HOW IT FEELS.
FINE. TELL ME, MADAME, SHALL WE FIND OUT WHY YOU'RE HERE?
DO YOU SUCCUMB TO MY WILL AND GRANT ME PASSAGE INTO YOUR MIND?
NO.
BUT DO YOU SUCCUMB TO MINE?

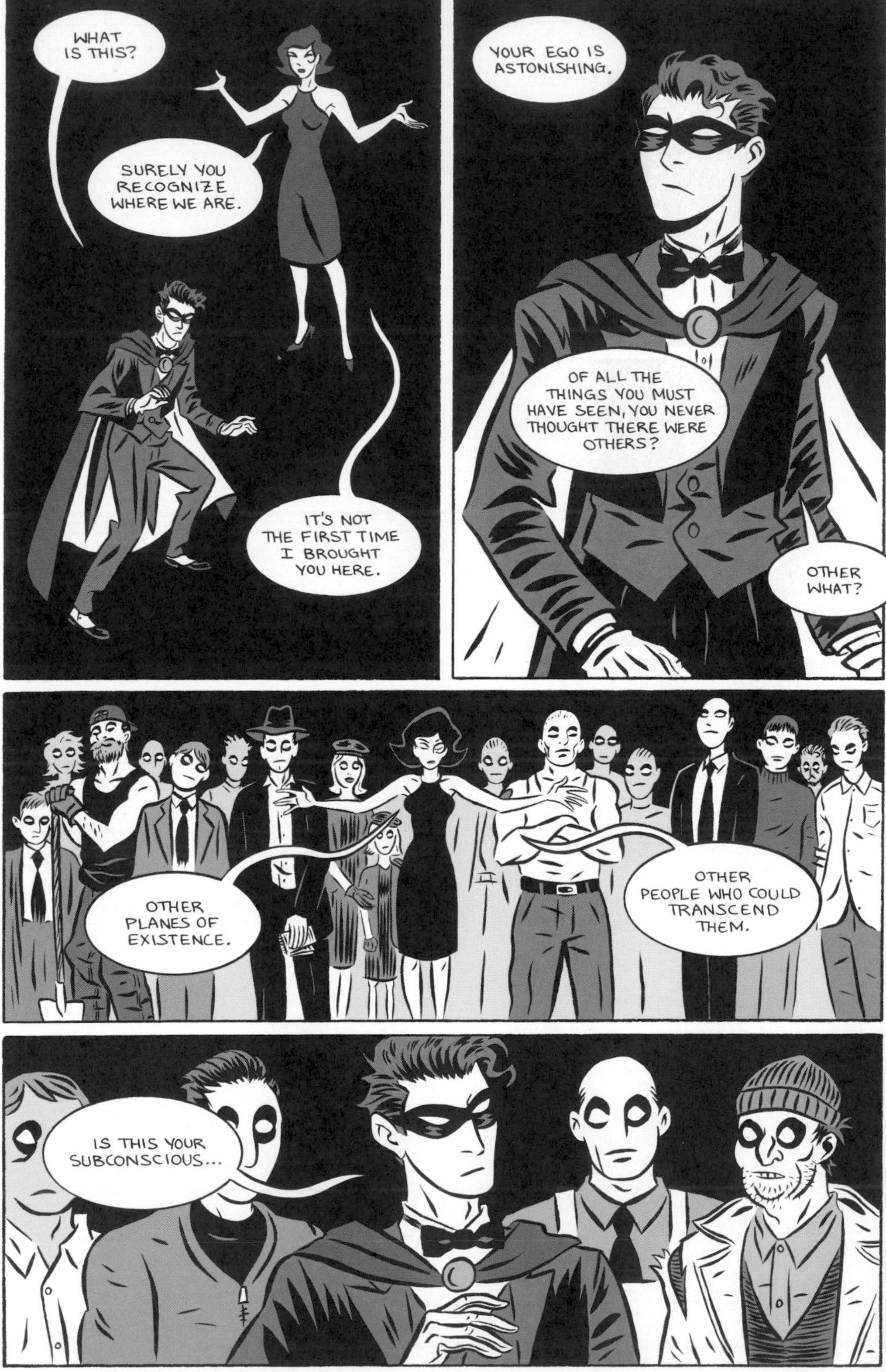
WHAT IS THIS?
SURELY YOU RECOGNIZE WHERE WE ARE.
IT'S NOT THE FIRST TIME I BROUGHT YOU HERE.
YOUR EGO IS ASTONISHING.
OF ALL THE THINGS YOU MUST HAVE SEEN, YOU NEVER THOUGHT THERE WERE OTHERS?
OTHER WHAT?
OTHER PLANES OF EXISTENCE.
OTHER PEOPLE WHO COULD TRANSCEND THEM.
IS THIS YOUR SUBCONSCIOUS...

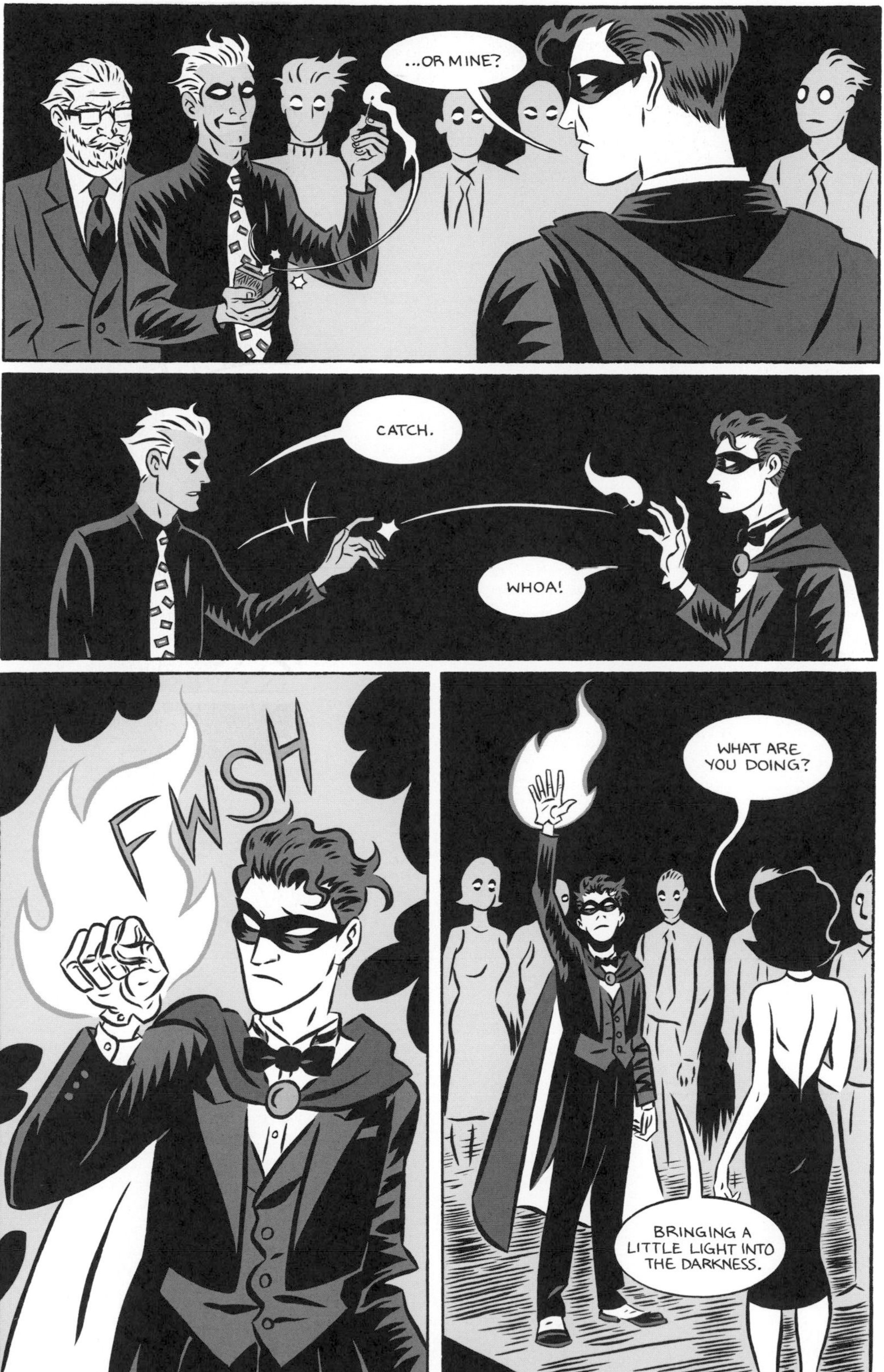
...OR MINE?
CATCH.
WHOA!
FWSH
WHAT ARE YOU DOING?
BRINGING A LITTLE LIGHT INTO THE DARKNESS.

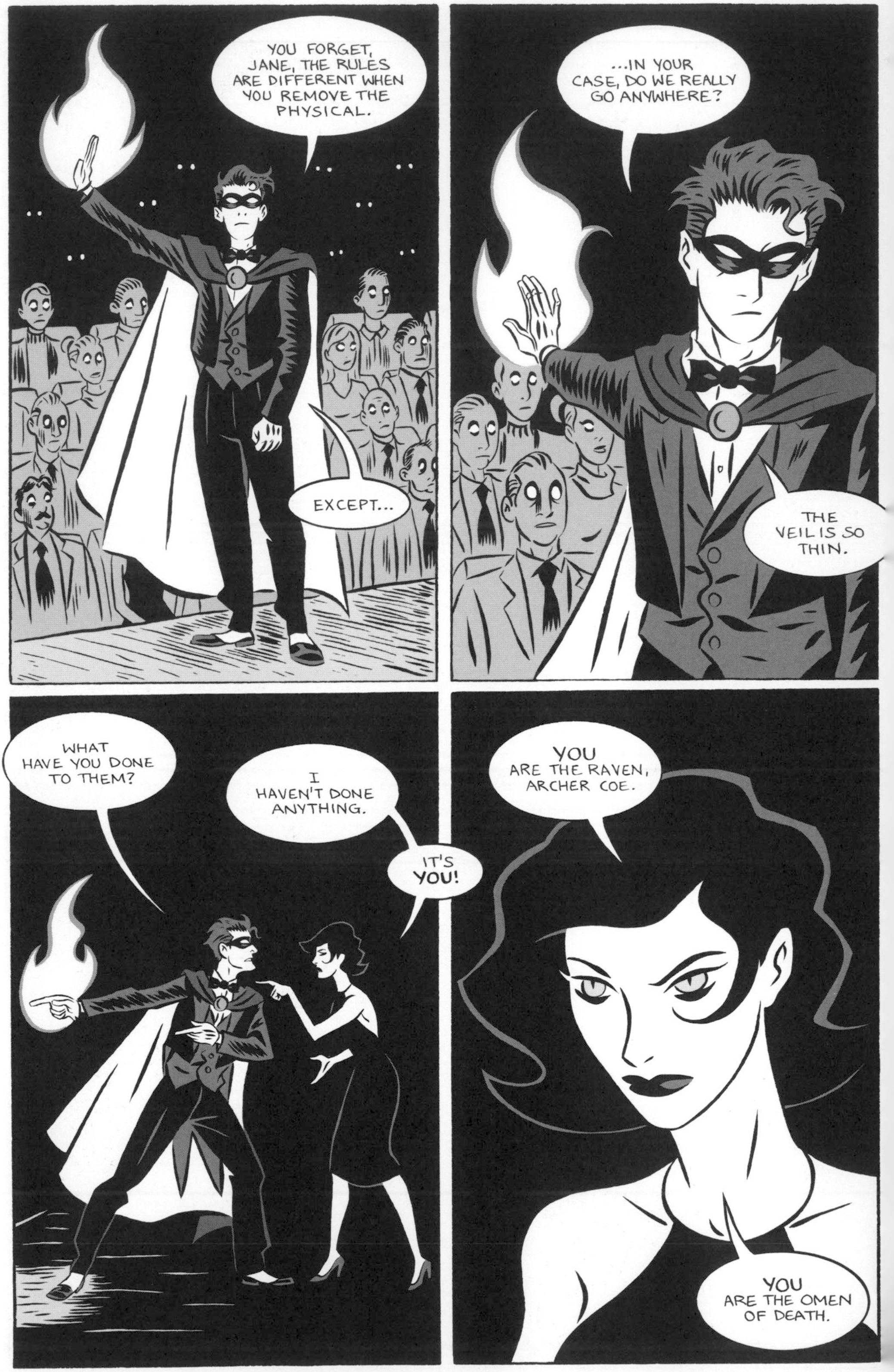
YOU FORGET, JANE, THE RULES ARE DIFFERENT WHEN YOU REMOVE THE PHYSICAL.
EXCEPT...
...IN YOUR CASE, DO WE REALLY GO ANYWHERE?
THE VEIL IS SO THIN.
WHAT HAVE YOU DONE TO THEM?
I HAVEN'T DONE ANYTHING.
IT'S YOU!
YOU ARE THE RAVEN, ARCHER COE.
YOU ARE THE OMEN OF DEATH.

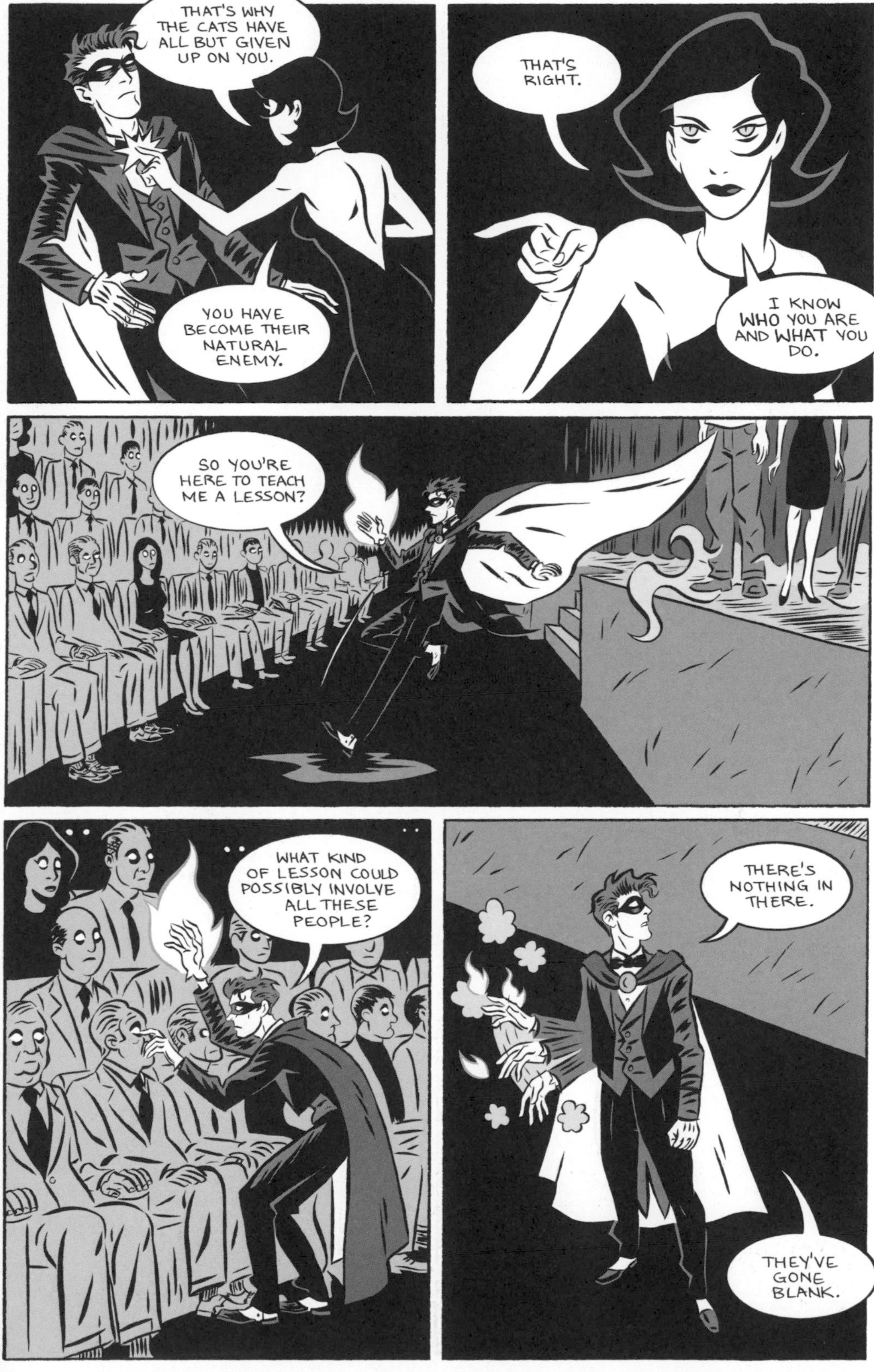
THAT'S WHY THE CATS HAVE ALL BUT GIVEN UP ON YOU.
YOU HAVE BECOME THEIR NATURAL ENEMY.
THAT'S RIGHT.
I KNOW WHO YOU ARE AND WHAT YOU DO.
SO YOU'RE HERE TO TEACH ME A LESSON?
WHAT KIND OF LESSON COULD POSSIBLY INVOLVE ALL THESE PEOPLE?
THERE'S NOTHING IN THERE.
THEY'VE GONE BLANK.

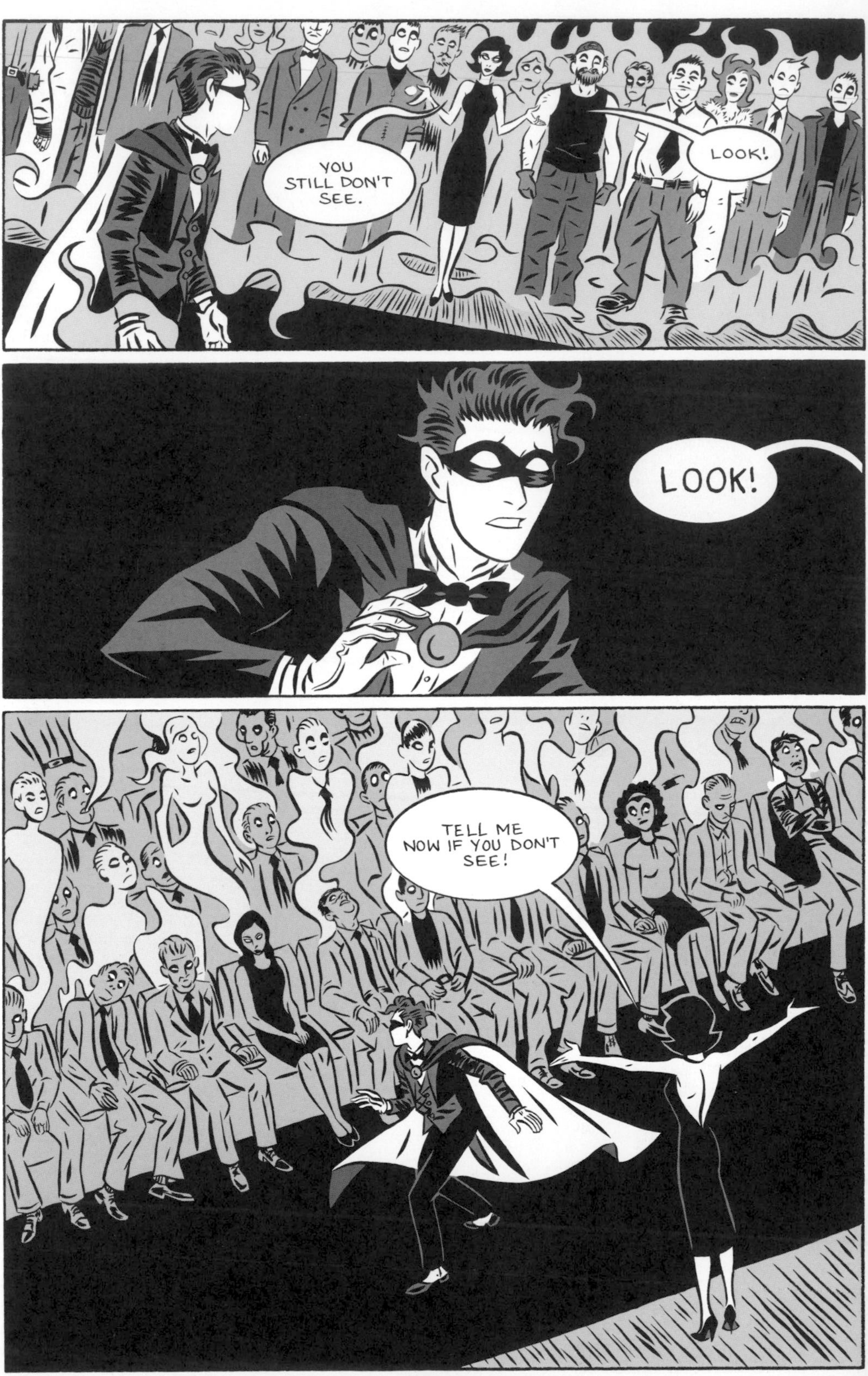
YOU STILL DON'T SEE.
LOOK!
LOOK!
TELL ME NOW IF YOU DON'T SEE!

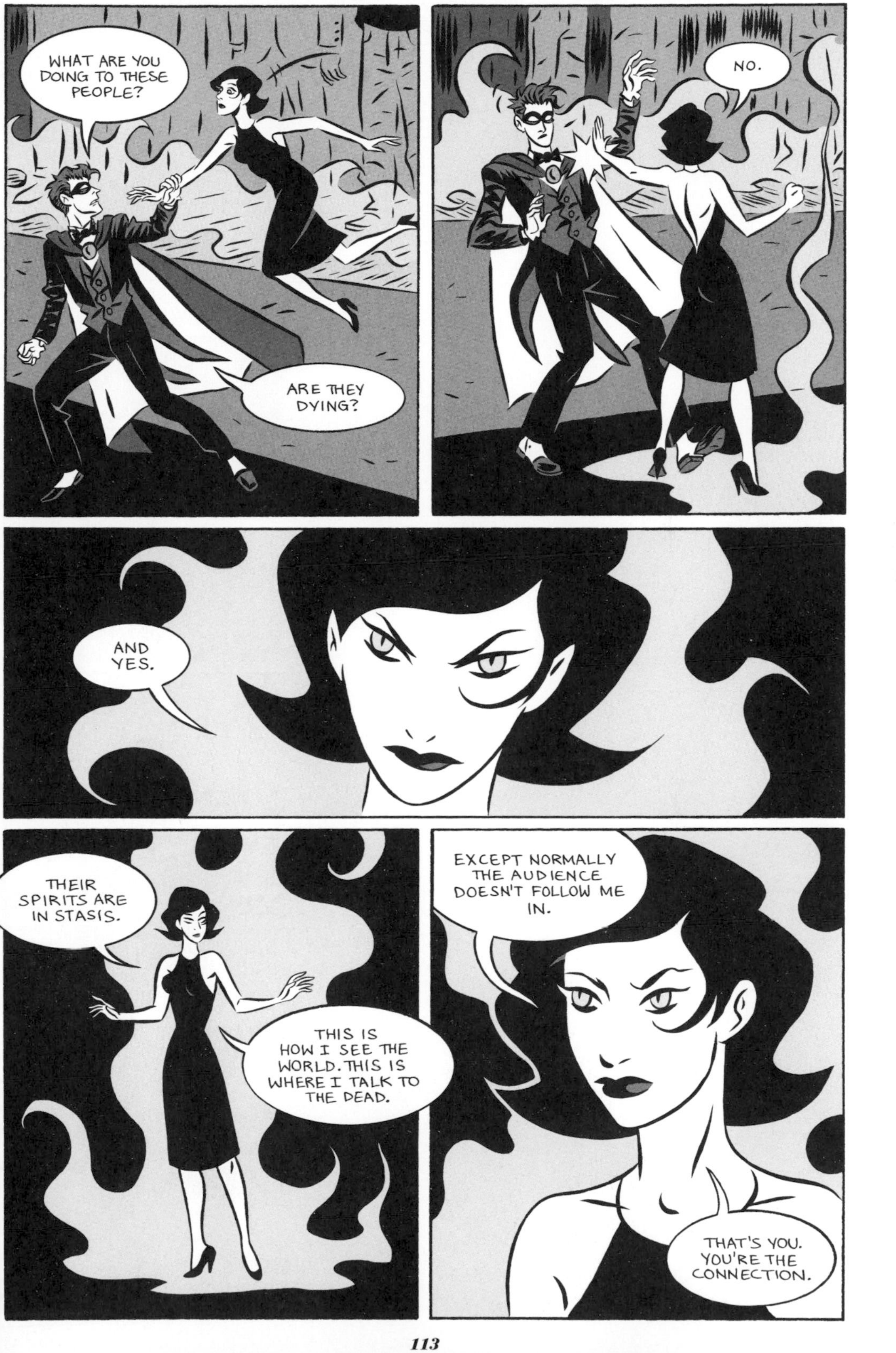
WHAT ARE YOU DOING TO THESE PEOPLE?
ARE THEY DYING?
NO.
AND YES.
THEIR SPIRITS ARE IN STASIS.
THIS IS HOW I SEE THE WORLD. THIS IS WHERE I TALK TO THE DEAD.
EXCEPT NORMALLY THE AUDIENCE DOESN'T FOLLOW ME IN.
THAT'S YOU. YOU'RE THE CONNECTION.

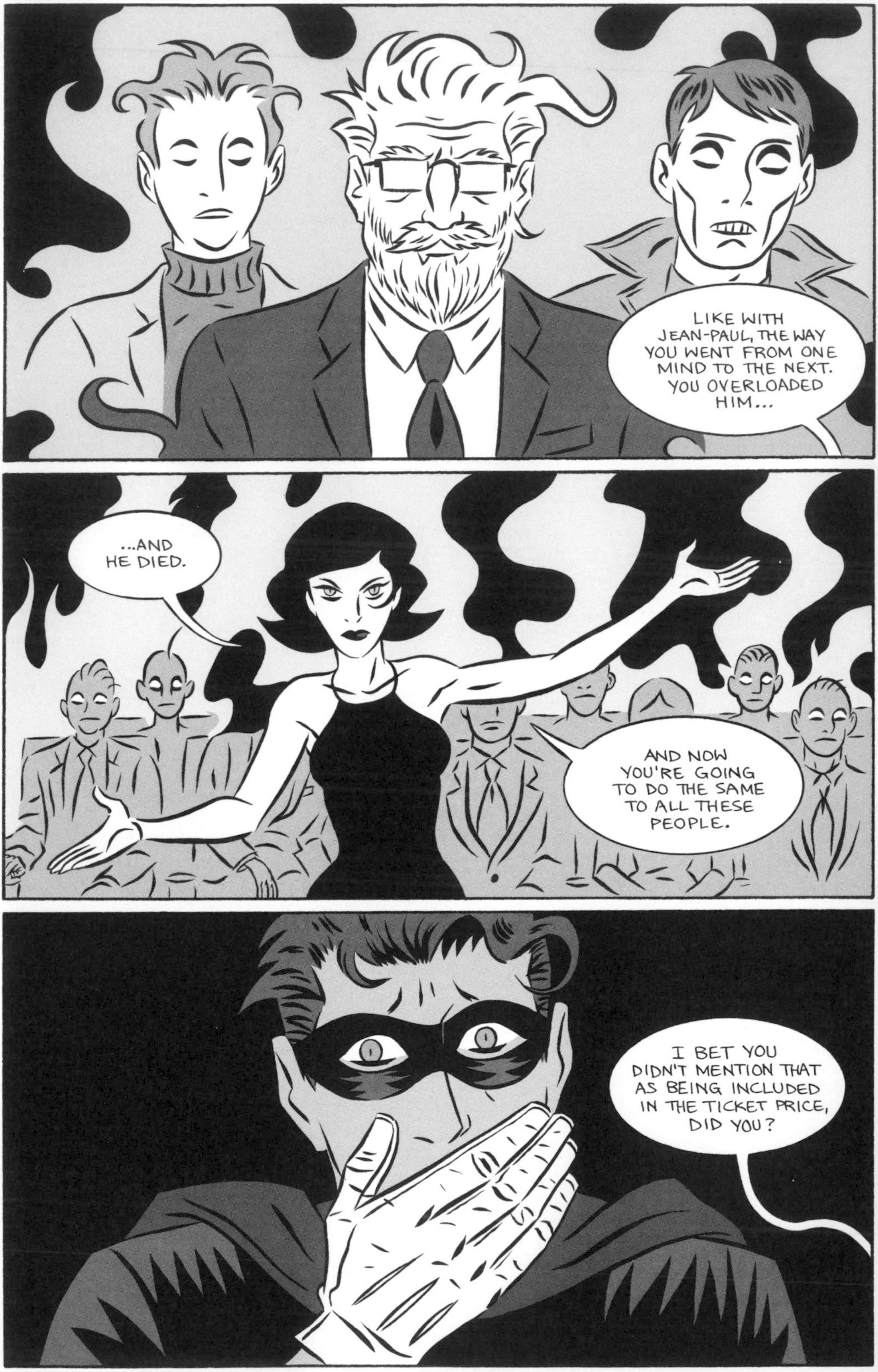
LIKE WITH JEAN-PAUL, THE WAY YOU WENT FROM ONE MIND TO THE NEXT. YOU OVERLOADED HIM...
...AND HE DIED.
AND NOW YOU'RE GOING TO DO THE SAME TO ALL THESE PEOPLE.
I BET YOU DIDN'T MENTION THAT AS BEING INCLUDED IN THE TICKET PRICE, DID YOU?

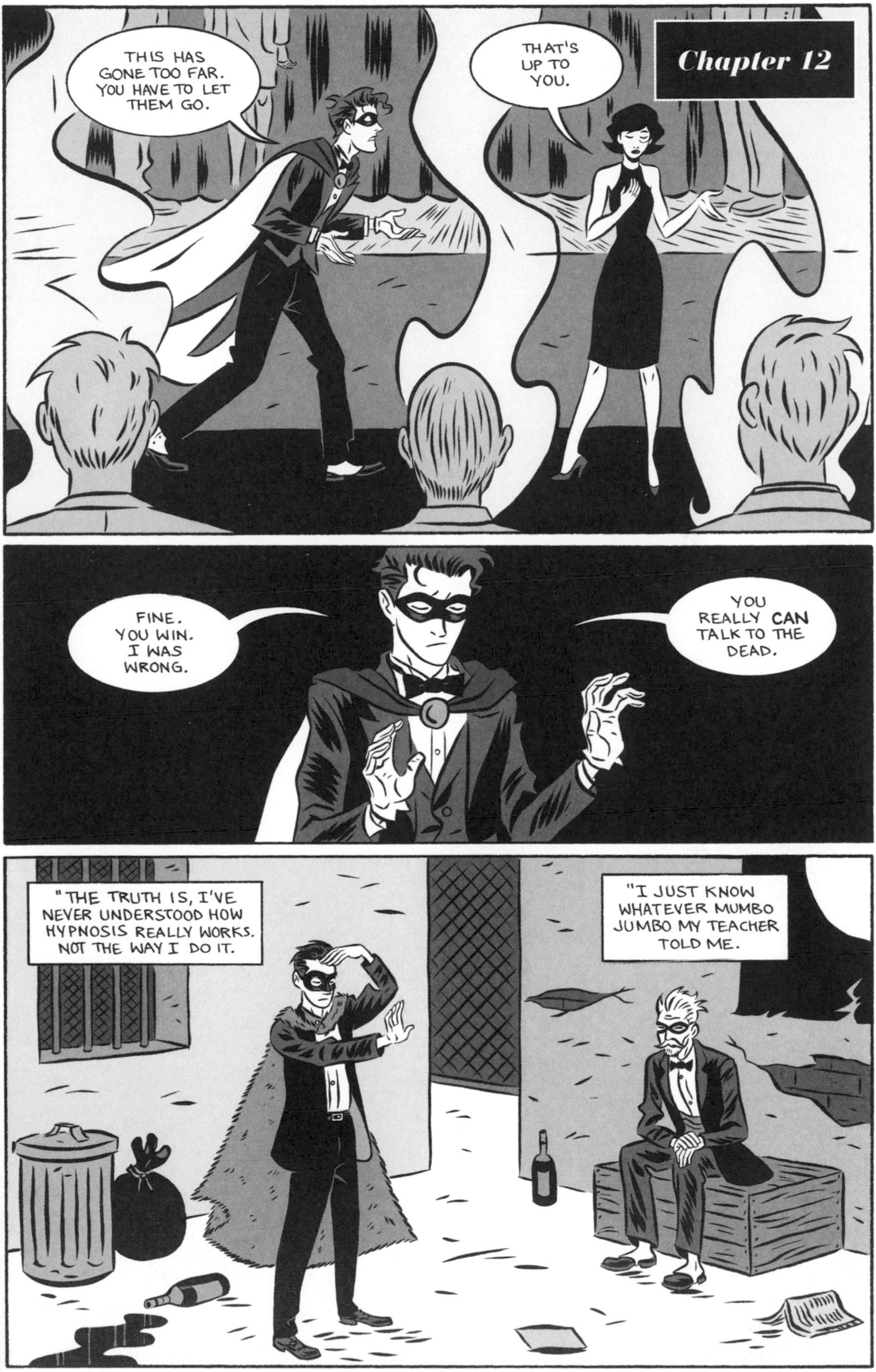
Chapter 12
THIS HAS GONE TOO FAR. YOU HAVE TO LET THEM GO.
THAT'S UP TO YOU.
FINE. YOU WIN. I WAS WRONG.
YOU REALLY **CAN** TALK TO THE DEAD.
"THE TRUTH IS, I'VE NEVER UNDERSTOOD HOW HYPNOSIS REALLY WORKS. NOT THE WAY I DO IT.
"I JUST KNOW WHATEVER MUMBO JUMBO MY TEACHER TOLD ME.

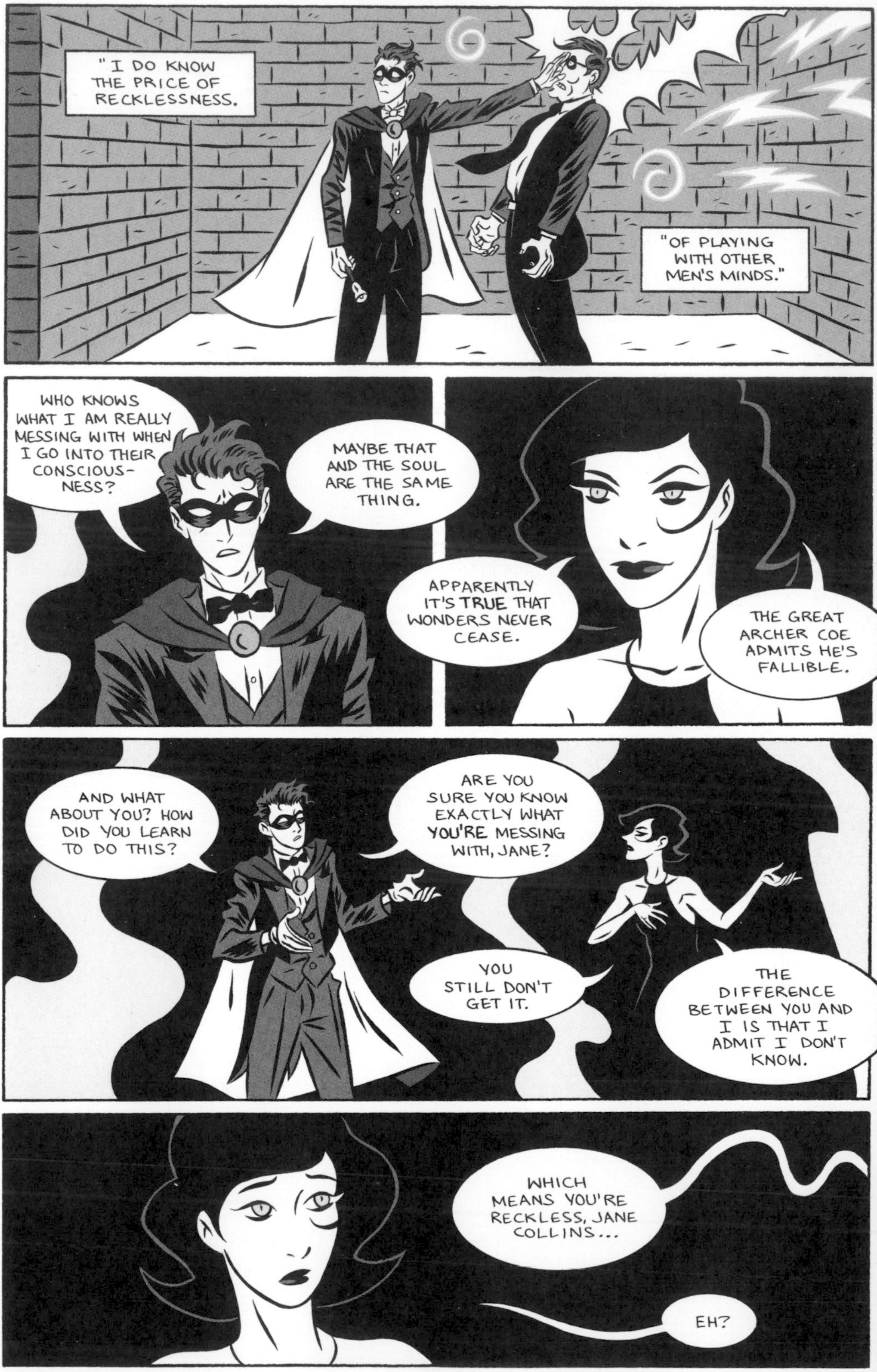
"I DO KNOW THE PRICE OF RECKLESSNESS.
"OF PLAYING WITH OTHER MEN'S MINDS."
WHO KNOWS WHAT I AM REALLY MESSING WITH WHEN I GO INTO THEIR CONSCIOUS-NESS?
MAYBE THAT AND THE SOUL ARE THE SAME THING.
APPARENTLY IT'S **TRUE** THAT WONDERS NEVER CEASE.
THE GREAT ARCHER COE ADMITS HE'S FALLIBLE.
AND WHAT ABOUT YOU? HOW DID YOU LEARN TO DO THIS?
ARE YOU SURE YOU KNOW EXACTLY WHAT **YOU'RE** MESSING WITH, JANE?
YOU STILL DON'T GET IT.
THE DIFFERENCE BETWEEN YOU AND I IS THAT I ADMIT I DON'T KNOW.
WHICH MEANS YOU'RE RECKLESS, JANE COLLINS...
EH?

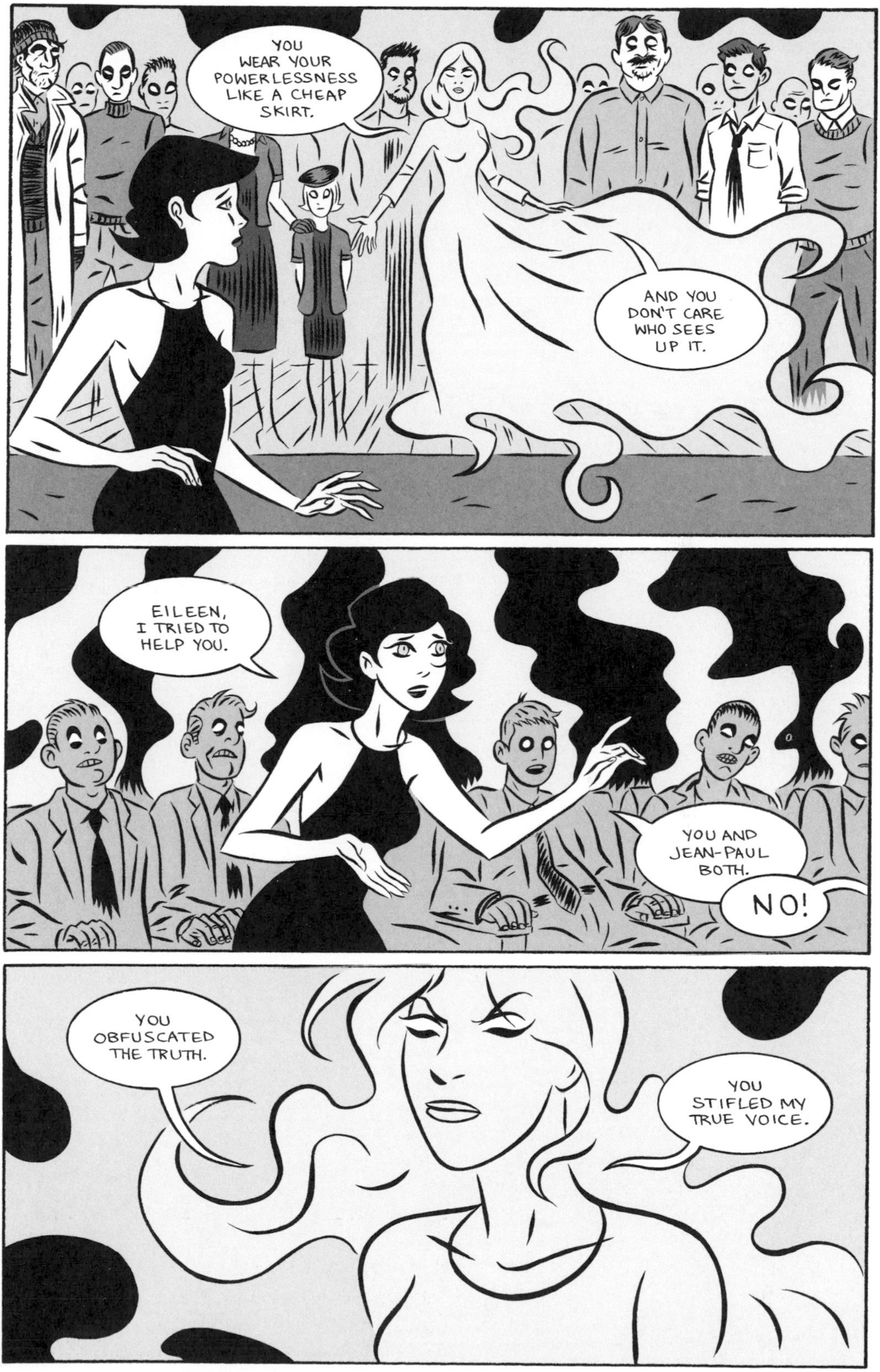
YOU WEAR YOUR POWERLESSNESS LIKE A CHEAP SKIRT.
AND YOU DON'T CARE WHO SEES UP IT.
EILEEN, I TRIED TO HELP YOU.
YOU AND JEAN-PAUL BOTH.
NO!
YOU OBFUSCATED THE TRUTH.
YOU STIFLED MY TRUE VOICE.

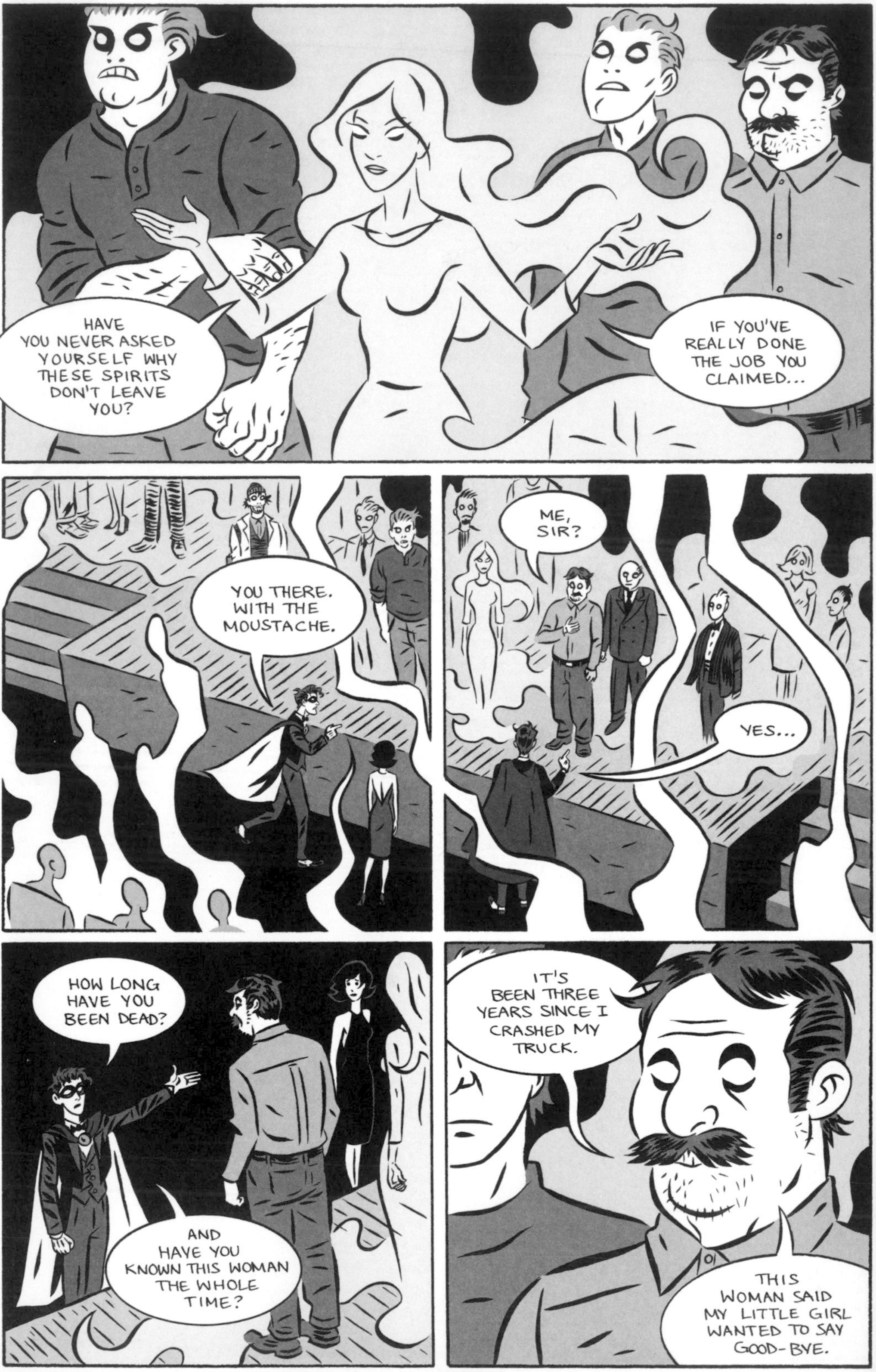
HAVE YOU NEVER ASKED YOURSELF WHY THESE SPIRITS DON'T LEAVE YOU?
IF YOU'VE REALLY DONE THE JOB YOU CLAIMED...
YOU THERE. WITH THE MOUSTACHE.
ME, SIR?
YES...
HOW LONG HAVE YOU BEEN DEAD?
AND HAVE YOU KNOWN THIS WOMAN THE WHOLE TIME?
IT'S BEEN THREE YEARS SINCE I CRASHED MY TRUCK.
THIS WOMAN SAID MY LITTLE GIRL WANTED TO SAY GOOD-BYE.

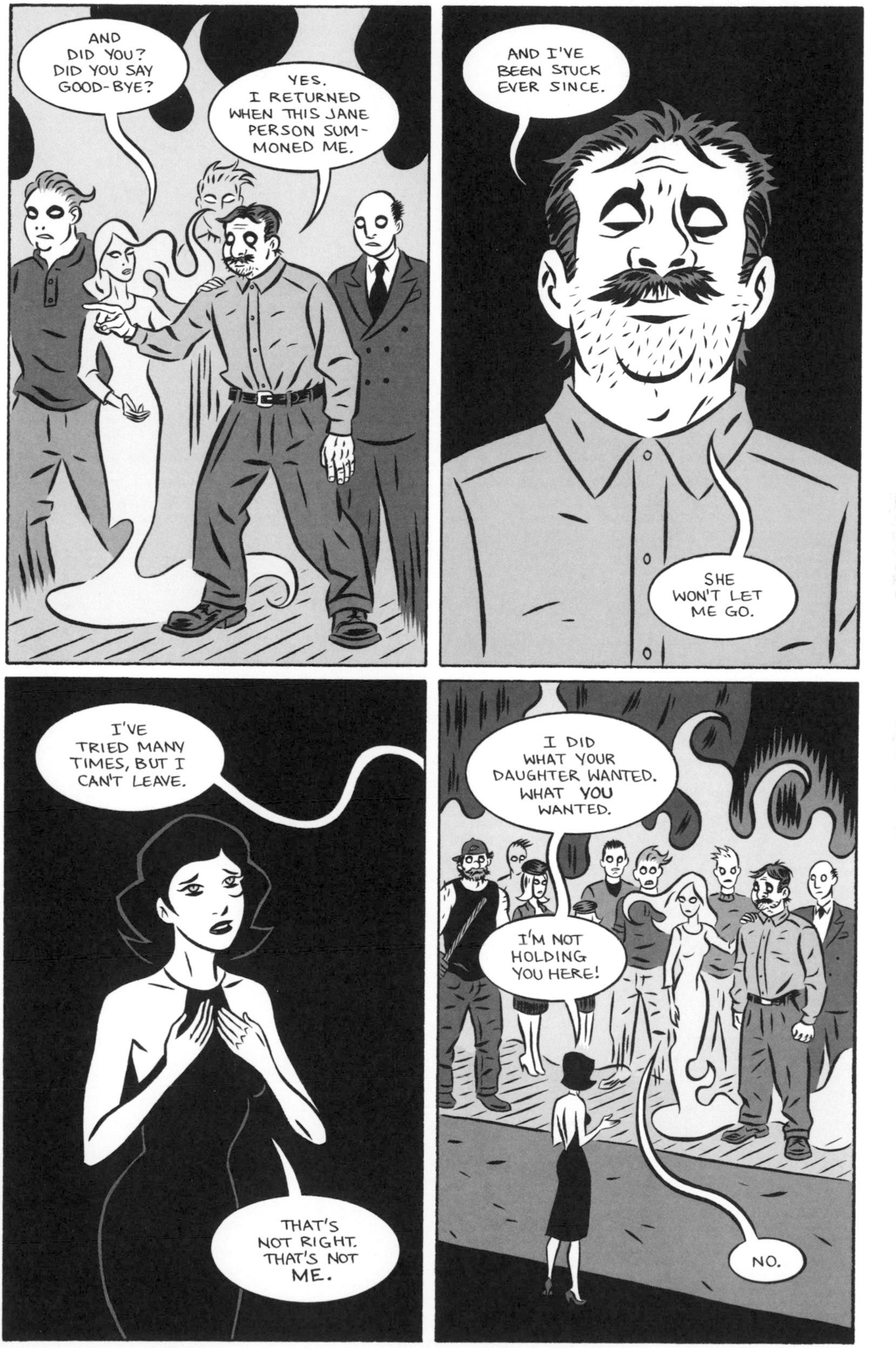
AND DID YOU? DID YOU SAY GOOD-BYE?
YES. I RETURNED WHEN THIS JANE PERSON SUMMONED ME.
AND I'VE BEEN STUCK EVER SINCE.
SHE WON'T LET ME GO.
I'VE TRIED MANY TIMES, BUT I CAN'T LEAVE.
THAT'S NOT RIGHT. THAT'S NOT ME.
I DID WHAT YOUR DAUGHTER WANTED. WHAT YOU WANTED.
I'M NOT HOLDING YOU HERE!
NO.

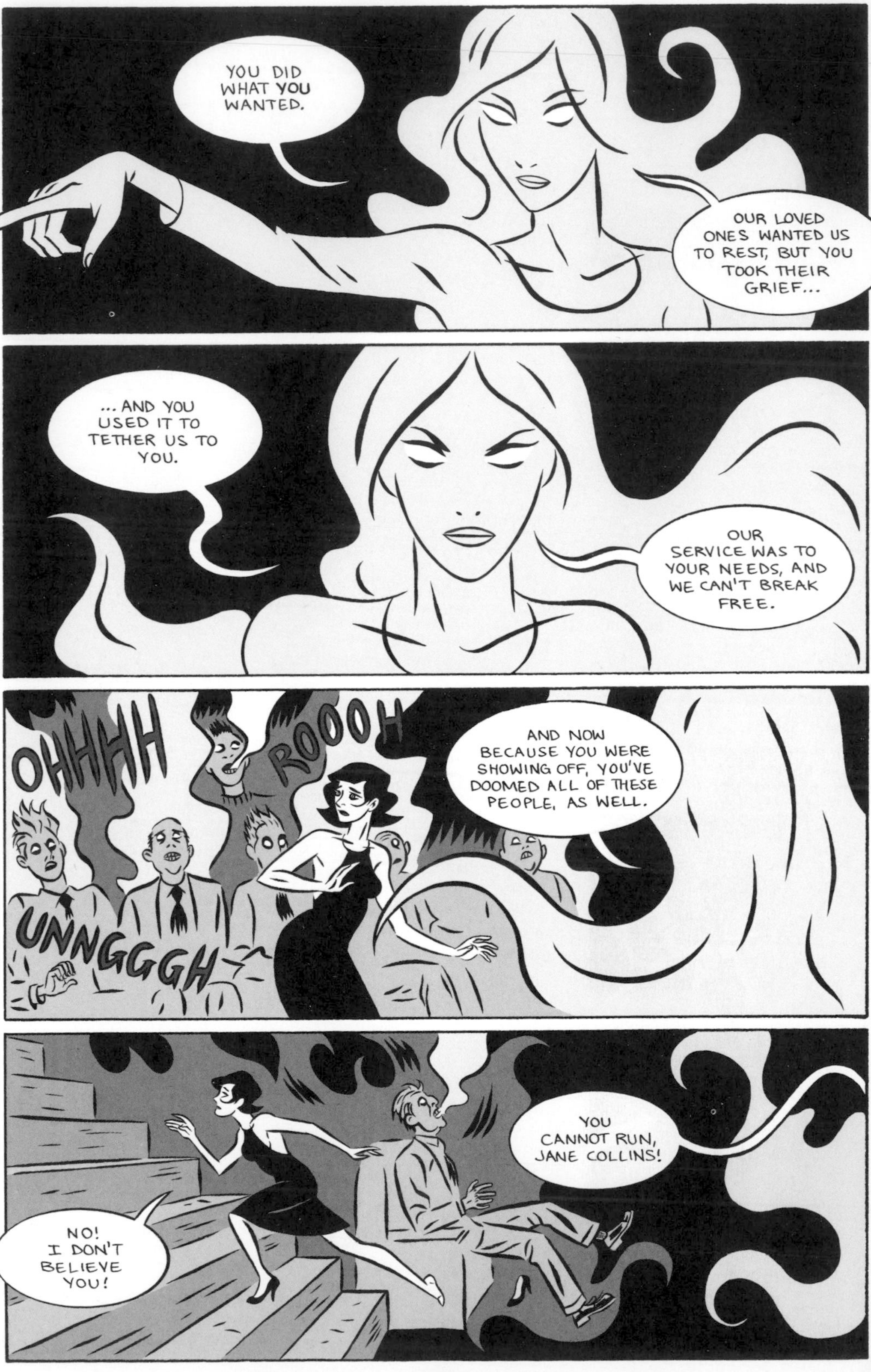
YOU DID WHAT YOU WANTED.
OUR LOVED ONES WANTED US TO REST, BUT YOU TOOK THEIR GRIEF...
...AND YOU USED IT TO TETHER US TO YOU.
OUR SERVICE WAS TO YOUR NEEDS, AND WE CAN'T BREAK FREE.
OHHHH
ROOOH
AND NOW BECAUSE YOU WERE SHOWING OFF, YOU'VE DOOMED ALL OF THESE PEOPLE, AS WELL.
UNNGGGH
YOU CANNOT RUN, JANE COLLINS!
NO! I DON'T BELIEVE YOU!

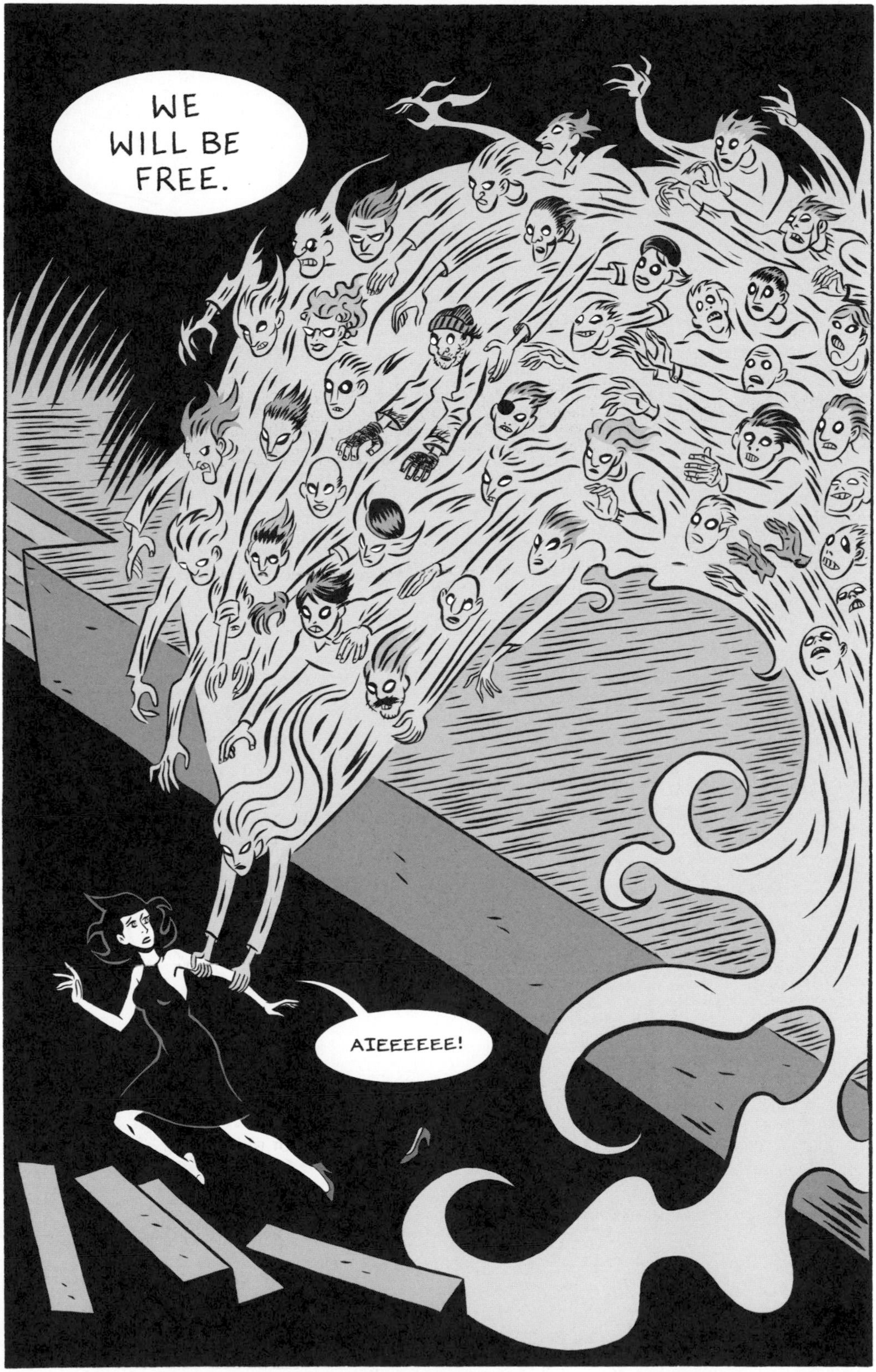
WE WILL BE FREE.
AIEEEEEE!

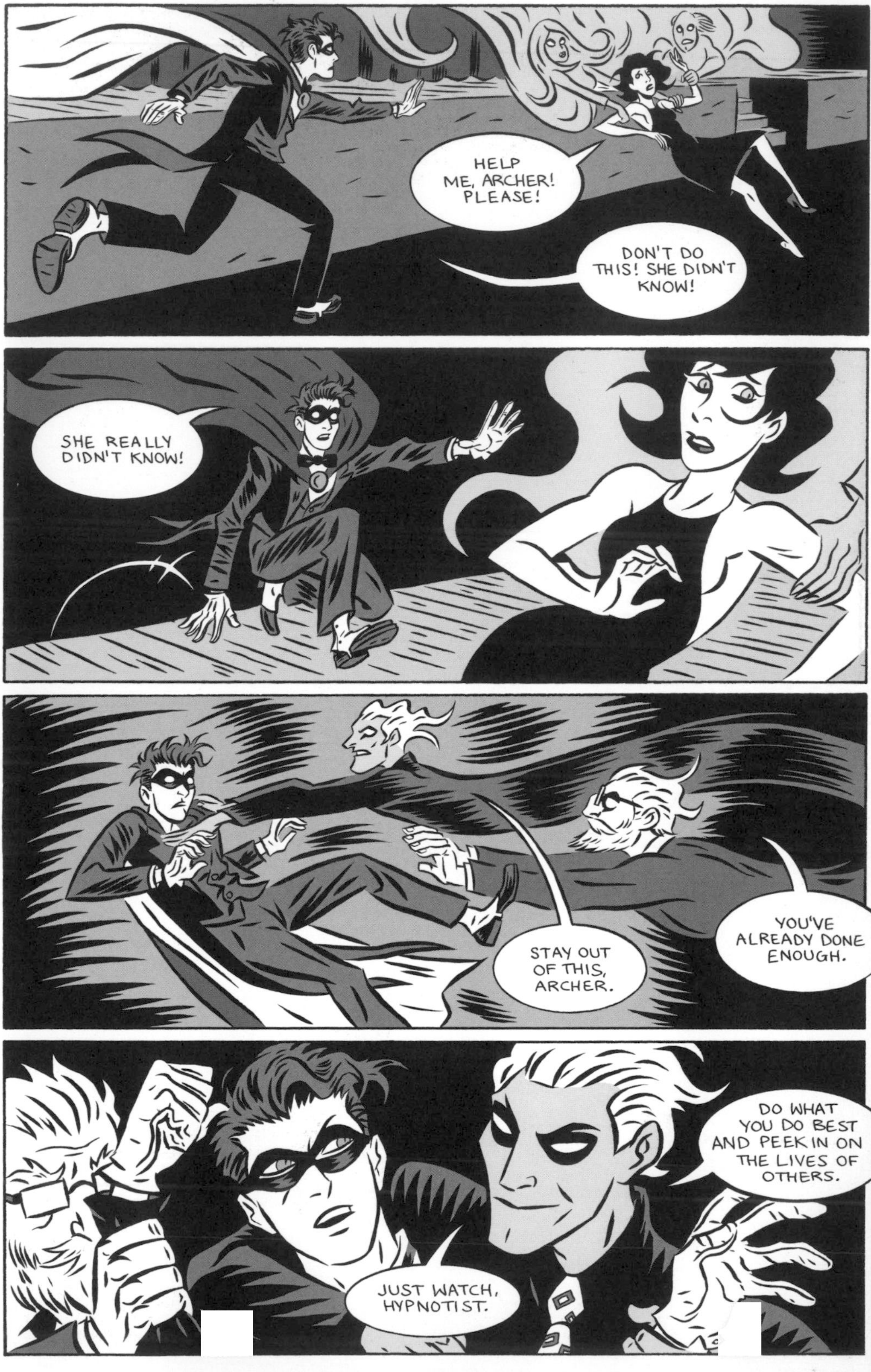
HELP ME, ARCHER! PLEASE!
DON'T DO THIS! SHE DIDN'T KNOW!
SHE REALLY DIDN'T KNOW!
STAY OUT OF THIS, ARCHER.
YOU'VE ALREADY DONE ENOUGH.
DO WHAT YOU DO BEST AND PEEK IN ON THE LIVES OF OTHERS.
JUST WATCH, HYPNOTIST.

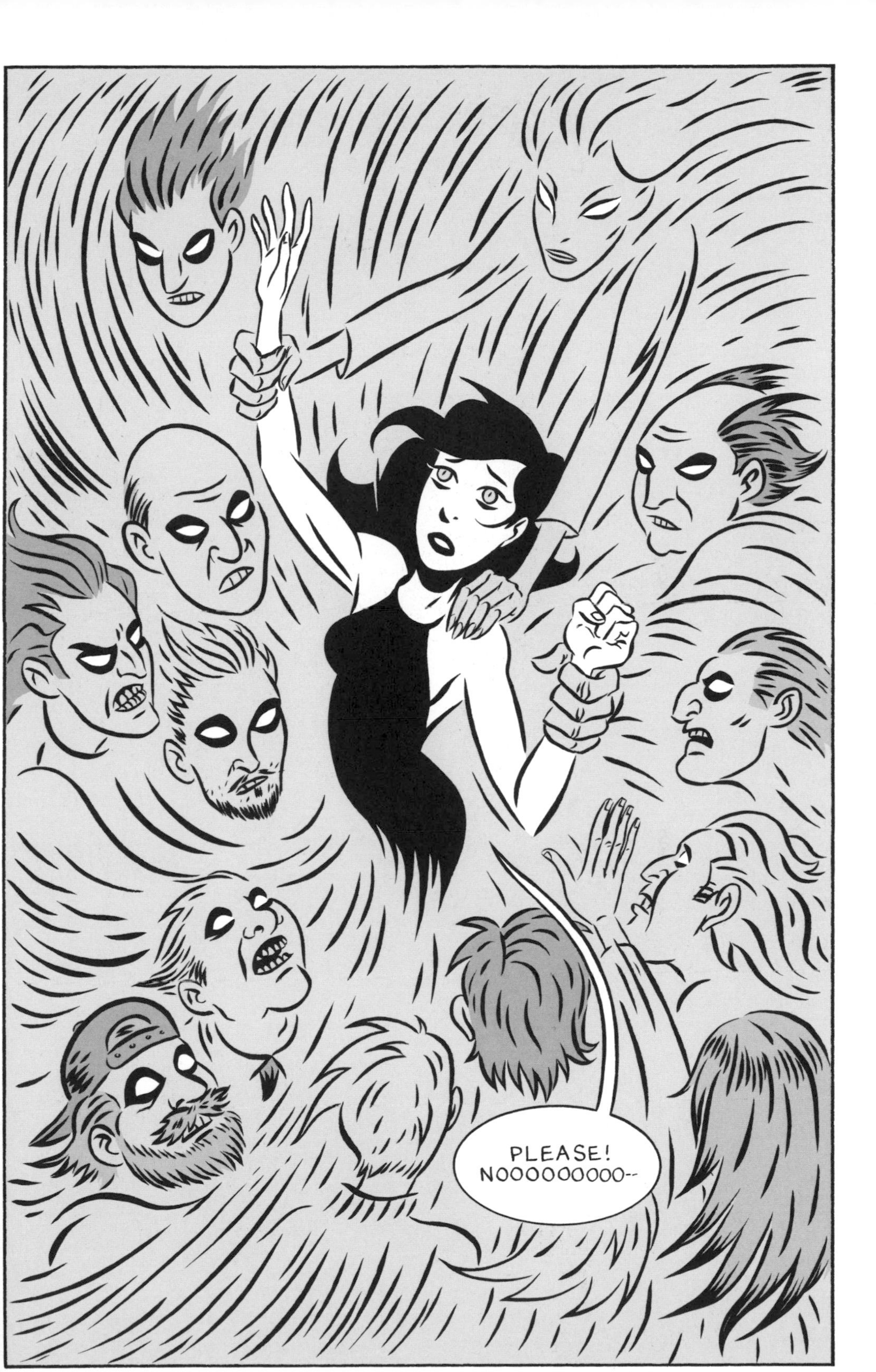
PLEASE!
NOOOOOOOOO--

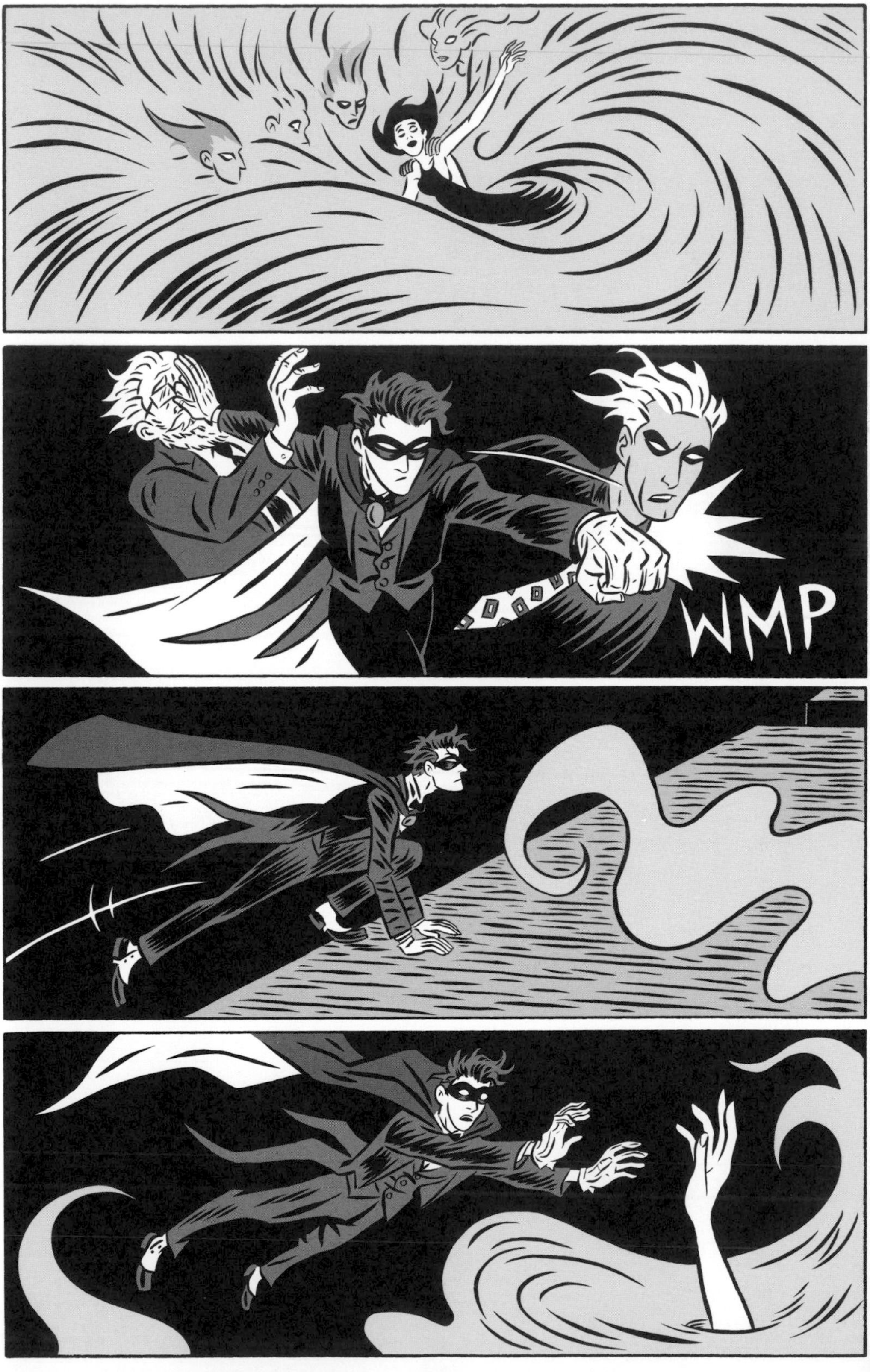
WMP

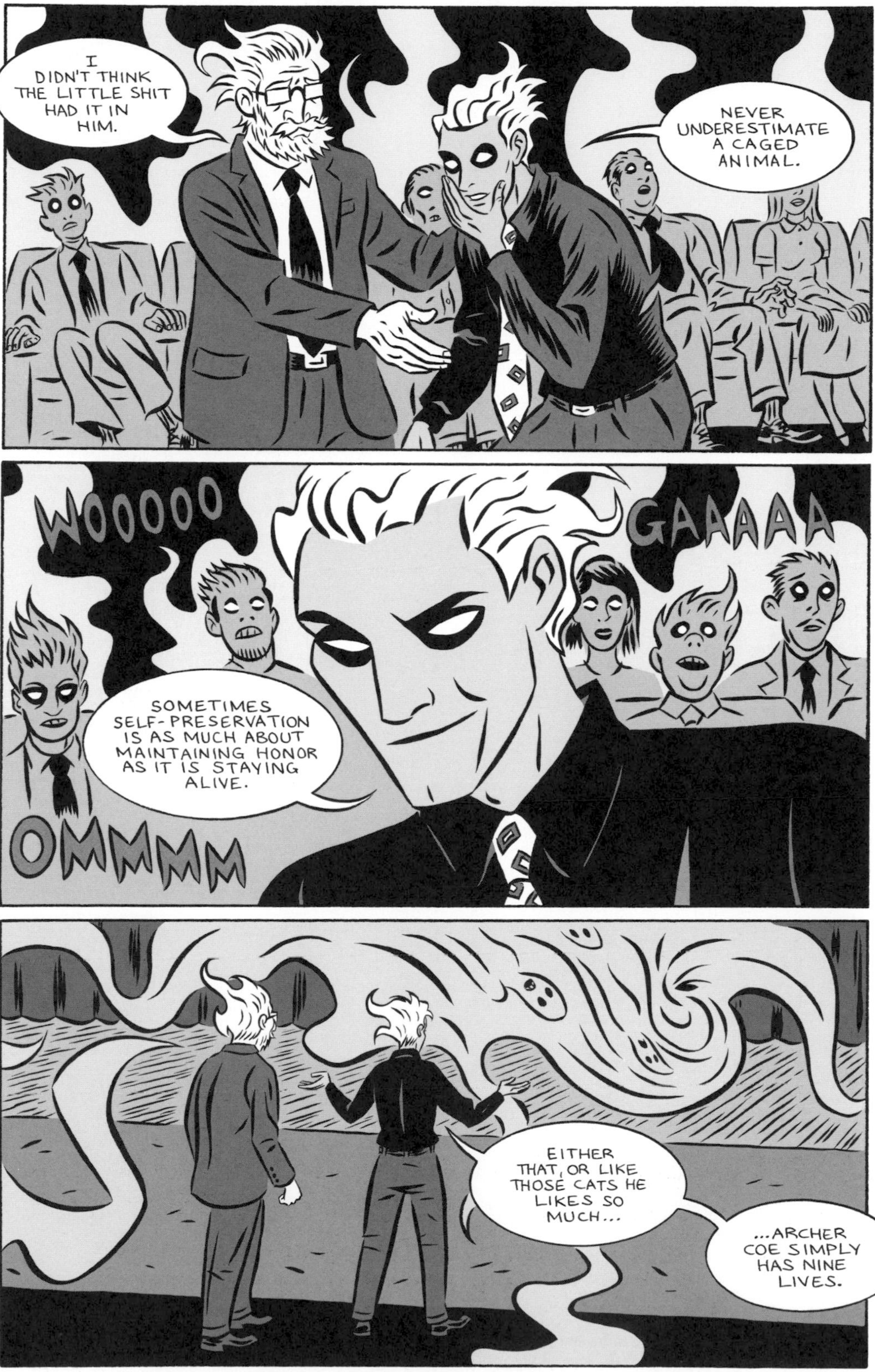

I DIDN'T THINK THE LITTLE SHIT HAD IT IN HIM.
NEVER UNDERESTIMATE A CAGED ANIMAL.
WOOOOO
GAAAAA
SOMETIMES SELF-PRESERVATION IS AS MUCH ABOUT MAINTAINING HONOR AS IT IS STAYING ALIVE.
OMMMM
EITHER THAT, OR LIKE THOSE CATS HE LIKES SO MUCH...
...ARCHER COE SIMPLY HAS NINE LIVES.

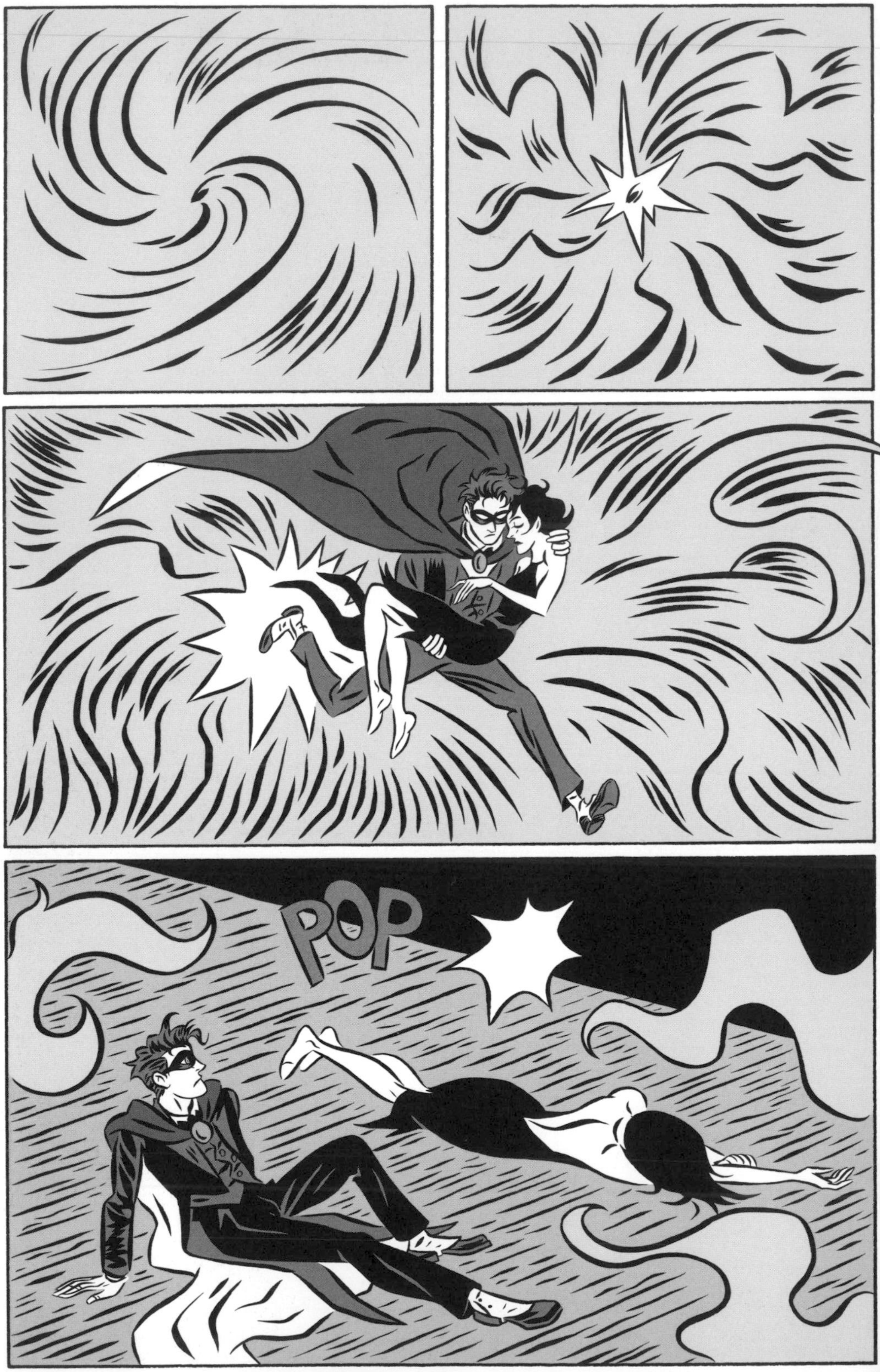
POP

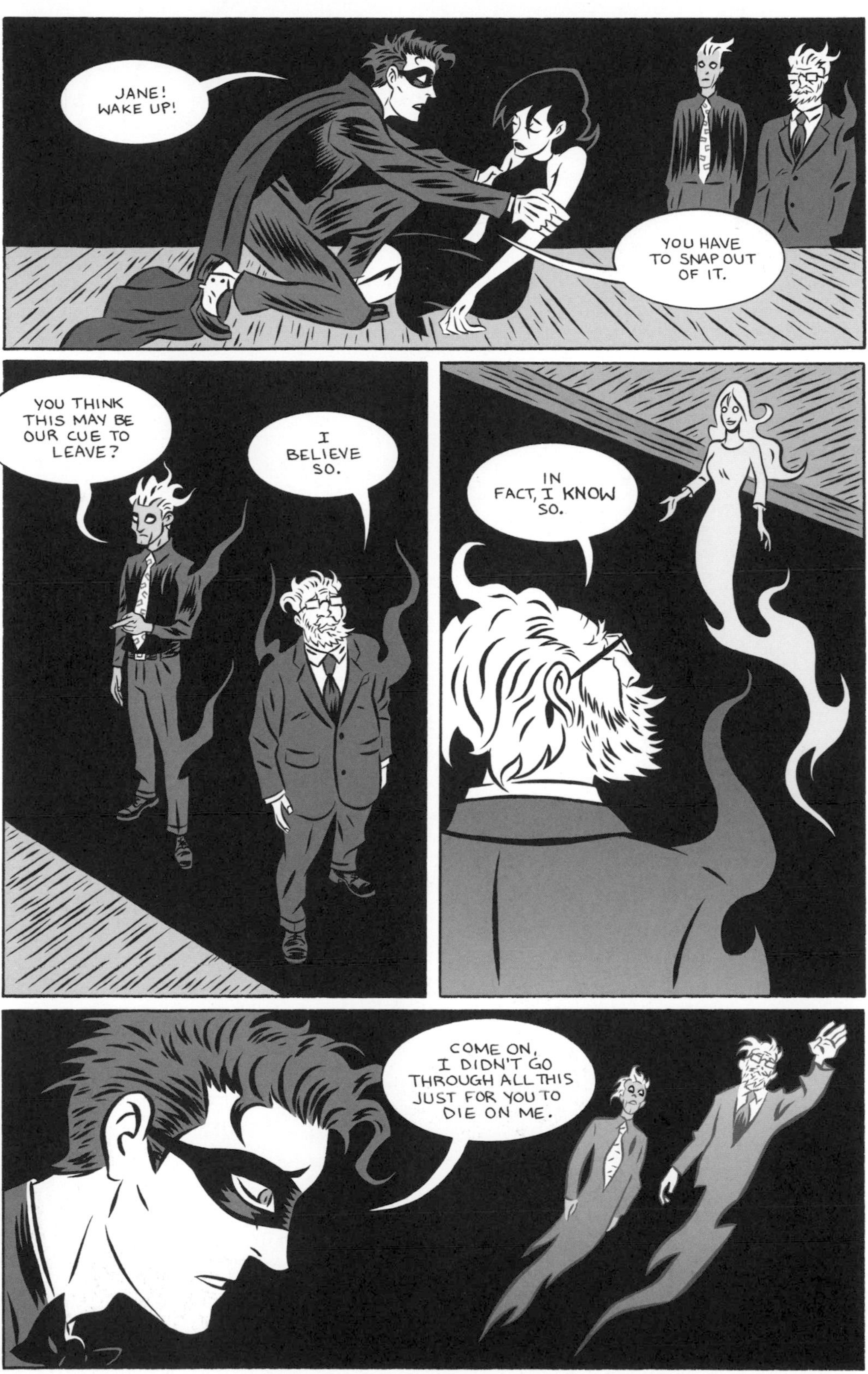
JANE! WAKE UP!
YOU HAVE TO SNAP OUT OF IT.
YOU THINK THIS MAY BE OUR CUE TO LEAVE?
I BELIEVE SO.
IN FACT, I KNOW SO.
COME ON, I DIDN'T GO THROUGH ALL THIS JUST FOR YOU TO DIE ON ME.

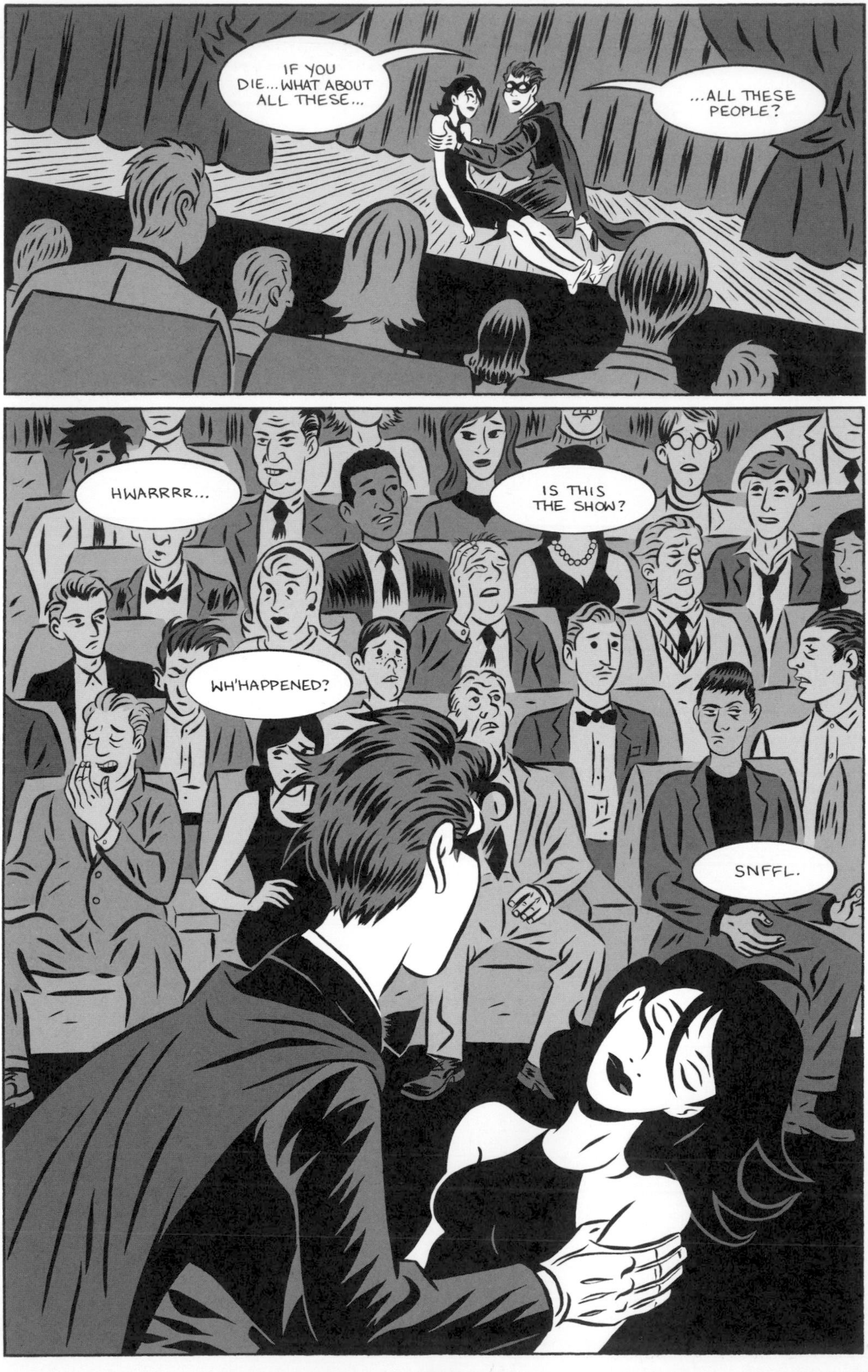
IF YOU DIE... WHAT ABOUT ALL THESE...
...ALL THESE PEOPLE?
HWARRRR...
IS THIS THE SHOW?
WH'HAPPENED?
SNFFL.

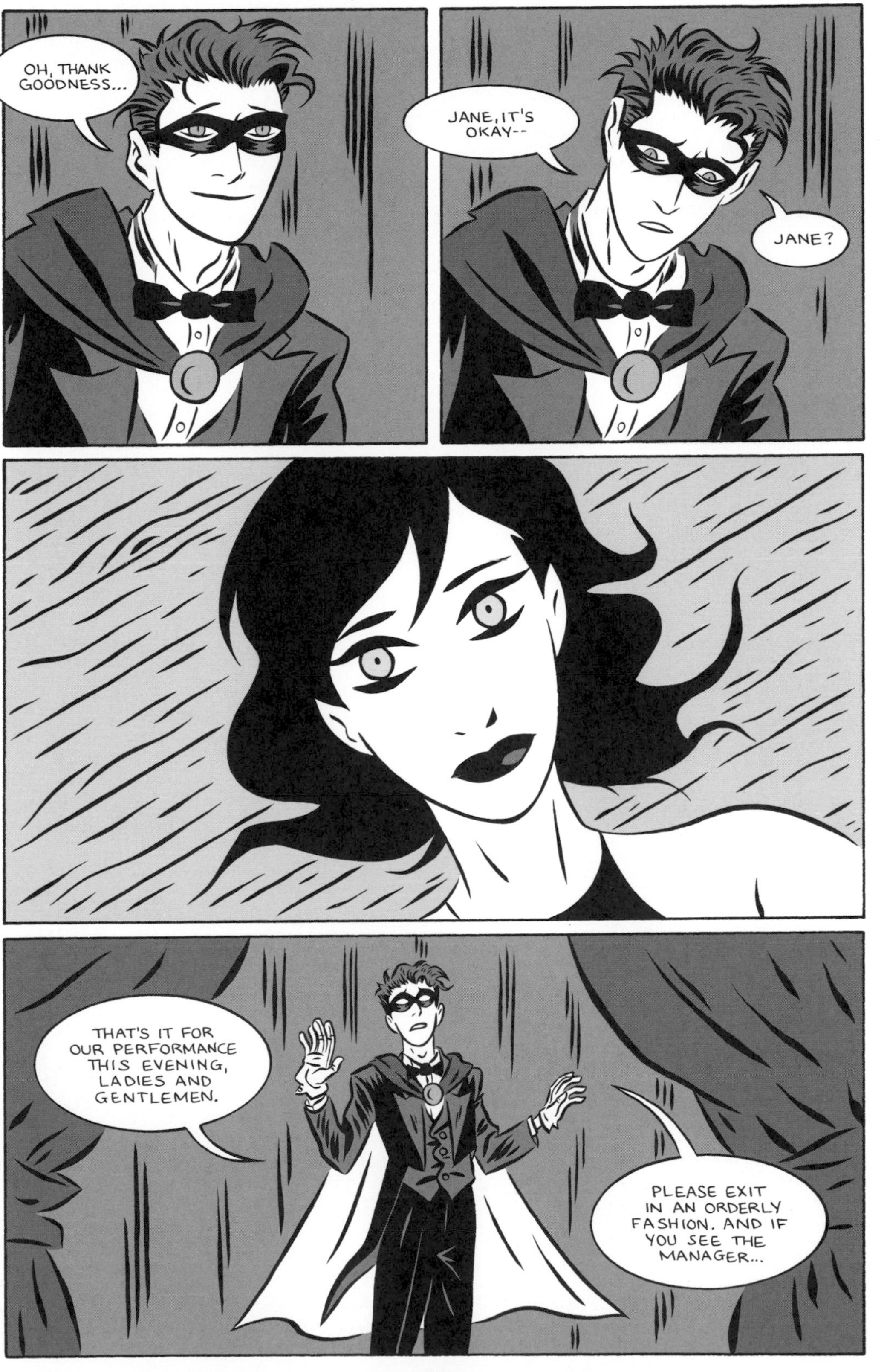
OH, THANK GOODNESS...
JANE, IT'S OKAY--
JANE?
THAT'S IT FOR OUR PERFORMANCE THIS EVENING, LADIES AND GENTLEMEN.
PLEASE EXIT IN AN ORDERLY FASHION. AND IF YOU SEE THE MANAGER...

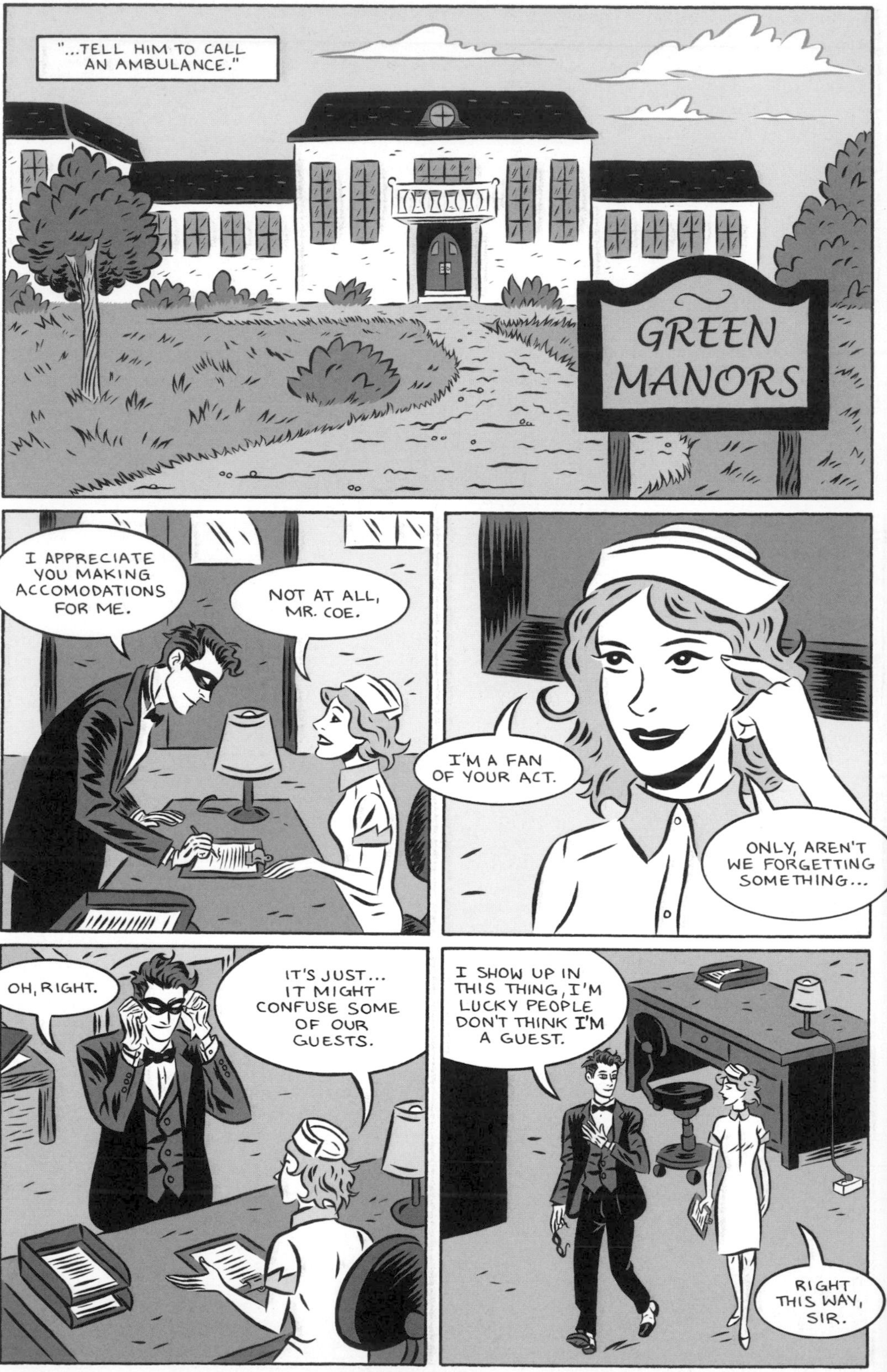
"...TELL HIM TO CALL AN AMBULANCE."
GREEN MANORS
I APPRECIATE YOU MAKING ACCOMODATIONS FOR ME.
NOT AT ALL, MR. COE.
I'M A FAN OF YOUR ACT.
ONLY, AREN'T WE FORGETTING SOMETHING...
OH, RIGHT.
IT'S JUST... IT MIGHT CONFUSE SOME OF OUR GUESTS.
I SHOW UP IN THIS THING, I'M LUCKY PEOPLE DON'T THINK I'M A GUEST.
RIGHT THIS WAY, SIR.

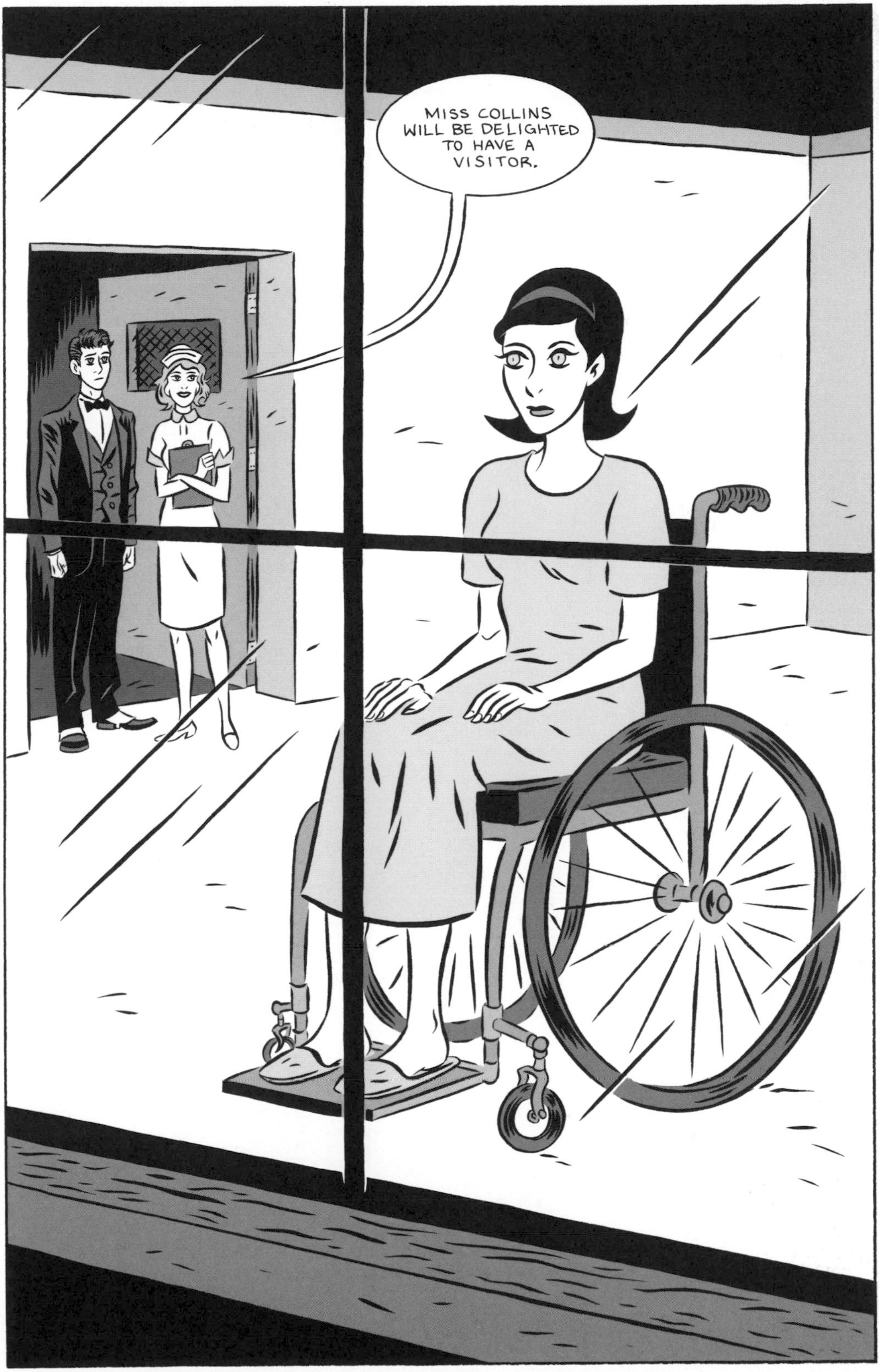
MISS COLLINS WILL BE DELIGHTED TO HAVE A VISITOR.

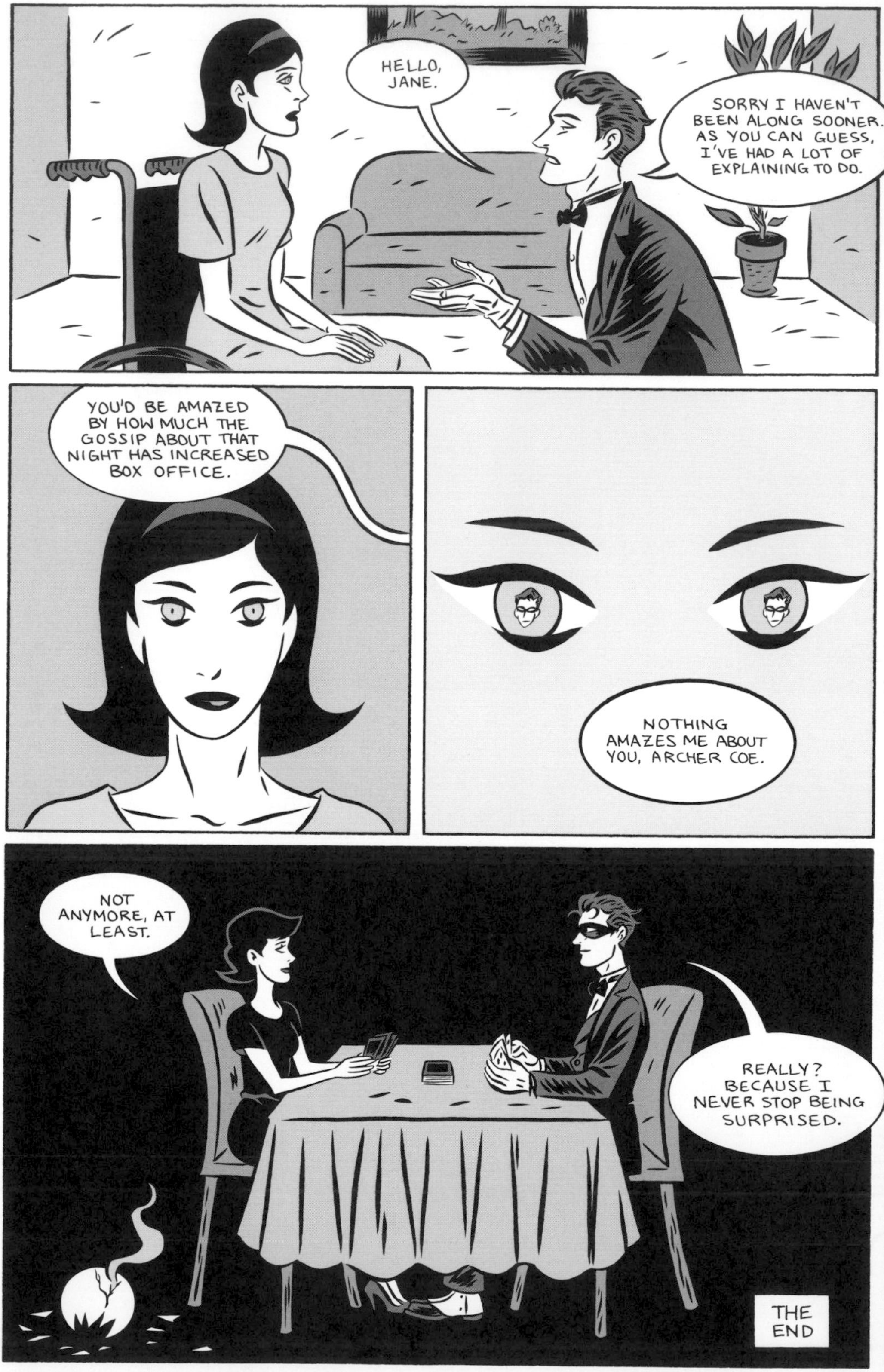
HELLO, JANE.
SORRY I HAVEN'T BEEN ALONG SOONER. AS YOU CAN GUESS, I'VE HAD A LOT OF EXPLAINING TO DO.
YOU'D BE AMAZED BY HOW MUCH THE GOSSIP ABOUT THAT NIGHT HAS INCREASED BOX OFFICE.
NOTHING AMAZES ME ABOUT YOU, ARCHER COE.
NOT ANYMORE, AT LEAST.
REALLY? BECAUSE I NEVER STOP BEING SURPRISED.
THE END

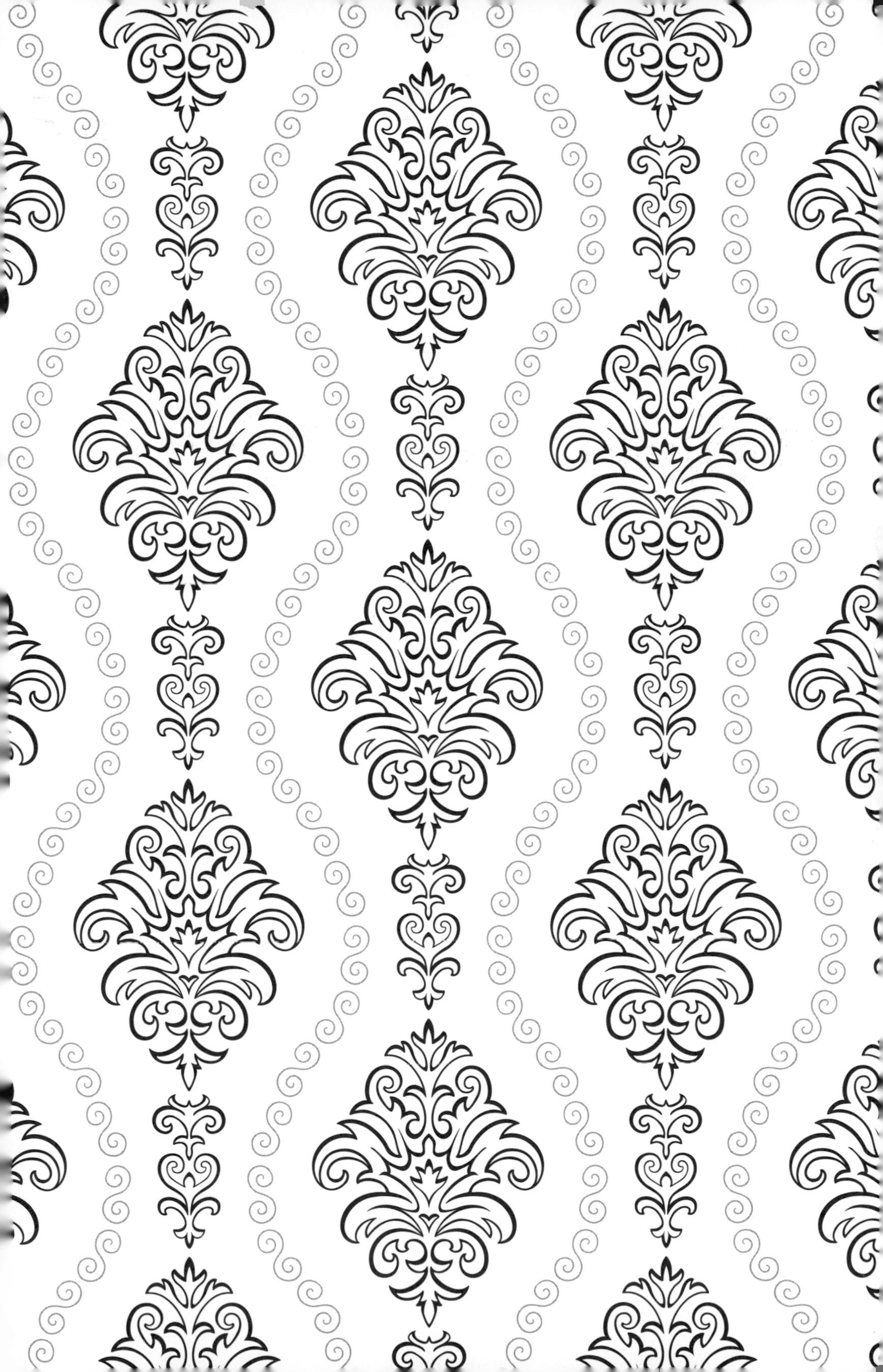

More Books from

Jamie S. Rich

THE MIND'S ARROW
ARCHER COE
THE THOUSAND NATURAL SHOCKS
JAMIE S. RICH
DAN CHRISTENSEN

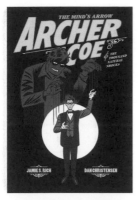

ARCHER COE AND THE THOUSAND NATURAL SHOCKS
Jamie S. Rich & Dan Christensen

160 Pages • Softcover
Black & White Interiors

ISBN 978-1-62010-121-6

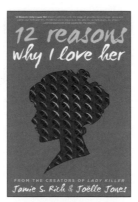

12 reasons why I love her
FROM THE CREATORS OF LADY KILLER
Jamie S. Rich & Joëlle Jones

12 REASONS WHY I LOVE HER: TENTH ANNIVERSARY EDITION
Jamie S. Rich & Joëlle Jones

184 pages • Hardcover
Black & White Interiors

ISBN 978-1-62010-273-2

YOU HAVE KILLED ME
from the creators of LADY KILLER
by JAMIE S. RICH & JOËLLE JONES

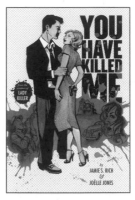

YOU HAVE KILLED ME
Jamie S. Rich & Joëlle Jones

192 Pages • Softcover
Black & White Interiors

ISBN 978-1-62010-436-1

A BOY & A GIRL
by Jamie S. Rich & Natalie Nourigat

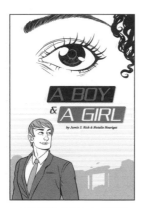

A BOY AND A GIRL
Jamie S. Rich & Natalie Nourigat

176 Pages • Softcover
Two Color Interiors

ISBN 978-1-62010-089-9

ARES & APHRODITE
love wars
JAMIE S. RICH & MEGAN LEVENS

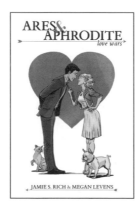

ARES & APHRODITE
Jamie S. Rich & Megan Levens

168 Pages • Softcover
Full Color Interiors

ISBN 978-1-62010-208-4

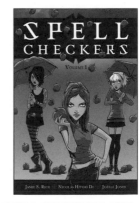

SPELL CHECKERS
Volume 1
Jamie S. Rich
Nicolas Hitori De
Joëlle Jones

SPELL CHECKERS, VOL. 1
Jamie S. Rich, Nicolas Hitori De, & Joëlle Jones

152 Pages • Softcover
Black & White Interiors

ISBN 978-1-934964-32-3

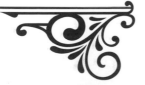

For more information on these and other fine Oni Press comic books and graphic novels, visit www.onipress.com.

To find a comic specialty store in your area, call 1-888-COMICBOOK or visit www.comicshops.us.

More Books from
Oni Press

"STUMPTOWN IS, FOR MY MONEY, THE PERFECT RUCKA BOOK."
$10
STUMPTOWN
GREG RUCKA • MATTHEW SOUTHWORTH

STUMPTOWN, VOL. 1, SQUARE ONE EDITION
Greg Rucka & Matthew Southworth
160 Pages • Softcover
Full Color Interiors
ISBN 978-1-62010-440-8

NOW A MAJOR MOTION PICTURE
ATOMIC BLONDE
WRITTEN BY ANTONY JOHNSTON
ILLUSTRATED BY SAM HART
ORIGINALLY PUBLISHED AS THE COLDEST CITY

ATOMIC BLONDE: THE COLDEST CITY
Antony Johnston & Sam Hart
176 Pages • Softcover
Black & White Interiors
ISBN 978-1-62010-381-4

PETROGRAD
PHILIP GELATT • TYLER CROOK

PETROGRAD
Philip Gelatt & Tyler Crook
264 Pages • Hardcover
Two Color Interiors
ISBN 978-1-934964-44-6

A DRAWN NOVEL
CAPOTE IN KANSAS
ANDE PARKS CHRIS SAMNEE

CAPOTE IN KANSAS
Ande Parks & Chris Samnee
160 Pages • Hardcover
Black & White Interiors
ISBN 978-1-934964-87-3

TUMOR
JOSHUA HALE FIALKOV & NOEL TUAZON

TUMOR
Joshua Hale Fialkov & Noel Tuazon
248 Pages • Hardcover
Black & White Interiors
ISBN 978-1-62010-326-5

OUR CATS ARE MORE FAMOUS THAN US
A JOHNNY WANDER COLLECTION
ANANTH HIRSH & YUKO OTA

OUR CATS ARE MORE FAMOUS THAN US: A JOHNNY WANDER COLLECTION
Ananth Hirsh & Yuko Ota
416 Pages • Hardcover
Partial Color Interiors
ISBN 978-1-62010-383-8

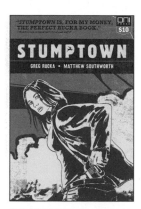

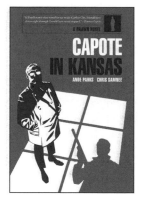

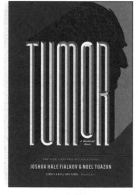

Jamie S. Rich is an author best known for his collaborations with artist Joëlle Jones on the graphic novels *12 Reasons Why I Love Her* and *You Have Killed Me*, as well as their acclaimed *Lady Killer* series. He published his first prose novel, *Cut My Hair*, in 2000, and his first superhero comic book, *It Girl and the Atomics*, in 2012. In between, he has worked on multiple projects in both mediums, including *A Boy and a Girl*, drawn by Natalie Nourigat, *Madame Frankenstein* alongside Megan Levens, and *The Double Life of Miranda Turner* with George Kambadais. In 2017, Jamie won an Eisner Award as one of the editors on the charity anthology *Love is Love*. He currently works at DC Comics.

Dan Christensen was born in California, grew up in Arizona, then moved to France. The first American to attend and graduate from the acclaimed ÉESI art school in Angoulême, he has since written and drawn several graphic novels, including *Riposte* and *Paranormal*. In addition to drawing comics, Dan works as a freelance translator for European comic book publishers Ankama, Lion Forge/ Magnetic Press, Dargaud, and Futuropolis, and has illustrated books for role-playing game publisher Hero Games.

He currently lives and works on the west coast of France. Visit his website at dcdrawings.blogspot.fr.